D0544117

THE JOURNEY

CONRAD JONES

CHAPTER 1

The sun was glaring down, making the air almost unbreathable. Beb was hot and thirsty; his black skin was wet with perspiration. There was no breeze to bring relief from the burning African sun. Across the road, in the trees, underfed cattle moved lethargically, flicking their tails to move the swarms of flies from their skin. The scorched earth was reduced to a terracotta coloured dirt, which would turn to mud in minutes when the rains eventually came. A minibus whizzed by, the radio blaring, leaving a trail of red dust billowing behind it. It was travelling at a dangerous speed, busing workers to the town of Monguno, where Beb was from. Black faces stared at him through the windows, some darker than others. Their eyes were filled with sorrow, staring blankly at the world outside as if all hope had been sucked from them. The bus hit a bump in the road and almost took off. It crashed back onto the road with a deafening clang. Some of the passengers looked frightened. He had never seen a local work bus travelling so quickly. They usually trundled along as if there was nowhere to be. Maybe the driver was running late, he thought.

'Hey, Beb,' his friend, Omar and Gamyu called from behind him.

'Hey,' Beb said, smiling as his friends caught up. They clapped a high-five and then gripped hands and locked fingers with practiced ease.

'Did you see that bus flying down the road?' Gamyu said, laughing.

'I have never seen a bus go so fast,' Beb laughed. 'I didn't think that they went that fast!'

'The driver is a crazy man,' Omar said, pointing to his forehead with his finger. 'Mad as a box of frogs!'

'When have you seen a box of frogs? Beb asked, sarcastically.

'Never,' Omar answered, putting his hands on his hips. 'But I know that they would be mad.'

'Why would they be mad?' Gamyu asked, confused.

'Because someone put them in a box, stupid!'

'That still doesn't explain why the bus was going so fast. I don't know why they want to rush to be in work!' Beb said.

'I would drive very slowly to work,' Omar agreed.

'The bus was packed too,' Gamyu said. 'Were they from, out of town?'

'I think so.' Beb nodded.

'Foreign workers?'

'I think so. There are more and more of them every month. My father says there will be no work for local people soon.'

Beb's father had told him that busing manual labour into the towns was big business nowadays. The indigenous population were becoming worried that their jobs would be taken by migrants from neighbouring countries. The border towns in the north of Nigeria had become an eclectic mixture of sub-Saharan migrants. Sectarian violence and civil war had driven millions from their homes into neighbouring countries where they worked the jobs that no one else wanted to do for a pittance.

'My father lost his job last week because they hired men from Mali for half the wages. Why do they have to come here?' Gamyu asked, angrily.

'My father says mostly it is because of Boko Haram,' Beb said, sounding as wise was a boy his age could. 'They are attacking villages and towns and killing lots of people. The people are too scared to go home, so they come here.'

Gamyu shrugged. He didn't look impressed by the answer. 'If they came here, my father would kill them,' he bragged.

'They have machineguns,' Beb said.

'That wouldn't matter.'

'Does your father have a machinegun?' Omar asked, raising his eyebrows.

'He would take one of theirs.'

'My father says they are very bad men,' Beb said, pressing home the point. He didn't think Gamyu's father would kill the Boko Haram rebels. In fact, he didn't think his father could kill anyone. He was a very small man with a withered arm. Beb wasn't even sure if he could hold a gun, but he didn't say anything. Lately, Beb had heard the news reports about unrest and conflict moving closer to their town and the grown-ups talked about it all the time. He thought that they worried too much. Grown-ups always worried about stuff. Don't do this, don't do that, don't do the other. Life seemed to be a constant battle between what he wanted to do and what he was allowed to do. Being an adult was like being the fun police. He couldn't wait to grow up so he could do whatever he wanted.

'How come you are off school?' Omar asked Beb

'They sent us home early.'

'Me too. My teacher said there's been trouble on the border.'

'Same for me.'

'Did you hear the news about all those schoolgirls being kidnapped?' Omar asked. Beb nodded but Gamyu shook his head. 'The television said they took three-hundred away.'

'Yes. My father said it was Boko Haram,' Beb said, nodding. His father was very clever and rarely wrong.

'How does he know?'

'He is always talking about them. One of the girls taken was my mother's niece,' Beb added.

'Really? You knew one of them?' Omar asked, pushing his index finger up his nose. He pulled out a green bogey and inspected it before rolling it and flicking it away.

'I don't know her. They are from near the border somewhere,' Beb explained.

'But she's your mother's niece?'

'Yes.'

'So, what relation is she to you?'

'I don't know. Just my mother's niece, stupid.'

'Funny man!'

'So, your father thinks it was Boko who took them?' Gamyu said, trying to get in on the conversation, although he had no idea what they were talking about.

'Probably. Boko are bad men.' Omar threw a stone at a tree as he spoke.

'The worst, my father says,' Beb agreed.

Beb thought his father was the font of all knowledge. Whatever he said was correct as far as Beb was concerned. He had finished his medical degree in London and worked in a hospital there for two years. Beb was very proud that his father has studied and worked abroad. No one else in Monguno had a degree from England. As far as Beb was concerned, his father was the cleverest man in town and that made Beb proud. He talked to Beb about things that he wouldn't discuss with his sisters. They were easily frightened. Beb and his father had discussed the activities of Boko Haram, the extremist militia that plagued the north-east of the country, attacking government targets and Christian settlements with increasing ferocity before disappearing like ghosts across the borders into Niger, Chad and Cameroon. They were also attacking the less fanatical Sunni Muslim communities, which was beyond Beb's comprehension. He did not understand why Muslims attacked Muslims. His father described it as being 'not Muslim enough'. Beb had heard him talking about the approaching violence to his mother in hushed tones, thinking their children were asleep. He also heard him talking on the phone to his brother, who was also a doctor and still lived in London. They talked for hours and his father would sigh and shake his head a lot during their conversations. Beb had never heard his father sound frightened before but he sounded increasingly concerned lately. He was the rock on which the family stood strong and it was unsettling to see him so worried. The cleverest man in Monguno should not be as rattled as he was. The fact that he was worried, worried Beb.

'My father is the same.' Omar agreed, poking his finger up the other nostril. This time he came up with nothing to show for his troubles. 'He talks about them all the time. My mother tells him to be quiet in case he frightens my sisters but he doesn't listen to her. She starts to sing whenever he talks about them so my sisters can't hear but he just talks louder, so she sings louder. It is like a madhouse sometimes. I don't know who is worse.'

Beb turned his head when he heard an engine revving loudly. A car approached at high speed, travelling way too fast to take the bend safely. It careered towards the curve, back end twitching in the dust; the driver nearly lost control. He managed to right the vehicle at the last moment and sped onwards towards town, honking the horn as he passed. The driver looked wide-eyed and focused on the road.

'Another crazy man. What is wrong with people today?' Beb asked.

'It is hot. People are crazy when it is too hot.' Omar threw another stone.

'It is always hot, you fool.'

'People are always crazy around here,' Omar shrugged. They laughed and kicked at the stones as they walked. Beb chuckled to himself. The man driving the car was in a hurry. He must have somewhere very important to be, he thought. Maybe he needed to get to the toilet quickly. Maybe they had all needed the toilet. There was nothing in town worth crashing into a tree for. And no one who lived there was in a hurry to do anything. Life was laid back. The town where they lived was a world away from the madness of the capital, Lagos; the politics of the capitol and the wars that raged in nearby countries seemed surreal to Beb. His family had been sheltered from the storms that raged across the continent. Beb's parents were industrious people, their father was a successful doctor and their mother a seamstress. They earned enough money to make sure that their children wanted for nothing. Beb and his three sisters knew little of the violence and poverty that epitomised childhood in Africa for millions of others. They were the lucky ones. Hunger was a stranger, their neighbours were friends and family and their water was clean and safe to drink.

'Where have you been today?' Omar asked Beb.

'Delivering some medicine for my father.' Beb picked up a stick and poked it into the dust, leaving a snake-like trail behind them. He turned around again when he heard a motorbike engine. The bike emerged from the trees and skidded around the bend at a dangerous speed, throwing red dust high into the air in a fan shape; then it straightened up and whizzed past him in a flash. The rider had a worried expression on his face and kept glancing behind him, probably checking for vehicles overtaking him, Beb thought. Maybe he was racing someone.

'Everyone seems to be in a hurry today,' Beb said, smiling. 'I want a motorbike when I am older.' It would make his deliveries easier and more fun too. Earlier that morning, his father had asked him to deliver medicines to the Christian minister, James, who lived a few miles away from the edge of town in an enclave called

Christown, inhabited by his flock. Beb's father had a clinic there twice a week in a small building which acted as his surgery. 'Girls like guys with motorbikes. Although, I don't think that I would ride it so fast. He was a crazy man.'

'I told you it is too hot today. It makes them crazy,' Omar said. 'Where did you take the medicines for your father?'

'To Reverend James.'

'The Christians?'

'Yes.'

'My father says that I shouldn't go there.'

'Why?' Beb asked, surprised. The Christians were a community of about sixty families, who had flourished there since the seventies. Many of them were treated by his father. Beb liked going to the village. 'I don't understand why he would say that. They are nice people.'

'He says they are different to us and that I wouldn't be welcome.'

'They pray differently but that is all.'

'Tell me what they are like?'

'They are like us!' Beb laughed. 'They have nice houses and they always have biscuits and home-made juice.' Beb's mother didn't cook biscuits. She said that they made people fat and that her daughters would not be fat. Finding a husband was difficult for fat girls, his mother explained whenever food was discussed. She warned Beb not to marry a fat girl as she would be expensive to feed. You need to marry a nice girl with all her teeth and her own job, she would say. Beb would listen politely and nod and his sisters would blush and giggle.

'My father would be angry with me if I went there.'

'If you got there, don't tell him, stupid,' Beb chuckled. He didn't understand why Omar's father was so wary of the Christians. 'If he met them, he wouldn't mind you being there.' Beb couldn't see much difference between the two communities. He shrugged and smiled and said, 'Go and see for yourself. They won't bite you!'

Beb had a smile that lit up his face. It made people feel relaxed with him. There was a hint of mischief in his eyes too. He was ten and tall for his age with gangly limbs and wide shoulders. Football was his passion and he was good at it. He was strong and fit and could play all day without becoming tired, if he was allowed. Reading was his second favourite pastime. His sisters, who were older, would pass him the books they had read. Reading books was a massive issue for the extremists. The way the Sunni Muslim schools were teaching students, especially girls, was attracting the wrath of Boko Haram. They didn't want girls to go to school. Beb's father had told him that Boko Haram translates to, 'Western education is a sin.' Reading anything but the holy book was a sin, they said. Beb couldn't comprehend that either. How could reading be a sin? His thoughts were disturbed by the sound of diesel engines approaching from the trees. This time there were lots of them.

'Can you hear that?' Omar said, excited. He squinted against the sun to see what was coming. 'What is going on today?'

'I don't know, Omar but something is wrong.' Beb turned and looked back down the dirt road, his eyes were narrowed against the glare. A cloud of red dust spiralled above the trees and it was moving quickly towards them. It was a convoy of some kind and that was very unusual. He was confused at first but instinct told him that they were in danger. Convoys were rarely good news. Beb looked around for a hiding place. 'Run, Omar!' Gamyu panicked and bolted down the road towards town, his shirt flapping in the breeze. 'Gamyu hide!' Beb shouted after him. There was no way he could make it to town before the oncoming vehicles did. It was too far.

'What is wrong with you, Beb?' Omar asked, calmly.

'Something isn't right. We need to hide, Omar. Run!'

Running from the road, Beb tried to climb a Marula tree. Its leafy branches offered him the best cover. As he clawed at the trunk, the engines grew louder. Beb jumped up and grabbed the lowest branch. His fingers closed around it and he pulled himself up. He pressed his sandals against the trunk to gain momentum and he was nearly there when the branch snapped and Beb crashed to the floor, landing on his back in the dust. The fall knocked the wind from his lungs and he couldn't suck air in. He felt like he had been punched in the kidneys. Sweat trickled into his eyes as he tried to push himself upright. Omar was standing next to the road, transfixed by the approaching convoy. He stood and waved at the oncoming vehicles, a wide smile on his face. Maybe it was government troops looking for the kidnapped schoolgirls? It was about time they did something about Boko, Omar thought.

'Omar!' Beb shouted. He sensed that the convoy was not friendly but Omar couldn't see it. Beb cupped his hands around his mouth. 'Hide, Omar. Get off the road!'

The first vehicle came around the bend in the road and he could see men with guns riding in the back, clinging to the roll-cage. He suddenly realised why people were driving so fast, they weren't in a hurry to get somewhere; they were running away. The pick-up truck roared towards them. Omar saw the guns and sunglasses too late but he was stranded and Beb couldn't help him. If he moved now, they would see him. He crouched behind the tree as the first pick-up truck sped by. His throat felt dry and his hands were shaking as a second vehicle appeared around the bend. A dark green army truck hurtled towards him; the bed of the truck was loaded with armed men. They held machineguns and were draped with bullet-belts. Some had berets and camouflage uniforms, others football shirts. They were not government troops, he knew that much. He saw machetes hanging from their belts and their mirrored sunglasses glinted in the sun. Beb couldn't tell if they were looking directly at him because he couldn't see their eyes. His breath was trapped in his lungs as he cowered behind the tree trunk. He dared not peer around it as four more personnel carriers roared by, loaded with militiamen. They were followed by a dozen more pick-ups. He heard two shots ring out and he put his hands over his ears. More troop carriers passed in a seemingly endless stream. It seemed like hours before the convoy had passed. The smell of diesel fumes filled the air, mixed with red dust; it was choking. Beb covered his nose and mouth with one hand and rubbed his eyes with the other as he waited for the sound of the engines to fade. He daren't move. It was at least ten-minutes before he broke cover, feeling vulnerable and exposed as he left his hiding place. There was no sign of Omar or Gamyu and he hoped that they had run and found a hiding place in the bush.

'Omar!' Beb shouted. There was no reply. He moved from one tree to another and called again. 'Gamyu!'

There was no answer from his friends. He looked both ways and tiptoed towards the road. The dust was settling and there was no more traffic. Sweat ran into his eyes as he moved stealthily from one tree to the next. His heart was pounding and his hands were shaking. He took a deep breath to calm his nerves and moved towards the edge of the treeline. As he reached the edge of the trees, he saw the broken body of his friend, Omar, face down in the dust. There was a bullet hole in his back and his limbs were bent and twisted at unnatural angles. A tyre mark ran from the base of his spine to his skull. Beb stifled his tears. He opened his mouth to shout for help when the sound of machinegun fire broke the silence and then the screaming began.

******

Esse, Beb's mother, was working at her sewing machine when the rebels swamped Monguno. When the first shots were heard, she thought it was a vehicle backfiring. The following short bursts confirmed her worst fears. It was persistent gunfire and it was coming from all directions. She knew her husband's worst fears had materialised. The rebels, Boko Haram, had come to Monguno. Her first thoughts were for her children. She needed to know where they were, find her husband Kalu and get them all home safely.

'Is that what I think it is?' one of her younger workmates asked. Her eyes were wide with fear. The sewing machines fell silent and the women gathered at the front of the workshop. They listened to the gunfire and watched the street for signs of the invaders. 'Is it Boko?'

'I think so,' Esse said, trying to keep her voice calm. She was the matriarch in the sewing shop; the other women were young and easily panicked. She had to set an example despite the burning desire to scream and run home to find her children. She knew the girls would be at home or on their way. Sometimes, they dawdled. She prayed that they were home safe. Her heart was pounding in her chest, thinking about them. The girls were vulnerable and naive. Beb was a different matter. Her son had no off-switch. He couldn't keep still and hated being indoors. She swore that he would sleep in the garden if he could. He was always off exploring and always late coming home.

She hoped that he was nearby, somewhere safe. More gunshots echoed down the street. 'It has to be them. I can't see any other explanation.'

'I heard that they had sent all the pupils home from school this afternoon,' another added. 'But they said it was a precaution because of trouble on the border, not near here.'

'Obviously, they were wrong. The trouble has come to Monguno,' Esse said, quietly. Kalu had said it would. His voice rattled around in her mind. She had been sceptical but he was right. 'We need to get home to our children immediately.'

'What do we do then, Esse?' a youngster asked.

'Yes, what do we do?' another asked, her voice high-pitched with panic.

'First of all, we stay calm. Get a grip of yourselves!' Esse said firmly, looking along the roads. She walked to the edge of the workshop, which was open to allow air to circulate. There were walls on three sides but the front elevation opened onto the street. She looked up and down the road. Vehicles were speeding passed in both directions and people were running, terrified expressions on their faces. 'What is happening?' she shouted to a neighbour who she recognised.

'It is Boko!' he shouted, without slowing. 'Go home to your children!'

'Pack up your things and go home,' Esse said, clapping her hands. She didn't require any more encouragement. 'Find your children and lock your doors until your men come home. Do not open your doors to anyone but your families.'

'Why are they here in Monguno? What do they want?'

'Whatever they can take,' Esse said, beneath her breath. Kalu had told her what Boko were responsible for. A cold shiver ran down her spine. 'Hurry up, now. Don't delay with silly questions. Go home as fast as you can!'

Suddenly, a convoy of trucks appeared from her left. Militiamen were hanging from the sides of the vehicles, their weapons glinted in the sun. The women stood still and watched as the convoy came to a standstill directly outside the small parade of shops. A dozen militiamen dropped from the trucks, aiming their weapons at the townspeople, before the convoy moved on to deploy troops elsewhere. Esse looked along the shopping parade. Traders and customers were trapped where the stood. It was too late to run. There were five small businesses operating there. A mechanic, a carpenter, a butcher and the sewing workshop. The fruit and vegetable stall next door had been there since she was born. Its owner, a wizened woman, who Esse knew well, was standing defiantly in front of her produce. She glared at the approaching troops, almost daring them to steal her goods.

'What are you doing here with your guns? You are not welcome here!' she called. 'We don't have anything for you! Get on your trucks and go back to where you came from and leave us in peace!'

A militiaman wearing a black beret and mirrored sunglasses, grinned from ear to ear. His teeth were white and straight. If had he been born on a different continent, he would have been a popstar. He approached the stall and picked up a melon. Using his machete, he cut into the flesh and then bit a chunk from it. He chewed it slowly and looked around.

'This is good, grandma,' he said, grinning

'I am not your grandma. You are a thug!'

'Why are you being so disrespectful, old lady?'

'Are you going to pay me for that or are you a thief with a gun?' the old woman asked, scathingly. 'You couldn't spell respect if you tried.'

'Pay attention, people of Monguno,' he shouted.

The rebel took out his pistol and raised it to her head and pulled the trigger. One side of her head exploded in a pink mist. Esse was covered in brain splatter. She touched her fingers to the pink goo and tried to wipe it off her cheek without going into a panic. Her hands began to tremble uncontrollably. She wanted to run. They had killed her without blinking an eye. The Boko knelt next to the woman's body. He snatched a gold chain from her neck and wiped the blood from it on her hair and then put it into his pocket. He took her takings bag from her waist and scooped out the money, stuffing the notes into his camouflage trousers. Kalu had been right. They were evil men.

'Unless you want to end up like grandma, you will be quiet and you will step out of your shops,' he looked around. 'Outside now!'

'We do exactly as they say,' Esse whispered to her workmates. Beads of sweat trickled from her temple. 'Do not resist them. Get outside.'

'Shut up!' one of the rebels shouted. 'Separate them and take them to the square.'

The militiamen began rounding people up. They were loud and aggressive and quick to lash out with their weapons. The butcher was floored by a blow to the back of his neck with the butt of a rifle. Esse didn't hear what he had said to them, not that it mattered. A man went to help him up from the floor and he was felled too. The rebels seemed to be enjoying themselves. Two soldiers walked into the workshop. They leered at the younger girls. One of them put his hand onto the breast of a teenager. He licked the side of her face with his tongue, leaving a sticky trail on her skin. The teenager couldn't believe that a man would touch her that way in public. Her eyes were fixed open in shock, her mouth dropped in shock. She tried to speak but her voice had deserted her.

'I like this one,' he said, pushing her against the wall. He pressed his groin against her. She closed her eyes and held her nerve. His breath made her feel nauseous; a mixture of tobacco and meat. 'I think she likes me too.'

'If you like her, take out the back,' his colleague said, matter of factly. 'Do it before the sergeant sees you.'

'Please don't!' the young woman sobbed.

'She is with child,' Esse said. Sweat ran down her back. She didn't want to speak, didn't want to stand out but she couldn't stand by and watch her young workmate being raped. 'You cannot touch her.'

'What are you saying, woman?'

'She is pregnant, leave her alone,' Esse lied. The soldiers turned and stared at her. She couldn't see their eyes but the menace was there nonetheless. Seconds ticked by in silence. She thought they would kill her. 'You shouldn't touch a woman who is with child. You know that it is a sin to take a woman who is already with another man's child. You cannot touch her!'

'Maybe we'll take you outside instead,' the soldier said, letting the young girl go. He sneered at Esse. She was tall and lean with bright eyes and high cheekbones, attractive for her age.

'What are you doing in there?' an angry voice shouted from outside.

'Nothing, sir.'

'What is wrong in there?' the rebel leader walked towards them, shouting at his men.

'Nothing, sir,' one of the men replied. 'We're on our way, sir.' He turned angrily to his colleague. 'I told you not to let him see!' he whispered.

'Shut up crying like a baby!' his friend replied beneath his breath.

'Get those women out here quickly!'

'We're coming, sir!'

'We do not have time for fooling around,' the sergeant scolded them. 'This town is not under control yet and until our captain says that it is, you will follow your orders to the letter, understand?'

'Yes, sir.'

'Get those women to the square immediately.' The sergeant shouted. 'You're wasting time!'

Esse and her workmates were herded onto the road and forced to walk quickly towards the square. The other traders were ahead of them, walking in a line. Esse tried to stay calm but the young women were crying. She put her arms around the youngest girl, who was sobbing; tears streaked her cheeks. Her stomach was twisted in knots as she thought about her children. She was desperate to reach them. There was no way to escape and get home. All she could do was hope that Kalu had avoided capture and that Beb was somewhere safe.

'Don't cry. Everything will be okay,' Esse whispered, her maternal instincts taking over.

'Shut up, woman!' a soldier shouted. His face was a twisted mask of hatred. Esse could feel the hatred oozing from the rebels. 'If you speak again, I'll kill you!' She thought twice about testing his resolve.

'I'm very sorry,' she muttered, avoiding eye contact.

'Move and keep your mouth shut!'

Esse squeezed the young girl to comfort her. All she could think about was what was happening to her family. Her daughters were young and attractive and she had seen for herself how the militiamen treated women. The thought of her children being raped was unthinkable, yet she couldn't clear it from her mind. She would rather they were dead than suffer that. The overwhelming feeling of total helplessness was smothering her. There was absolutely nothing that she could do. Her limbs were shaking and her hands were trembling. She wanted to let go of her emotions but she couldn't crumble. She wondered if she would ever see her family again.

****

Kalu was visiting an elderly patient on the outskirts of town when the shooting started. He knew immediately what it was and who was responsible. He checked his mobile phone for a signal and cursed under his breath when he saw there was no coverage in this part of town. His eldest daughter had a mobile, much to the contempt of his son, Beb and her younger sisters. He had drawn a line in the sand on her last birthday. She was allowed the phone and could use Facebook with her friends, under the supervision of her mother, Esse. The other children would be allowed the same privilege when they reached her age. Kalu sent a text message quickly.

'GET YOUR SISTERS AND GO HOME!'

He knew Beb was out of town at Christown and he hoped that he had heard the shooting and hidden somewhere.

'I need to go home to my family,' Kalu told his patient. He stood tall. His shaven head was sheen with perspiration. 'Keep taking the tablets and the infection will shift.'

'Thank you, doctor,' his patient replied. 'What is all the shooting, is it Boko?'

'I think so,' Kalu said, packing his medical bag. His white shirt was open at the neck, tucked into his khaki trousers. 'Let's hope that I'm wrong but to be on the safe side, I need to go home to my family and make sure they are okay. You need to lock your door and stay inside. Do not go out for anything and do not open the door, okay?'

'Okay, thank you.' His patient offered a gnarled hand. Kalu shook it. 'Good luck, Kalu. I'll pray for you and your family.'

'Good luck to you.' Kalu walked to the front door and looked outside. People were running here and there, self-preservation pumping through their veins. The gunshots were much closer already and he could hear engines approaching. He stepped out and closed the door behind him. The sound of the lock being slid home came from the other side. He tucked his bag under his arm and sprinted across the road. Bullets whistled above his head and he had to duck. Fifty yards to his right, a woman screamed and collapsed in a heap. He could see that she was heavily pregnant. She rolled onto her back and clutched at her stomach, her hands slick with blood.

'Help me!' she cried weakly. 'Please help me! My baby is coming!'

Kalu thought about his family, his wife, his daughters and his son. He thought about ignoring the stricken woman and heading home to them without stopping to help her. The thought was alien to everything he had done in his life. Helping others had always been his priority. He turned and ran to her, kneeling to help. As he opened his medical bag and applied a pressure pad to a glancing wound on her stomach, the first Boko vehicles appeared from the corner of the street. Soldiers deployed from the trucks and began to herd the townspeople. A militiaman approached him and gestured with his machinegun.

'Move over there, now!' he ordered.

'This woman is having a baby,' Kalu said. 'I'm a doctor.'

'If you don't move now, you will need a doctor. Get over there!'

'Keep pressure on the wound,' Kalu said into her ear. She nodded, eyes filled with tears. 'I'm sorry,' Kalu said, standing.

'I like that watch,' the Boko said. Kalu looked at his wrist. His father had given him the Omega when he had graduated from university. He didn't want to part with it. 'I said, that I like that watch.'

'I heard you. It was a gift from my father.'

'You can take it off or I can cut your hand off and take it?'

Kalu capitulated and unfastened the clasp. He handed the watch over without a word. The watch disappeared into a grimy pocket and the rebel gestured with his head.

'Move!'

Kalu raised his hands above his head and stepped onto the road, joining the ragtag bunch that was being jostled towards the town square. He looked over his shoulder at the pregnant woman and hoped that she would be left alone to deliver her baby. The Boko was standing over her. A burst of automatic gunfire dashed his hopes and silenced her moans. He closed his eyes and looked away from her dead body and tried to focus on finding his family. He couldn't save everyone. They were his priority now.

****

Oke avoided making eye contact with a group of boys who always hung around near the market, kicking a football. They looked at her and her sisters, Isime and Kissie whenever they passed them, making lewd comments or trying to be funny. Mother had warned the girls that young boys only wanted sex and nothing more and until they were married, they were to stay away from them. Oke was old enough to recognise the hunger in their eyes but her younger sisters were still too young to understand. The boys whispered and giggled as they approached. What she didn't realise was that they were laughing at their hair and clothes. The girls looked like triplets, despite their age difference. Their hair was braided close to their scalp in cornrows and their long grey dresses were identical. They were pretty girls but a little aloof with the poorer kids.

'Ignore them,' Oke said to her sisters.

'Who?' Kissie asked, looking around for a potential offender. She had been thinking about what would be for tea and had no idea what Oke was talking about. Boys weren't on her radar. She couldn't see anyone to ignore.

'Hold my hand and cross the road,' Oke told them. She looked each way and they crossed, just as the first shots were heard. They reached the other side and stopped. Kissie had her mouth open. Isime looked up at her older sister for an explanation. A text message pinged her mobile. She looked at it and started to shake. It was from her father.

'We need to go home, quickly.'

'What is wrong, Oke?'

'Father says we need to go home immediately.'

Oke knew that her father didn't panic unnecessarily. He had been wittering on about the rebels in the west for as long as Oke could remember. Her mother used to roll her eyes to the ceiling every time he mentioned them. It looked like he had been right. As machinegun fire began to intensify, the first trucks appeared, sealing off both ends of the road. There was nowhere to run. Oke froze to the spot. She waited to see what would happen. A woman tried to run and a soldier raised his weapon and shot her in the back.

'He shot her,' Kissie whispered. 'Is she dead?'

'I don't know, Kissie,' Oke whispered back to her.

'Who are they?' Isime asked, clutching her schoolbag tightly. 'What do they want?'

Oke looked around as troops jumped down from the trucks, firing their weapons in the air. To their right was a service road, which ran behind the market. She thought about running away for a second until soldiers turned into the other end and blocked it. Her mother had warned them to stay somewhere public if anything bad happened. She told them that when things turned violent, being in a public place was safer.

'It is Boko Haram,' Oke whispered. The rebels were rounding people up. Anyone who questioned them was shown no mercy. They watched as a teenage boy was beaten with the end of rifle until his face was a bloody mess. 'We must do as they say until we can see a way to run, okay?'

'I'm scared,' Kissie said. 'What will they do?'

'They will steal things, father says,' Oke said, squeezing her hand tightly. She didn't want to tell her the truth about what father said about them. He said that they were rapists and murderers, not to Oke herself but she had heard him talking to his brother on the telephone. She was old enough to know that three pretty, young girls needed to stay in a public place. The soldiers were moving towards them, herding a group of twenty or so townspeople. She felt their eyes on them as they neared. Two of the rebels looked at each other and grinned. Oke knew the seriousness of their situation.

'Hey girls,' a young soldier called to them.

'Do not look at them,' Oke whispered.

'Hey girl, I like you,' the soldier persisted.

'What does he want,' Kissie asked.

'Just ignore him.' Oke was starting to panic.

She looked around for help. A large woman, who she recognised waved her hand. Oke knew that she worked with her mother sometimes.

'Oke,' she hissed. 'Get over here near me.'

'Cameela,' Oke said, smiling nervously. She pulled her sisters towards her. 'I'm so glad we saw you.'

'Come and walk with me,' Cameela said, shepherding the girls around her as if they were her own. 'Are you okay, little one?' Kissie hugged her as if her life depended on it. The Boko men looked disappointed. The young girls were no longer alone and vulnerable. 'Do not make eye contact with these animals,' she whispered.

'Where are they taking us?' Isime asked, her eyes wide with fear. The Boko men were scary, their eyes covered with mirrored sunglasses, machetes and machineguns glistening in the sunlight. They had never seen anything like it. 'What do they want?'

'They want us to go to the square,' Cameela said, looking around nervously.

'Why?' Isime asked.

'Will mother and father be there?' Kissie asked. She looked close to tears.

'You there!' a teenage soldier barked. He pointed at Cameela with his gun 'Hey, I like your daughter!' Oke felt his eyes all over her. He was leering like a fool. Cameela didn't turn her head. She ignored him. 'I am talking to you, woman!'

'That soldier is talking to you,' Isime said, frightened.

'Shush, Isime! Ignore him,' Cameela said, looking forward, never acknowledging the soldier. 'We stay with the group, no matter what they say. If they separate us, we are in trouble. Ignore them until we get to wherever they are taking us, understand?' The girls nodded that they did. 'He is no older than you and some fool has given him a machinegun. They are the most dangerous. Do not answer him no matter what he says!'

'You there! Woman with the children, stop!' the soldier shouted louder. He was crossing the road towards them, intercepting their path. 'I am talking to you!'

Cameela picked a different track and kept on walking. She held the girls close to her hips. Some of the townsmen sensed the danger and moved closer to them. They formed a human wall around the girls.

'They are children. Leave them alone,' one of the men in the crowd shouted. The boy soldier didn't know who had said it but it had angered him.

'Who said that?' the young soldier said, turning.

'They are children, you dog!' someone else called out.

'Who said that?' the boy snapped. The crowd moved on, ignoring his frustrations. 'Say that to my face, whoever said it!'

'What is your problem, stupid boy!' another voice called out from the back of the crowd. The Boko pointed his machinegun into the group but couldn't identify a target. His anger was rising and he felt foolish. The townspeople were making an idiot of him, disrespecting him.

'Who called me stupid?'

'You are stupid,' a woman near the back taunted him. The soldier turned on his heels quickly but couldn't tell who had said it.

'Keep walking and mind your business!' the soldier barked at one of the townsmen. He slapped him hard on the back of the head. The man turned to retaliate but Cameela put her hand on his shoulder.

'Don't give them an excuse to kill you,' she said in his ear. 'That is what he wants. Keep walking.' He listened to her and stepped back.

'Keep moving all of you! I am talking to this woman.' The group kept moving, shuffling around the girls to make it awkward for him to get near them. Cameela didn't look sideways once. She focused on a spot in front of her. 'I am talking to you, woman!'

'She doesn't want to talk to you. Leave us alone!' Kissie shouted. Oke put her arm around her and her hand over her mouth.

'Shush, Kissie!'

'You're not going to get near them,' another townsman said, stepping close to the girls. There were nearly a dozen people huddled around them now. All walking, all blocking access to Cameela and the children. 'If you didn't have that gun, I would snap you.' Another voice said from the crowd.

'What did you just say to me?' the young Boko growled. His face was creased with frustration. The townsman didn't make eye contact with him. He continued to walk towards the town square, shoulders touching the next man, protecting the women.

'You're going to have to kill all of us to get near those children.' A voice from the group added. The Boko glared into the crowd but he couldn't see who had said it.

'Who said that?' he shouted again. The crowd ignored him. Some of the other soldiers were watching the situation, smiling at each other. It appeared to Cameela that the young rebel was not popular amongst his peers. 'Who said that?' The group kept walking.

'You won't touch those children, idiot,' a townsman said, loud enough to be heard.

'Who called me an idiot?' the Boko shouted, his face flushed with anger and embarrassment. 'Who was it?'

No one replied and the crowd walked on. Despite his weapon, the boy felt defeated, like a baby hyena too small and weak to bring down a buffalo from the herd. He saw his colleagues laughing at him and slowed down his step, allowing the group to move away.

'Keep walking!' he shouted as his parting shot. Cameela felt a sigh of relief as he gave up and dropped back. She looked down and smiled at Kissie, rubbing her hair gently. The girls were attractive and young and very vulnerable. Keeping them safe would be a mammoth task. She could only hope that Kalu and Esse were safe.

****

Beb covered the distance to town quickly, using the cover of trees, the bushes and the occasional outbuilding. The was no sign of Gamyu. The closer to town he got, the louder the gunfire became. He could hear men shouting and women screaming. A dog barked somewhere in the madness. The staccato retort of weapons made him flinch with each shot fired. He had to get home to his family. Panic was driving him on; fear was telling him to turn and run the other way but the urge to reach his kin was overwhelming. Running into the trees and hiding until the soldiers left was the sensible thing to do but he couldn't do that. His mother and his sisters would be frightened. He had to find them.

As he approached town, the dust road changed to tarmac and the trees became sparse. A line of single-storey buildings marked the edge of town and he took a deep breath before running towards them. The gunfire was deafening now and the sound of screaming women curdled his blood. He could see the faces of his mother and his sisters in his mind. A high pitched scream pierced his soul, spurring him on. He kept low and sprinted behind the buildings, tears filled his eyes, blurring his vision. The image of Omar crushed in the dirt was branded into his psyche. Leaning against a wall, he sucked in the scorched air and closed his eyes and listened. The gunfire was no longer constant but it was still close. Intermittent bursts rang out, echoing from the walls. Angry male voices shouted instructions, but he couldn't make out what they were saying. Their dialect was unfamiliar. Beb edged his way along the wall to the end of the building. He peered around the corner and looked at the next street. Gamyu was sprawled face down on the road. His lifeless eyes stared back at Beb. Blood was weeping from a dark hole in his forehead, forming a congealing puddle on the tarmac. Flies crawled around the jagged wound, gorging on the warm liquid. Beb was mesmerised as a blow-fly disappeared into the bullet hole; morbid fascination had him transfixed.

The sound of an engine made him duck. He looked through one eye, not daring to show his face and saw an old Volvo speeding down the street. It didn't slow as it hit Gamyu, sending his body into a spin beneath it. A pick-up truck was on its tail. The three men on the back were aiming AK-47's and firing sporadically. The back window of the car exploded and the Volvo veered violently to the right and crashed into a low concrete wall, mounting it before coming to a complete standstill. The wall disintegrated and the vehicle rocked; the back wheels were on the road, front wheels spinning in the air. Beb watched in horror as the pick-up truck screeched to a halt behind the Volvo and the militiamen jumped onto the road. They aimed their weapons into the Volvo as they approached, shouting at the driver to get out of the car. The driver's door opened and Beb saw him raise a pistol. A shot rang out and a militiaman crumpled to the ground as a bullet ripped through his midriff and blew a hole in his back as it exited. The soldiers retuned fire. A volley of machinegun fire rang out and the Volvo driver dropped from his seat onto the road, blood spreading from his wounds. He fell twitching in the dirt next to the man he had shot.

Beb felt his limbs turning to stone as shock and fear gripped him but he couldn't look away. The militiamen ran to the passenger door and pulled it open. That side of the vehicle was hidden from his view but he heard a woman and a young girl screaming as they were dragged from the car. The young girl was dragged away from her mother and thrown into the pick-up. Her mother cowered in the dust and cried for help. Beb knew that no help was coming. Machete blades flashed in the sun and her screams reached fever-pitch before falling silent permanently. He heard the men laughing. They thrashed at her body long after she had stopped screaming.

Beb turned his eyes away and hid behind the wall, his body trembling. His breathing was fast and shallow as his brain tried to erase what he had seen. The woman's cries resounded around his mind. He closed his eyes and didn't move until the pick-up had moved on and the sun had gone down on the horizon. He wasn't sure how long he waited there but he physically couldn't move a muscle. Pins and needles cramped his limbs. The darkness didn't bring peace with it and the soldiers didn't leave. The gunfire and screaming carried on although it was moving away to the west towards the town square. Beb was desperate to get to his family. He decided to use the cover of darkness to move through the unlit streets. It would hide him while he navigated the alleyways and snickets that he knew so well. He was about to run to the next street when he heard the click of a gun being cocked and a bright light blinded him.

'Move and I'll blow your head off!' a voice said, from the shadows. Beb raised his hands and closed his eyes and waited to die.

18

CHAPTER 2

A mile away in the town square, Beb's family had been separated, tied up and forced to kneel on the road. The inhabitants of the town had been separated into six groups. Men and boys, women and girls, children and the elderly. The youngsters were herded into one unruly group, many sobbing for their parents, older siblings caring for younger ones. Militiamen barked at them when the volume became too loud. The adults were forced to kneel in rows on opposite sides of the square. Kalu looked around and tried to find his family. Sweat trickled down his back, fear and the heat made his heart beat wildly. He had followed the birth of Boko Haram in the news and knew it was made up from kidnapped orphans, disenfranchised teenagers, religious fanatics and organised criminals. The criminal element controlled the group using ideology, while profiteering from their raids, mostly by selling people into the slave trade. In a poor country, people were the most valuable currency available. Kalu knew why they had been separated. Old men and women had no value. They would be slaughtered like cattle or left in a ghost town to starve to death. The men of fighting age would be offered a choice, join Boko Haram and convert to ISIL ideology or die. It wasn't much of choice but it was a better choice than the women would be offered. The females would become slaves to be abused or sold onto traffickers. Youth was the most valuable asset. Young people had a value. Young women were valuable to the sex trade; young boys would become soldiers for their cause.

Kalu was sick to his stomach with fear. He spotted his daughters huddled together across the square. It offered him some cold comfort. His eldest was fourteen and attractive, the middle girl a year younger and the youngest just twelve. The thoughts of what would happen to them were twisting his mind. They would be sex slaves until they were too old to be attractive. It would be a life of relentless horror, a tortured groundhog-day. He could hardly think straight. The feeling of helplessness was suffocating. The only positive was that he had sent Beb to Christown. He had to hope that his boy was somewhere safe for now.

An angry voice echoed across the square. One of the soldiers guarding the youngsters was growling at a little boy. Kalu had treated the boy recently and recognised his face. He remembered he was about six-years-old. The boy was standing with his hands covering his groin. He was sobbing uncontrollably. A dark patch was spreading across his pants. Kalu was sickened when the guard hit him across the face, knocking him to the ground.

'Don't strike a child, you bastard!' a woman called.

'The child needs the toilet!' someone shouted.

'We all need the toilet,' another added.

'How can you hit a child, you coward!'

The soldier scowled at the women and kicked the child in the ribs. The groups of women began to wail. Their cries were deafening. Angry voices protested at the cruelty and the townsmen became restless. One man stood and broke free of the kneeling prisoners. He ran awkwardly across the square, hands tied behind his back. Kalu recognised that it was the boy's father. A young militiaman raised his machinegun and aimed at him as he ran.

'No! Do not shoot him,' a voice called out. The Boko leader pushed the gun barrel upwards, pointing at the sky. 'What is wrong with you, man?' he snapped. 'This man is tied up.' He shouted at his soldier, shaking his head in disgust. 'We don't shoot men who are tied up!'

'Yes, sir,' the soldier mumbled.

'Do you understand why?'

'Not really.'

'We do not waste bullets on men who are tied, idiot! Use your machete.'

The boy's father was nearly across the square. His son was crying and calling for him. The women were chanting his name as if he was an athlete approaching the finishing line. Kalu watched in slow motion as the Boko leader stepped forward blocking the way. He unsheathed his machete and held it before his face; a twisted smile touched his lips as he raised the blade and swung it down in a vicious arc. The boy's father anticipated the blow and he dodged right, narrowly avoiding the blade. It glinted in the torchlight as it whistled by his head. The Boko leader lost his balance and stumbled, falling onto his knees, which brought a deafening cheer from the townspeople. The desperate father staggered to his distraught child. He knelt to comfort him and his son wrapped his arms around his neck tightly. The women howled with delight. Kalu felt joy and pain at the sight of the father risking all to comfort his son.

The Boko leader stood up and dusted himself off. He approached the man, shaking his head. He raised his machete again. The boy's father stood and glared at him, eye to eye. The Boko leader snarled and brought the machete down onto the father's skull. The crowd fell into a stunned silence as the father's knees folded beneath him and he toppled sideways into the dirt. His son was roughly peeled from around his neck and tossed onto the road like a ragdoll. One of the older children scurried to him and picked him up, returning to the group quickly. The little boy was beside himself and couldn't be consoled. Kalu closed his eyes and felt stinging tears running down his cheeks. He knew that this was only the beginning.

CHAPTER 3

Nearby, James Cisse, the spiritual leader of Christown, was standing in the observation tower, watching muzzle-flashes lighting up Monguno against the night sky. His townspeople were in their houses, preparing for an attack, praying that the Boko rebels wouldn't venture from the neighbouring town. When the attack had started, he had spoken to the regional Inspector General on the telephone, who had said that he was aware of the Boko Haram attack on Monguno and that they couldn't get government forces there until late afternoon the following day. James knew that meant that no one was coming to help. The government troops had a knack of arriving when the rebels had gone. He didn't like to say that they were purposely avoiding direct conflict with the well-armed militia, but it did seem uncanny how they always turned up when they had left. They preferred to act on intelligence and pick up individuals or small groups, who could be tortured and brutalised as an example to the Boko leaders. Not that the Boko leaders took any notice. The execution of a few stragglers here and there was to be expected. The government took the safest option. They didn't want a real fight against Boko troops. The rebels fought with conviction and didn't fear death. They had nothing to lose. The government troops were low paid and wanted to go home to their families unhurt. The truth was, Monguno and the surrounding communities were too remote to protect. James believed that no one in power cared anyway. Monguno was a poor community with no commercial value to the government.

When the gunfire had started earlier, six men from his congregation had taken the children away from their enclave and had hidden them a few miles away in the bush. Another four men had taken the women, who were fit enough to walk, in the opposite direction towards the hills, where they would wait until James sent word that it was safe to return. James had tried to prepare his community for such an attack but all the training in the world couldn't prepare them for the real thing. Practicing didn't instil the sheer terror that they would feel when the sound of gunfire and humans screaming drifted across the village. He knew that they were vulnerable as a community. Recently, since the rise of Boko Haram, being a Christian in the north of the country had become dangerous. Boko were wiping out entire villages of Christians indiscriminately, selling the females into the slave trade.

James phoned the authorities, to no avail and then scaled the wooden tower with his town councillors and they listened to the attack in the distance. They had built the tower to give them a view of the road and the surrounding area. There was one road in and one road out. They could see vehicles approaching from miles away. It was built to give them some time to prepare if danger approached. If Boko decided to leave Monguno town and head in their direction, they would have ten minutes to hide the elderly and the sick. It wasn't long but it was better than nothing. He closed his eyes in silent prayer. Maybe the rebels didn't know about their community; he prayed they didn't but it was an unlikely summation. The Boko leaders were tactically sound and geographically savvy. They had to be to be able to roam the north as freely as they did and then vanish when government troops arrived.

A nudge in the ribs startled him. He opened his eyes and glanced at his colleague. Then his eyes focused on a column of headlights. They were travelling on the road from Monguno, heading towards them.

'Go now!' James ordered. 'Make sure all the weak are hidden. Get the men and head for the trees to the east. Get as far away as possible and do not come back, no matter what you hear.'

'What about you?'

'I must stay with the elderly. Don't worry about me, get our people away.'

The councillors scurried down the ladder and sprinted across the dirt road, knocking on doors. The townsmen came out of their homes with torches and rucksacks of food. Some carried rifles. They moved from house to house, street to street with practiced ease taking the sick and elderly to the hiding place. Within five minutes, James could see their torches flashing in the trees beyond the village moving away to safety. He could hear engines approaching; they were close now. It was time to climb down and take his place with the weak and vulnerable members of his flock. They had been made comfortable in a hidden corridor between two wooden barns. From the outside, it could not be seen and it was wide enough and long enough to hold fifty or so people comfortably. They had enough food and water to last until the next morning. James couldn't see the point in storing more. If the rebels found the town deserted, they would loot it and leave and the sick and elderly would be safe. If they stayed and searched it thoroughly, they may find them, in which case, they were dead anyway. They were too weak to travel quickly so they needed a plan to hide them and that was the best plan that he could come up with. Like any plan, until it was tested, the worth was anybody's guess.

James slid down the ladder and landed at the bottom with a thump. He could see the beams of the headlights searching the trees as the vehicles approached. He crouched low and sprinted across the dirt road which ran from north to south through the village. The barns were to the west, only a few hundred yards away. The single-storey houses would be between him and the intruders. When he knew that he was out of sight, he stood upright and sprinted towards the barns. He opened the door of the first one and slipped inside, closing it behind him but he didn't lock it. A door locked from the inside would give the game away. The wooden structures were high and wide, with vaulted ceilings. They were used to store sacks of rice, the farm equipment and animals if the rains were bad. James put his head against the door and listened. The rumble of vehicles told him that the rebels were on the edge of the community. He had plenty of time but the sound of gunfire gave him a sense of urgency. The rebels were announcing their arrival. James ran to the far end of the barn and knelt in the dirt. He tapped three times on a wooden hatch, which was almost impossible to see, especially in the dark. Muffled noises came from the other side. Hushed voices drifted to him.

'It's James,' he whispered.

A bolt clicked loose and the hatch creaked open. James ducked through it and looked around. Candlelight flickered, illuminating the occupants in an orange glow. The faces that looked back at him were old and haunted, frightened and exhausted. He smiled at them and some of them smiled back, some didn't.

'Close the hatch and blow out the candles,' James whispered. 'They're here.'

CHAPTER 4

B eb was blinded by the torchlight. He heard footsteps approaching him and squinted to see who it was. A blow to the head with the butt of a machinegun sent white lightning flashing through his brain. He sensed that he was falling but couldn't do anything about it. His jaw hit the ground first, sending another shockwave of pain through his mind. Pain coursed like electricity from his teeth, through his jawbone up into his brain, making his eyes water. He felt warmth trickling from a wound on his forehead and the coppery taste of blood filled his mouth. Someone grabbed his arms, pulling them painfully behind his back, tying his wrists together. His shoulders felt like they would pop from their sockets. He was yanked up, half dragged, half carried and dumped in the back of a pick-up. As they dumped him down, his head hit the metal bed, numbing his senses further. The voices around him were young and aggressive. He drifted in and out of consciousness as the engine started and the vehicle moved. The night air was cool on his skin. His eyes flickered open and he looked at the star-studded darkness above him, like black velvet bejewelled with tiny diamonds. Its beauty belied the violence that created it. His father told him that chaos and violence had created the universe and it suddenly felt that they still reigned on Earth. His world had been shattered and he couldn't see it improving any time soon.

Beb closed his eyes and drifted off away from the pain in his head. He woke when the vehicle stopped suddenly, wheels skidding noisily. The young men standing on the bed lost their balance and they shouted angrily at the driver and the driver responded with a tirade of abuse. Beb heard the tailgate being dropped and rough hands grabbed his ankles, yanking him towards the edge. He thought they might stop as his head and shoulders neared the tailgate but they didn't. They dragged him clear of the truck, his hands still tied behind his back. He felt the sensation of falling through a void and the back of his head hit the tarmac with a sickening crunch. He heard his father shouting his name. His familiar voice, cut through the others. Women were wailing, children were crying; it sounded like a scene from hell. He glanced around him. It didn't just sound like it, it was a scene from hell, he thought. As unconsciousness enveloped him, he decided that if he didn't wake up again, it wouldn't be such a bad thing.

Kalu watched as the militiamen dragged Beb from the pickup. He was dropped three-feet onto the back of his head. In the torchlight, he could see that his face was covered with blood. He was motionless as they dragged him across to where the young men were being held. They didn't realise he was just a ten-year-old boy because he was tall for his age. Boko didn't care about their age anyway. If he was strong enough to carry a machinegun then he would be forced to do just that, even if he was only ten. Kalu stared up at the stars and cried. He was distraught, his stomach tied in knots. The despair was debilitating. He had no idea if his son was alive or dead, his daughters were distressed and he had no idea where his wife was and there was absolutely nothing that he could do to help them. He felt like screaming until his heart exploded.

'Kalu,' a voice whispered from behind him. Kalu glanced over his shoulder. His neighbour, a carpenter, shuffled closer to him. 'Keep your hands still,' he whispered. Kalu felt cold steel on his skin as his neighbour cut him free. 'Don't move until I tell you. When I do, move backwards towards the alleyway. They cannot catch us all.'

'Are you out of your mind? I'm not leaving my children here,' Kalu whispered. He sounded ungrateful but could not think about running away from them. 'I cannot leave them.'

'Some of the other men feel the same. They're going to attack the Boko men. They will all be shot and killed but the decision is yours. You can't help your family when you're dead. Keep your hands behind your back, stay still and don't move until I say so.'

Kalu felt the rope fall away and he rubbed his wrists. The militiamen guarding them were distracted, chitchatting, smoking and drinking from a bottle of rum that they had looted. So much for being devout, Kalu thought. They were devout when it suited them. He looked around at the group of his fellow townsmen. There were sixty or so of them, all familiar faces. They were family men, not warriors but their sons and daughters were in peril and that changed the dynamic. Men change when their families are threatened, their boundaries shift; peaceful men could become killers. Kalu had no idea what he was going to do when the signal was given but he knew that he couldn't do nothing. If he ran to his children, he would be mowed down by the machineguns before he got ten yards. If he ran away, he would be hunted like an animal. He might make it, he might not. If he did, maybe he could arm himself and return although it seemed pointless. What could he do against so many armed men, trained to fight? What could sixty townsmen do against them? His mind was racing. Questions sprang from nowhere, most remained unanswered. Was it better to die running away or to die trying to fight for his family or was dying simply futile? Before he could answer that question, shots rang out. A militiaman fell to the ground and the square was silenced for long seconds, another shot rang out and a second militiaman dropped, then suddenly the square disintegrated into chaos.

'Move now!' a voice shouted. Kalu didn't know who it was but the group of townsmen rose as one. Men ran left and right, some ran in circles, unsure where to go. Some ran towards the guards but most ran away towards the alleyway behind them. Kalu was frozen to the ground, indecision held him. He heard the militiamen men shouting as two more of their group were shot dead. There was a sniper somewhere. From the corner of his eye, he saw muzzle flashes on the roof across the square. A townsman with a rifle was offering his neighbours the chance to escape before it was too late. Kalu admired his spirit. He had more courage than most. The militiamen were focused on where the shots were coming from and had their backs to Kalu and his neighbours. Half a dozen men hit them from behind like a human tidal-wave and they were overpowered quickly, their weapons taken and turned on them. Kalu watched one of his neighbours smashing the butt of a machinegun into the face of a Boko until it was unrecognisable as human.

The women realised that the men were free and they stood and ran in all directions. Some ran to their children, some attacked the guards with just their teeth and nails. Over three hundred townspeople reacted in unison and the militiamen were in disarray. The decision to send half of the convoy to Christown was an arrogant one. They thought they had total control of the town but they had underestimated the inhabitants of Monguno. The Boko leader barked orders from the back of a pickup and his men opened fire indiscriminately with no concern about hitting their own men. They had to supress the uprising before they lost control completely.

Kalu saw his wife stumbling through the crowd about fifty-yards away and he ran towards her, head down, crouched low. She was wandering in circles calling for her children. When he reached her, she looked at him as if he was a stranger. Her eyes were wide with fear; tears streaked her cheeks.

'It's me, Esse!'

'I thought you were dead,' she gasped, holding him tighter than she had ever held him before. 'I thought they had killed you. I couldn't see you!'

'I'm okay, Esse. We need to move, now!' Kalu said, taking her hand and pulling her through the chaos. 'The girls are there,' he said, pointing. 'I'll get Beb and meet you at the surgery. Take the alleyways and go to the backdoor. Do not stop for anything, understand?' Kalu touched her face. 'Do not go to the house. They will search the houses first. Do you understand me?'

'Yes.'

'Are you sure you understand, Esse?'

'Yes,' she said, nodding.

She glanced at the mayhem around her and then ran towards where her daughters were. Her heart stopped in her chest when she realised they had gone. One minute they had been there, the next they were gone. She looked left and right but couldn't see them. People were running all around her, gunfire echoed from the walls and the panicked screams were deafening. She looked around desperately for Kalu but he had vanished into the melee. Someone bumped into her, almost knocking her over. A woman fell in front of her but no one stopped to help her. Esse reached down and pulled her up before she was trampled to death. She gathered herself and ran to where the girls had been sitting. As she broke free of the crowd, she turned full circle. Her heart was pounding as she searched the panicked faces in the crowd. A soldier ran towards her, machinegun raised. He was screaming orders that she couldn't understand. The man next to her collapsed in a bloody heap as he opened fire. A gunshot from above rang out and the militiaman staggered backwards, clutching his chest. His eyes met hers as the light faded from them and he toppled forwards, dead in the dirt.

Then she saw them. They had run to their brother and were kneeling over Beb; Kalu was with them. He looked up and saw her and waved for her to run. Kalu picked up Beb in his arms and they ran towards an alleyway, the girls close to him, hanging tightly to his shirt. Esse caught up with them and put her arms around her daughters as they ran. Gunshots roared and bullets exploded against the rendered walls, showering them with plaster and stone. They bent double and ran blindly as fast as they could into a dark alleyway, which led away from the square.

The surgery was a half-mile away through a network of narrow alleys and backyards. As the family weaved their way through them, the sound of gunfire was fading, the screaming less pronounced. They heard engines and men shouting as the militiamen gathered themselves and tried to roundup their prisoners. Their vehicles prowled up and down the streets, crisscrossing the town to recapture people but the element of surprise had escaped them. When they first arrived, they had swamped the town and overwhelmed the naïve inhabitants with shock and terror. Corralling them had been simple then, but now the townspeople had dispersed and would keep running in every direction. Recapturing them would be impossible. They could hear the militiamen shouting at each other, anger and frustration filled their voices. The family kept moving steadily, stopping only when a vehicle passed the entrance of an alleyway. They were hidden by the darkness as they weaved through the lanes in silence. The streets were deathly quiet, their friends and neighbours hiding from Boko Haram.

Kalu slowed as they neared the back of the surgery. The streets of the tiny commercial area were deserted. The workshops and retail units were in darkness. He led them through a gap in some bushes, into the carpenter's yard. The walls were high and the locks on the gate were communal. A makeshift roof covered the area. Kalu laid Beb on the ground and took the keys from his pocket. He fumbled through them until he found the right one. The slightest noise made his heart race. Opening the lock, he bent and released the bindings from his wrists. Then he picked up his son. Beb moaned weakly.

'Is he coming around?' Esse asked.

'Yes,' Kalu said, smiling. 'Come on. Keep quiet.'

'Why are we here at the surgery, father?' Kissie, his youngest asked. 'Why don't we go home?'

'The rebels will search our homes first, Kissie. They will come and search here eventually but not yet. We don't have long to prepare.'

'Prepare for what?' she persisted.

'We need to get ready to travel and we need to do it quickly,' Kalu whispered. 'Now be quiet and get inside.'

'Travel where?' Esse asked, in a whisper.

'We need to go north. Away from here,' Kalu answered, as he struggled with Beb. 'We can work out where exactly on the way. We need to go north tonight.'

'North? Where to?' Kissie asked.

'That doesn't matter for now. We must leave.'

'You are upset, Kalu. He is upset; He isn't making sense,' she said, turning to her daughters, trying to calm them. 'It has been very distressing for everyone. Take no notice of him while he is upset.'

'Are you blind or stupid, Esse?' Kalu said, leaning against the wall. He sighed and shook his head. Pinching the bridge of his nose between his fingers, he tried to shake the weariness from his bones. 'I am not upset, Esse. I have watched our townspeople being herded like cattle to be slaughtered or sold into slavery. Did you not see what I saw?' Esse looked away, tears on her cheeks. 'Did you see it or not?'

'Yes. I saw it,' she admitted, reluctantly.

'Then you understand why we have to leave here.'

'How long do we have to go away for?' Kissie asked.

'I don't know the answer to that, Kissie. It won't be safe until Boko are stopped by the government. It could be months; it could be years. We may never be able to return.'

'We can't just leave our home, father,' Kissie said, holding back the tears.

'Did you not see what I saw,' he asked his daughters. 'Do you not know what those men would do to you before they sell you as slaves? They will rape you. Not one of them, all of them!'

'Kalu!' Esse hissed. 'There's no need to frighten them.'

'Oh, I think they should be very frightened right now. We all need to be frightened.' He looked at each one in turn. 'This boy here in my arms is your brother, Beb. Take a good look at him and then tell me that I am not thinking properly because I am upset.' The females looked at each other sheepishly. 'You have no idea how close you came to being taken away and sold to the traffickers.' The girls looked suitably rattled, 'Now, enough of this nonsense, get inside, please.'

'Surely, they will go soon when they realise everyone has run away,' Esse argued with his logic. 'They have never bothered us before. They might not come back, Kalu.' Kalu took a deep breath.

'Do you believe that they will leave Monguno emptyhanded?' Kalu asked her calmly. 'Do you think Boko will leave this as it is?' She couldn't look him in the eye. 'They cannot leave emptyhanded. Their reputation would be in tatters.' Esse looked sad and confused. 'Someone shot their men and their prisoners are all over the place. They will raze the town to the ground and kill everyone in it. We must leave.'

'This is our home, father. We can't just leave,' his eldest, Oke said. An explosion in the distance made them duck. They looked to the east and the horizon was lit by an orange glow. Kalu looked at their faces in turn as if to say, '*I told you so.*' But he didn't say it. Kissie started to weep.

'It was our home but it isn't anymore. They will burn everything down and kill anyone who remains. That is just what they do when things don't go their way. This town will be on their bad list forever. They will kill anyone who comes back and make sure that it is never rebuilt. We knew this would happen eventually. Now it has, we must leave.' Kalu waited for a response but none came. There was no more argument. 'Hush now and help me to get Beb inside.'

Esse opened the door and ushered the girls inside. The smell of antiseptic hung heavily in the air. Kalu pushed his way into his surgery and placed Beb on his treatment table.

'I need to stop the bleeding,' Kalu whispered. 'Push that trolley over here.' Esse reached for the light switch. 'Don't turn that on, Esse!' he hissed. She realised what she was doing and nodded, blushing. Their middle daughter, Isime pushed the trolley for her. Kalu washed his hands and cleaned up the wound before stitching it closed neatly. Beb was coming around, his face contorted in pain.

'How are you feeling?' Kalu asked.

'My head hurts,' Beb moaned. His memory began to clear. 'Where's mother?'

'Right here,' she said, leaning over to kiss his face.

'And the girls?'

'We're here too,' Oke said, holding his hand. 'You're going to have a nice scar. It will make you look like a warrior.' Beb smiled as she kissed him. 'How are you feeling?'

'Okay.'

'What happened to you?'

'I was coming back from Reverend James's when Boko arrived. They killed Omar, father,' Beb said. 'They shot him in the back and ran over him with their trucks. I told him to run but he didn't.'

'I'm sorry about Omar, Beb. They're evil men,' Kalu said, stroking his head.

'I need to tell his mother that he is dead and where he is,' Beb said, trying to sit up. 'His family will be looking for him.'

'Stay where you are, Beb,' Kalu said, holding him gently. 'We cannot go to his mother now. Boko have overrun Monguno. Nowhere is safe. We have to pack and leave tonight.'

'But what about Omar's body?'

'There are many bodies lying untended tonight, son. We can't help them all.' Kalu looked around his family. 'Truth is we can't help any of them now. We have to leave right now.'

'What about my sister and her family, Kalu?' Esse asked. 'We must find them.'

'And what about our friends?' Kissie added.

'Listen to me, Esse,' Kalu said, firmly. 'Boko will be moving door to door, street by street until everyone in town is captured or dead. We must leave and head north. We must leave now and we don't have time to help anyone else and we don't have time to argue. Your sister and her family and everyone else who escaped will be doing the same thing. They will all head north. You and Beb and the girls are my only priority. Once we are safe, we can try to find them but not before.' Esse folded her arms and sighed. The girls stood huddled together with their mother, too traumatised to move away from Beb.

'There's nothing more to do for you now, son. It will still hurt for a while and you'll have a headache but you'll live. It is a good job you have a head like a coconut.' They all laughed. Kalu put his hands on his hips and looked at his girls. 'I need you to be strong for your mother,' he said, kindly. 'I have been preparing for this for a long time. We will be okay if you do what I tell you to do. Listen to me and do not question my decisions no matter how bizarre they may seem at the time, understand?' They looked at their mother and then each other and nodded that they did. 'Esse, take the girls into the back room. Here is the key to the stockroom. You will find six rucksacks full of supplies and another bag with my medical equipment inside. Grab them and bring them back and while you are there, open the back door. Don't make any noise.'

'Okay,' Esse said, surprised at how assertive he could be. She was impressed with her husband's calmness and more impressed with his foresight. She paused before she left the room. 'Kalu, can I ask you a question?'

'Quickly.'

'Where are we going to go?'

'Europe,' he said, quietly. Esse had no idea how far that was but she nodded her head and did as she'd been asked. The girls stood, open mouthed. 'Go with your mother, quickly!' The girls filed out in silence. Kalu winked at Beb and Beb winked back, a smile lit up his bruised face. 'We'll be okay, Beb.'

'I know, father.' His father was the cleverest man in Monguno. If he said that they would be okay, then they would be okay.'

CHAPTER 5

Reverend James and the elderly and infirm from his community, waited in the darkness between the two barns. They could hear the trucks approaching and the rebel troops trawling the streets. Christown was a ghost town; its inhabitants vanished into the bush surrounding it. There was nothing to steal and no one to capture. Voices called out, echoing from the distance as they searched the unlocked houses and left them emptyhanded. The owners had few possessions, none worth stealing at any rate. What little money they had was on their person or hidden in the bush. The Boko Haram would leave with nothing and hopefully never return. At least that was the plan.

Reverend James was sitting on a crate, his fingers squeezed the bridge of his nose. His eyes were closed, his hearing tuned into the slightest sound. He could hear doors being opened, militiamen shouting into empty houses, furniture being tossed around and then doors slamming. It would be a fruitless search for them and they would be angry. Being outwitted would make a saint annoyed and there were no saints in Boko. James had planned it to the letter. If Boko invested the manpower and money to travel to a remote area like Monguno, it needed to pay dividends. They couldn't rob, torture, rape and kill when there was no one there. His scorched earth approach would certainly deter them from venturing that far again. The longer the fruitless search went on, the angrier they would become. And then there was their hierarchy to consider. Returning from a mission emptyhanded would be a personal failure and failure wasn't tolerated in the African militia, whatever their politics. The repercussions would be swift and brutal.

A rebel truck turned onto the street, its headlights pierced the minute cracks between the planks, illuminating specks of dust like tiny fireflies floating on the air. They heard the engine slow to idle as the militiamen climbed down and began their relentless search again. The sounds of wood splintering and glass shattering drifted to them. Their frustration was becoming more evident; the unnecessary destruction of property clearly audible. He heard a bottle smash and then the whoosh of flames. James got a whiff of smoke, tinged with petroleum. He had seen enough petrol bombs thrown to know what they smelt like. They were torching everything as a punishment for running away. James thought the mentality of it was mind-bending. Stay and be tortured, maimed, and sold into slavery or we'll burn down your homes. Their homes were poorly built structures with sporadic electricity supply and basic sanitation. The choice for the inhabitants was a simple one. Burn down our houses if you like but we won't be here. That aside, he was very concerned that the fire was so close. There was a narrow street between the residential buildings and the barns, which was designed to act as a firebreak but if the fire leapt the gap onto the farm buildings, he wouldn't be able to rescue his people from the smoke and flames. He listened as the truck crept closer and closer to them; all the time the smoke thickened. His people covered their noses and mouths with their clothes. He crawled between them, reassuring them in hushed tones that everything would be alright and that God was with them. Taking a bottle of water, he encouraged them to sip theirs. He didn't want a coughing fit to give away their position. The sound of the barn door being wrenched open brought them all to a standstill. They froze in the blackness like statues, not daring to breath. James prayed silently for their deliverance. The sound of his blood being pumped around his body was deafening. Rivulets of sweat trickled down his back. Three sets of footsteps entered the barn. The men ripped tools from their fixings and smashed anything that was breakable. All the animals had been released into the wild; better to try and recapture them than let Boko feed on them or slaughter them for sport but some of the goats must have lingered nearby. From behind the barn they heard machinegun fire and angry voices and then the sound of the animals squealing followed by silence. James knew that they had slaughtered the goats. The destruction of the interior of the barn had been halted by the gunfire but it began again in earnest once it had died down. The air was becoming thick with black smoke, burning their lungs and stinging their eyes. He heard the militiamen muttering to each other as they left the outbuildings. Peering through a knot in the wood, his heart sank when he saw burning torches thrown onto the wooden roof; flames leapt and crackled from one building to the other. He knew that they had only minutes to escape and the rebel truck was still outside. The voices of the rebels were clearly audible. He poured water onto his shirt-tails and put the wet material over his nose. The others followed suit but he knew it would only give them relief for a short time. They had to escape their hiding place, which had turned from refuge to tomb in minutes. Shots rang out from the distance. A firefight was raging somewhere beyond their enclave. It was coming from the direction of Monguno. Maybe the government had sent troops after all. He listened as the militiamen mounted the truck and the engine quickened, readying to move. His hands were on the bolt to open the hatch when an elderly lady succumbed to the smoke and began a coughing fit. One of the men nearby put his hand over her mouth to quieten her. James was sweating profusely as he listened.

'Stop the truck!' a voice shouted.

'Did you hear that?'

The engine quietened and James heard boots thud on the ground as the troops jumped down from the truck to investigate. As he peered through the spyhole, he watched the militiamen lining up, weapons aimed at the barns.

'Where did that come from?'

'From the barn.'

'I thought you searched it!'

'We did. Someone must be hiding in there.'

'Let them choke to death,' another voice called. James could see it was the driver. 'Hurry up! We need to go back to Monguno, now!'

The soldiers looked at each other, cocked their machineguns and then opened fire at the fragile wooded structures. James closed his eyes as bullets smashed through the walls.

CHAPTER 6

Kalu ran his fingers through Beb's hair and smiled at him. He turned and walked to his desk, pulling it away from the wall. Beb watched, fascinated as his father rolled up a threadbare rug and uncovered the floorboards. Kalu knelt and took a screwdriver from the bottom drawer of his desk. He used it to unscrew one of the boards and then lifted it clear to reveal the crawlspace beneath.

'What are you doing, father?'

'Emptying the emergency bank. Our journey will be an expensive one and there won't be many cash machines along the way. At times like this, cash talks.'

Kalu reached into the dark void, his arm disappeared to the shoulder. He grabbed a rucksack and pulled it up onto the floorboards. The door opened and Esse and the girls stepped in, each carrying a rucksack. They looked at their father crouched on the floor, confused expressions on their faces.

'What are you doing, Kalu?' Esse asked.

'Put the bags down here,' Kalu said, pointing to the space in front of him. Esse and the girls placed the bags on the floor. 'Each of us has a bag to carry. It is your bag to look after. Do not leave it for one second and do not give it to anyone else to look after. It is yours,' he explained. 'You must guard your bag as if your life depends on it, because it does. There's enough food and water in each one to feed one person for one week if it is rationed sensibly.' He opened the rucksack that he had retrieved and tipped the contents onto the floorboards. The girls gasped. Esse put her hands to her mouth as rolls of green dollars tumbled out. A small cloth bag hit the floorboards with a thump. Then Kalu took six mobile phones out and placed them on the floor next to the money. The last items were an old Smith and Wesson .38 revolver and a box of shells.

'What are you doing with a gun, Kalu?' Esse asked, her voice almost a whisper. She sounded shocked.

'It is to protect my family. I bought it in case of an emergency. This is an emergency.'

'I don't like guns.'

'Good. You shouldn't like guns. No one should. I don't like them either but it is coming with us nonetheless.'

'Where did you get all that money from?' Esse gasped.

'I have been changing money into American dollars every month and saving it for years; it was to send the children to university or in case of an emergency. This is an emergency,' he repeated. He separated the bundles of cash and put one bundle next to each bag. The remaining rolls were put back into his rucksack. Then he opened the cloth bag and tipped twelve gold Krugerrands into the palm of his hand. 'Now listen to me. We're going to try to fly to Europe from Morocco. From Europe, we can contact my brother and get visas to visit him in London. Once we are in London, we can apply for asylum.' He paused to look at their faces. They looked frightened and confused. 'If my plan breaks down and we get separated along the way, each of you has a phone, one coin and enough cash to get you passage across the Mediterranean to Europe. If, and only if we get separated, then you turn your phone on and find the others. Each phone has the other phones stored in the memory. We have one charger in each bag but we won't be able to charge them very often. We will not turn the phones on unless we are lost, understand.' They all nodded. 'The gold coin is your very last resort. Hide it well and tell no one about it. People will hurt you for the food and water that we carry but they will take your life for gold and dollars, understand me?' he asked. They all nodded, their eyes wide and frightened, full of uncertainty. 'You all know how to find north using the stars. We're going to head north together and we're going to stay together but if something happens and you find yourself alone, keep heading north to the sea and use your phone to find the others.'

'I'm scared, mother,' Kissie said, almost in a whisper. She clung to her mother's hip. Esse put her hand on her head to reassure her.

'You are scaring me, never mind the children, Kalu.' Esse glared at him. He was used to her glare. Sometimes it was enough to quieten him but that was only to keep the peace. Tonight, was not the time to back down. An explosion nearby confirmed that.

'We're all scared, Kissie,' Kalu said, holding out his hand. She grabbed his fingers and squeezed. 'I am not trying to scare you. All I am telling you is what to do if we are somehow separated. We have to plan for every event, okay?'

'Okay, father.'

'Do not worry. We will not be separated,' Esse said, firmly. 'I will not let any of you out of my sight.'

'Your mother is right, we won't get separated, we'll be fine,' Kalu agreed. 'But we have a backup plan, just in case.'

'I don't want to be separated,' Kissie sobbed. A tear broke free. 'I just want to go home.'

'I want to go home too, father,' Oke agreed.

'Me too,' Isime whispered. 'But I know we can't,' she added, hugging her older sister. 'Boko will take us from our family, Oke. We will never see them again. We can't go back can we, father?'

'No, Isime. We can't. We need to leave to be safe. We'll head for Morocco first but if we can't cross the border, we'll head for the sea.'

'How far is it to the sea, father?' Beb asked, quietly.

Kalu took a map from the rucksack and spread it on the floor. He gestured that they should come closer. 'If we can't cross the Moroccan border, we will go north through Niger and then follow the border between Algeria and Libya, heading for Tripoli; it's about two and half thousand miles.'

'Two and half thousand miles?' Esse mumbled, shaking her head. 'You make it sound like it is just down the road! How are we going to travel that far with four children?'

'We can do it. We have no choice. It's our only option.'

'Why can't we go south?' Oke asked. 'At least we will be in our own country.'

'She's right,' Esse said, 'We need to stay in our country. We cannot take four children two and a half thousand miles. It is madness.'

'South is through Boko territory; nothing but war and extremists. Our country is imploding and if we don't leave tonight, we may never have the chance again. If you want to live as free people in peace, then listen to me.' Esse took a deep breath and nodded. She knew that her husband was right. He was an intelligent man. That, said, she couldn't stop her brain from desperately seeking another option. 'This is our only option.'

'Okay, okay,' she agreed. 'What is your plan?' Esse asked.

'When we leave here tonight, we're going to walk from here, to here through the bush,' Kalu said, pointing to the map. The road was about ten miles north of Monguno. 'Boko will have patrols around the town on the main roads. We will bypass the Boko patrols by walking through the bush and then we will drive up the Kukawa-border road from here.'

'Drive what? We cannot go home and get the car.' Esse frowned. 'What are we going to drive in?'

'I have a vehicle stored in a barn, there in Marte.' Kalu pointed to the map.

'What vehicle?'

'An old Land Cruiser. I bought it two years ago and hid it there, just in case this ever happened. I hoped that it wouldn't but it has.'

'So, you bought an old Land Cruiser and hid it in a barn and didn't tell me?'

'Yes. Chika the mechanic has been checking it for me every month and I have enough fuel stored there to get us to the coast. It is an old vehicle but it will get us to where we need to go.'

'And where is that exactly?' Esse seemed miffed.

'Wherever we can get a flight to Europe. We'll have to keep our options open.' He paused. 'We can buy tickets online when we get there. We'll try and fly from Morocco to the European mainland.'

'What about passports?'

'They're in the truck.'

'In case of an emergency?' Esse mumbled.

'Yes,' Kalu said, a half-smile touched his lips. 'In case of an emergency.'

'How did you know this would happen, father?' Beb asked. He was impressed. His father was the cleverest man in the village. Probably the cleverest in Nigeria.

'I didn't know that it would happen. I guessed that one-day Boko would come to Monguno and I planned for us to escape. Now, can we stop talking and get moving, please?'

'All this planning you have done, Kalu. Why did you never tell me about all this planning?' Esse asked, frowning. They were close and she felt betrayed somehow that Kalu had kept secrets from her. 'Why all these secrets?'

'Esse, you worry about everything. You have a big heart and you even worry that you worry too much. I didn't tell you because I hoped that the government would get a grip of the rebels and we would never ever need to use them.' He smiled and shrugged. 'I put some safeguards in place to protect my family, just in case the worst happened. It has happened. We don't have time for this now. We need to leave.'

'Do we have to cross the desert, father?' Beb asked, recalling a geography lesson.

'Yes. There is a road that will take us across.'

'This is madness,' Esse said, shaking her head. 'We can't just head off across two thousand miles even if you do have a vehicle.'

'Do you want to travel north as a family and have a chance to remain free or travel east to be tied up like dogs to be sold, with Boko Haram?' Kalu, said shrugging. 'It is a simple choice because we have no choice.' The steel in his voice didn't go unnoticed. He was a kind, gentle man normally but his delivery had changed dramatically. 'Now, listen to me, all of you. No more arguments.'

No one spoke. Even Esse remained tight-lipped.

'When Boko invade a town, they put soldiers on the all the roads out of town to stop people escaping. We're going to walk through the bush to Marte on the Kukawa-border road.' He pointed to the map again. 'It will be a long walk in the dark but we will be safe as long as we leave now.' He looked at each of them in turn. 'We need to go. Pick up your bags.'

No one moved.

'Pick up your bags!' he snapped, loudly. The girls did as they were told. Esse stood stoic and glared at him. 'If you want to be angry with someone, Esse then look out of the window at the fires.' He opened the shutter a fraction. The horizon was glowing orange. 'Be angry with them, Esse. Be angry with the men who shot Omar, not me.' A tear ran down her cheek. She bit her bottom lip to stop from breaking down. Her children were watching her and she had to be brave. She knew Kalu was right. 'Now, pick up your bag and let's take our children to someplace safe, before it is too late, shall we?'

'Yes,' she said, nodding. She wiped her nose with the back of her hand and composed herself. 'I am very proud of you, Kalu,' she said, walking to him and kissing him on the cheek. 'You are a good father and a good husband.' She looked into his eyes and kissed him again. 'Now, hurry up. We must leave here. We're wasting time. We need to get moving,' she added.

Kalu raised his eyebrows, rolled his eyes and nodded. Inside, he sighed with relief. 'I'm hurrying, Esse. Let's go.'

CHAPTER 7

James fell backwards as the wooden planks exploded into splinters. He heard cries of pain, cries of fear and cries of outrage as bullets ripped through the walls and continued without slowing into the bodies beyond them. Warm liquid splattered against his face and despite the darkness, he knew it was the blood of his neighbours. The volley seemed to go on forever and it was all he could do to keep down against the ground and pray that none of the bullets would find him. Eventually the shooting stopped and the barn fell silent. The flames from the roof were casting the scene with a flickering orange glow. He heard moaning nearby and then he heard footsteps approaching the barn.

'Hey! Stop wasting bullets, you idiots. We need to go now!'

'Most of them are dead. Let the others burn!' another voice shouted. James could see silhouettes through the bullet holes on the front elevation. The men outside were peering inside.

'I'll leave them a present too,' someone else said. James saw something thrown through a hole in the wall and heard a thud in the dirt. The soldiers jogged back to the truck and the engine revved and then a grenade exploded.

There was a blinding flash and a deafening blast and the concussion wave stunned him. He heard moaning from the far side of the room and he heard the truck pulling away. The fire had taken a hold on the roof and embers were beginning to fall on the dead and injured. Long minutes went by before he could compose himself to move. He pushed himself up onto his elbows and reached for the bolt, sliding it open with a clunk. The smell of burning flesh reached him. Before he could push the hatch, it flew open and hands reached in and grabbed him by the shirt, dragging him through the narrow opening and into the barn. Punches and kicks rained down on him as he was pulled across the dirt.

'Did you think we had gone, fool?' A voice shouted at him. James felt his watch being stolen and his chain was snatched from his neck. 'I'll take them and look after them for you,' the voice sneered.

'Look at his clothes,' someone spat in his face.

'He is a preacher.' Another voice growled.

'Check if anyone else is alive in there!'

James was dragged out of the burning barn and dumped unceremoniously onto the street. Strong hands grabbed him by the shoulders and forced him to his knees. He tried to see what was going on in the barn and received a punch to the side of his head for his troubles. Bright lights flashed in his mind and he shook his head to clear the fog of pain. He could hear the cries of the dying from inside the barn. His eyes were stinging, his vision blurred.

'Help them, please!' James pleaded, coughing smoke from his lungs. 'Get them out!'

'They're all dead or dying,' a militiaman said, leaving the barn and closing the huge door behind him. 'Let them burn!'

'You can't leave them like that. Help them, please!' James asked the man who appeared to be in charge. He was wearing a camouflage vest and a red beret. His sunglasses reflected the fires. The man grinned coldly and shook his head. 'They are old and sick, please help them!'

'If they are old and sick, then it doesn't matter if they burn '

'Please, don't do this!'

Part of the roof that covered the hiding place collapsed, sending a shower of embers skyward. The flames retreated for a few seconds and then leapt forward and upwards with a whoosh and a deafening roar. There was a backdraft and a column of flame climbed above the building. The crackling of wood being devoured by flame was like the sound of firecrackers exploding. James closed his eyes and said a silent prayer as the cries of the infirm fell quiet. No one could survive the inferno. His faith was being tested to the limit and it was difficult to believe that his God was listening. The heat from the burning buildings became unbearable and the rebels dragged him further down the street. They forced him to his knees again. He heard a petrol lighter click and the smell of cigarette smoke drifted to him. It had been five years since he had smoked a cigarette but the urge to smoke one now was overwhelming. He stared at the Boko leader as he sucked on his Marlborough. Orange flames danced on his mirrored lenses.

'There may still be people alive,' James said, calmly.

'It's already too late. They're all dead.'

'Please.'

'Where are your people hiding?' the Boko leader asked, ignoring his pleas. James shrugged and stared at the floor, deflated and defeated. 'Tell me where the women and children are and I'll let them live. If we must go into the bush to find them, we will hurt them.' James looked at him for a second and then looked at the star-studded sky. Grey smoke spiralled upwards, carrying ash and burning fragments. He thought it ironic. Life was fragile. One minute a community lived in harmony, the next it was gone in a puff of smoke. There was no act of God to blame, no demonic influences responsible. Man's inhumanity to man was the cause. Nothing more and nothing less. 'I will not ask you again. Where are they hiding?'

'I honestly don't know where they are,' James said, shaking his head. 'They are in the bush somewhere. We tell them to keep moving. Your guess is as good as mine.'

One of the militiamen walked over to the officer and whispered in his ear. Both men looked at James, their eyes boring into his mind. The leader pondered what he had been told and nodded his head.

'So, they are in the bush.'

'Yes.'

'Okay!' the Boko said, happily. 'Let's go to your house and wait for them to come back, shall we?' he added. James was speechless. The thought that the rebels might wait it out had not crossed his mind. He had planned for a hit and run style attack. He opened his mouth but nothing came out. 'You look shocked. What is wrong?'

'Nothing,' James muttered.

'Did you think that we would leave so soon?'

'I didn't think anything.'

'We have come to stay. I like this town.'

James didn't have a clue what he was talking about. He remained silent.

'Are you the leader here?'

'No. We don't have a leader. There is a town council.'

'A town council?' he smirked. 'How very democratic.'

'We try to be.' James felt nervous and frightened. Sweat poured from his forehead and top lip. He felt that the Boko was toying with him, waiting for a reason to pounce.

'There is always a leader. Always,' a sly smile touched his lips. 'There is always a voice that people listen to when a decision needs to be made. I think you are that voice.'

'You're mistaken.'

'You are a man of God.'

'Yes.'

'Your house is the house next to the church, isn't it?' the leader said, grinning. James didn't reply but he nodded. There was mischief in the rebel's eyes, like it was a game. Like a cat playing with a mouse. 'You are reasonably young and fit yet you stayed with the old people. Why only you?'

'I stayed to comfort them. They were old and frightened.'

'Did you tell them that God was with them, watching over them?'

'Something like that,' James answered in a whisper.

'How did that work out for you?' he smiled again. Suddenly, the smile was gone. His eyes became cold and dark. 'Let's not waste any more time. Only a man with a sense of responsibility to the community would do that. I believe you are their leader, their reverend?' he asked calmly. 'There may be a council but you are the voice that they listen to.'

'I don't...'

'Lie to me again and I'll kill five of your people when they return.' The Boko leader smiled. 'No messing about. You are the leader here.'

'Yes,' James admitted with a sigh. 'I am.'

'Good. Now we have established that, let's go to your house and wait for your people to come back from the bush.' The leader waved his hand and a truck engine started, somewhere in the darkness beyond the orange glow. Headlights blinked and then illuminated six other trucks filled with troops. He hadn't realised how many troops they had brought. They had only seen three sets of headlights but there were many more. James felt sick. He thought he had tricked the rebels but they had fooled him. One of the trucks trundled towards them; the driver had his head out of the window as it approached, sunglasses on despite the darkness. 'Hide the trucks in the bush behind the church and spread the men out to the west.'

'Yes, sir.'

'I want you to drive your truck back towards Monguno with the lights on. Then turn around and drive back with the lights off. If anyone is watching from the bush, I want them to think we have gone.'

'Sir?'

'The people will come back soon, especially if they think we have left the town. They will be tired and hungry by now.' He looked down at James and grinned. 'You thought we had gone didn't you, reverend?' he gloated. 'Your people think that we're stupid, don't you?' James didn't answer. There was no correct answer, so he deemed it best to say nothing. 'Go now and spread the men out,' he said to the driver. 'Keep your eyes peeled and your ears open. They will be out there somewhere.'

'Yes, sir.' The truck revved and then reversed down the road, choosing to take the long way around to avoid the burning barns, which were on the point of collapse.

'We will take a stroll to your house, shall we?' the Boko leader said, smiling coldly. He gestured to his men and they dragged James to his feet, his arms pushed painfully up his back. The rebel soldiers reeked of sweat and tobacco. He could feel the hatred oozing from their pores. They despised him because of his religion. 'You can tell me all about your people.' He lit another cigarette. 'How many families live here?' James didn't want to answer any question that could endanger his people. He didn't think that question could put his community in more danger than it was in already. He was praying that the men in the bush would send scouts to make sure the rebels had left before bringing the women and children back. 'You can tell me, reverend. What is the harm in answering my questions?'

'There are sixty-three families,' James mumbled. The rebels, half carried and half dragged him. As they moved away from the burning buildings, the night air became cold on his skin. He turned to look over his shoulder when he heard the barns collapse. His heart felt heavy as he thought about those inside. He had known them all his life. To meet their end in that way seemed unfair. He felt sick inside. When their families returned, they would be devastated. He would find it difficult to look them in the eye and say sorry. The guilt was already weighing him down.

'Sixty-three families. That is impressive, reverend.'

James coughed smoke from his lungs. His eyes were still stinging. He could feel his legs trembling with fear.

'Are they all Christians?'

'Yes.'

'You are the last Christian community in the north now, you know?' the Boko said, conversationally. 'I should say you *were* the last really, shouldn't I? Past tense,' he laughed.

'Our community is of no threat to your people. We are a peaceful community. We mean you no harm,' James said, trying to appeal to a sense of humanity, although he knew he was clutching at straws. There was a glint of evil in the rebel's eyes. 'We have no issue with other religions.'

'We do, I'm afraid. We have major issues.'

'Surely, we should be able to live in the same country and coexist.'

'If only we could all say that and mean it and stay within our own little communities and live and let live. The world would be a better place, wouldn't it, reverend?' the Boko leader took a deep drag of his cigarette. He looked at James and removed his sunglasses. 'What is your name?'

'James. What is yours?'

'My name doesn't matter. It hasn't mattered for a long time. My men call me captain. That will do.'

'Captain it is. I think that we could negotiate here, captain.'

'Negotiate?'

'Yes.'

'Negotiate what?'

'My people's safety.'

'Why do you think we're here, James?' the captain asked, crushing his cigarette in the dirt. His tone had changed. His eyes narrowed and the corner of his mouth seemed to twitch. James shrugged and shook his head. It was another question with no correct answer. Better to say nothing than to offend a man with a machinegun and a machete hanging from his waist. 'Do you think we're just thieves and robbers?'

'I don't judge you or your men. What I think doesn't matter.' James rubbed his wrist where his watch had been unconsciously. What else were they? 'You are soldiers fighting a war, aren't you?'

'A holy war!'

'It is to you. Who am I to judge you or your men?'

The captain looked at him and smiled. He nodded his head and pointed his index finger at him.

'You're being diplomatic. I can see you're an intelligent man with a sense of responsibility,' the captain said.

''We only want to live in peace.'

'Peace is a commodity that we cannot give yet but we will eventually.' The captain stared into the trees. 'We are not here only to steal from you.' James didn't comment. Once again there was no right thing to say. Saying the wrong thing would be fatal or painful, probably both. 'Unfortunately, funding our activities is very expensive so, we have to take what we need to fund ourselves.'

'We have nothing of value.'

'You have people.'

'You take people from their homes and sell them to traffickers and you think that is okay?' James said. As soon as he said it, he thought better of it. He decided to backtrack. 'Surely, that can't be right?'

'Let me put it this way to you,' the captain said. He stroked his beard thoughtfully. 'Would you and your people come under our umbrella and live as we do?' James tried to find the right words but couldn't.

'The answer that you're looking for is no.' He pointed his finger at James. 'You would not conform to our beliefs because you have your own.' He paused and stroked his beard again. 'So, what do we do with people who don't conform, who don't believe, who won't embrace our beliefs?' he asked, looking at James for an answer. 'We could kill everyone, who doesn't believe but we don't. If they choose not to convert then we sell them. What is wrong with that?'

'You sell them into slavery. It is cruel, especially for the women.'

'It is a means to an end. People have a value, Christian women especially. Times are changing, James. Our message is spreading and gathering pace; it is only a matter of time before we win and, in the meantime, we have to finance ourselves.' James shook his head at the thought of the women being sold into slavery. He couldn't stomach the idea. 'Don't be too hard on yourself. You cannot fight against the inevitable. We will leave some of our people here in your town; to repopulate it. Your people will be offered the option to stay and convert.' He shrugged and gestured with his head. 'Of course, your church will be demolished and replaced. We will inhabit this area and Monguno and our people will flourish here. In five years, nobody will remember that you were once here. Our message will spread, one town at a time, region by region, country by country. You are in the way of progress, reverend and we wipe out anything in the way.'

'So, you are going to populate Monguno and our village with your own people?'

'Yes. That is why we are here. We need towns close to the border. The government doesn't send troops this far north. From here we will take the towns to the south.'

'If that is your plan, then take the town and let us walk away from here.' James said, stumbling. He fell heavily to his knees. The smoke had made him weak and disorientated. The rebels pulled him to his feet again. The captain looked at him, confused. 'It would be easier for you.'

'I don't understand you?'

'Let me take my people and walk away from this town. You can keep it. We will relocate, as you put it.'

'Where would you go?' the captain asked, frowning. He shook his head as if the idea was insane.

'North. I would lead them north across the border. And I would promise never to return here.' James said. He looked the captain in the eyes. 'I am serious. Let us walk away from here.'

'You are forgetting my need to fund our activities. There is nothing here worth taking. I would need compensation for my troubles. I must pay my men, clothe and feed them and put fuel in our trucks. Your people will be sold to pay for this.'

'I can give you money, if you let my people go free,' James said, nodding his head. 'I can give you money and some valuables from inside the church. Let us walk away from here in peace.'

'Valuables from inside the church?' the captain grinned. James nodded. 'Search the church,' the captain snapped. He looked at James and studied his face. 'We can take your valuables without making deals.'

'It is hidden.'

'Is it indeed?' The captain gestured to his men to take James to the church. They carried him towards it. The Boko soldiers opened the double doors and stomped inside, a look of distaste on their faces as if entering a Christian church would cause them to melt like a vampire in sunlight. The captain stepped into the arched doorway and looked around. It was a simple wooden structure with a vaulted ceiling and exposed joists. At the far end was a highly polished altar draped with white silk. Above it, hung a large wooden crucifix. Rows of narrow pews were separated by a single isle, which ran down the middle. There was no sign of any gold or precious metals. 'Take that thing down,' he said, pointing to the cross. Two of the men climbed onto the altar and ripped the crucifix from its fixings. The sound of wood splintering reached James outside. He knew this was the beginning of the end. It fell against the wall with a loud thud, that echoed from the walls.

His men tipped the altar over with a clatter. They looked underneath it and inside it and shook their heads to indicate that there was nothing there. The captain turned and looked at James. He shook his head and grinned and then checked his watch.

'You're wasting my time and time is precious to me.'

'I will tell you where it is if you give me your word that my people can go free,' James said. He sounded confident, assertive even, despite being far from comfortable. 'You can have the town. Do as you please with it. Populate it as you like but let us go in peace.'

'How much?' the captain asked. He slapped James hard across the face. James was shocked by the change of tact. He spat blood onto the floor. 'How much money do you have?'

'I'm not sure.' James mumbled. Another hard slap rocked his head sideways.

'Let us say that I am considering your proposition,' the captain said, smiling. He squeezed James' cheeks between his fingers and thumb. 'I need to know if it is worth my while.' He poked his index finger hard into James' left eye. James cried out and tried to pull back but the men holding him were too strong.

'Please, captain!'

'I'm asking you for the last time. How much money do you have?'

'Enough,' James said, panting. He had to remain calm. If he buckled now, all was lost. He tried to compose himself before answering. 'Let us walk away and I will give you the money.'

'You need to tell me where it is now,' the captain said, punching him hard in the stomach. James was doubled over, winded. He couldn't catch his breath.

'I can't do that,' James said, shaking his head. Saliva dribbled from the corner of his mouth. A hard slap shook him. Tears escaped from the corner of his eyes.

'Where is the money?'

'I can't trust you to let us go.'

'I don't see how you think that you have a choice,' the captain said, bending down towards his face. 'Unless you are stupid, you must see that you are not in any position to bargain with me.' Another slap split his lip. Blood trickled down his chin. 'Where is the money?'

'Please, Captain!' James gasped. 'It is a genuine offer.' He spat blood again. 'All I want is for my people to leave unharmed. Let us leave in peace.'

'Give up the church valuables as a gesture of goodwill. I need to know that you're not lying to me.' The captain grinned and pointed his finger again. James flinched, thinking he was going to poke his eye again. 'Tell me where they are and we can talk about it. Give me something to work with.'

James thought about it. He couldn't see how on earth he could broker such a deal but it was the only chance that they had. There was no way to trust the captain but he had to try. A slim chance was better than no chance at all. He looked to the heavens for divine intervention but none was forthcoming.

'Last chance.'

'The silverware is in my house.'

'Silverware?' the captain said, frowning.

'Yes.'

'No gold?'

'We don't have gold. We are a small community.'

'Where is it?'

'There is a cupboard in the living room.' James said, a knot tightened in his stomach. Had he given it up too soon? He felt like he had made a mistake as soon as he said it. 'Next to the table.'

'Is it locked?' the captain asked, surprised.

'We have no need for locks here,' James answered.

The captain gestured to the house next door. Three of his men went inside. After a few tense minutes, they returned with a box and placed it on the ground in front of the captain. He opened it and looked inside. It was obvious that he didn't know what he was looking at.

'That is a baptismal bowl and jug, our chalices, candlesticks, ciboria and a communion set. It cost over five-thousand dollars.'

'Five-thousand?' the captain said, nodding. He didn't look too impressed. 'Second-hand silver isn't worth much nowadays. Especially religious shit like this. It appeals to a very limited market. It is scrap. I'd be lucky to get a thousand for the lot.' He closed the box and took out a cigarette. His zippo clicked as he lit it and sucked deeply on it. 'You're going to have to do a lot better than that.' He paused and turned his back to him. The huge crucifix was leaning against the wall at an odd angle, looking more like a X than a cross. 'How much money is there?'

'I have some cash but I need assurances.' James swallowed hard. His throat was parched. Negotiations weren't going as planned. He was losing any grip that he had on proceedings. 'May I have some water, please?'

The captain nodded and one of his men placed a canteen to their captive's lips. James gulped greedily from it. When he was done he looked at the captain. 'Thank you.'

'Where is the money?'

'I need promises.'

'Cut out his left eye,' the captain said, turning to walk away.

'No, no, no!' James panicked. 'Okay, okay! I'll tell you.'

'Where is it?' the captain said, not turning around. He watched the treeline, searching for shadows moving. Somewhere in the bush his prize was hiding. He would round them up like sheep and send them off to be slaughtered, doing the world a favour.

'There is an emergency fund in the church,' James said. The captain eyed him suspiciously. His men had searched it. 'It is all the cash that we have. There is a hatch in the floorboards where the altar was.'

Two of the rebels ran into the church. The sound of wood cracking drifted to them from inside. They returned at a jog with a metal cashbox.

'The key?'

'In my back pocket.' James said. He felt like all his chances were ebbing away. Any leverage that he thought he had was evaporating before him. The keys were removed and the captain opened the box. He looked at the small roll of green dollars and then looked at James.

'What is this?'

'Five hundred dollars,' James said, nodding. 'We keep it in there just in case someone from the community needs a loan. It is just our cash float.' He tried to justify the trifling amount. 'We have more money elsewhere obviously, but it is a gesture of goodwill, like you said.'

'How much more?' the captain asked, stuffing the dollars into his pocket. He looked at James, angrily, punching him in the guts again. This time James vomited, almost choking as he tried to suck in air. The captain gave him a few minutes to recover. 'I asked you how much?'

'I'm not sure exactly. I would have to check online to be accurate.'

'Online?' the captain turned suddenly. 'What do you mean, online?'

'The money is in our bank account. I can check the amount and then transfer it to you once you have let us go.'

The captain shook his head and snorted. He looked at his men. Their faces were creased with laughter. James looked at them and saw nothing but contempt in their eyes. He felt like he wanted a big hole to swallow him up. Fear and embarrassment made him blush red. He felt like he had been stupid, pathetic even to try to deal with the Boko. Had he really believed that they would let them walk away?

'Let's be clear. You have no cash here?' the captain asked, slowly. He looked into James' eyes. James shook his head. 'Nothing at all?'

'No.'

The captain punched him hard on the nose. There was an audible crack as the small bones snapped. Blood poured from both nostrils. James felt lightening bolts flash in his brain. His head rocked backwards and his eyes rolled in his head.

'And you think that you are going to walk away from here for five-hundred dollars, a few trinkets and the promise of a bank transfer?'

'Yes,' James dribbled.

'How many bank accounts do you think we have?' the captain said, turning to his men. His men laughed raucously. A wide grin crossed his face. 'Have any of you brought your cheque books?' he joked. The men laughed louder. James felt the tension building. He was paralysed by fear. His throat was dry, like sandpaper. 'Maybe you could write us a cheque James?' James looked at the floor. He couldn't answer. It did seem ridiculous now. 'Could you write me a cheque, James?'

'No.' James looked up. 'I can make it a cash transfer to a Western Union.' His voice was garbled, difficult to understand. 'You could pick up the cash from there.'

The captain appeared to contemplate the idea. His eyes were focused on something inside the church. He shook his head and walked towards the house.

'Enough of this. Do you have food in your house, reverend? I need to eat,' he said.

'What about our deal?'

'What deal?'

'I thought we had a deal!'

'Tie him to that cross,' the captain ordered, boring of the reverend.

'No!'

'Tie him to it and hang it above the door of the church. When his people come back, I want them to see what will happen to those who defy us.'

'Please, captain!' James shouted, panic in his voice. A blow to the head stunned him. 'We can negotiate!'

'Cut out his tongue,' the captain ordered. 'I don't want to hear him whining anymore. James cried out; it was a howl of desperation. 'If you have any money to give up, reverend, you will give it to me now.' The rebels held James down and forced open his mouth. A razor-sharp blade sliced through the pink flesh and his pleas became a muted gurgle. His tongue was tossed into the dirt still twitching. His eyes rolled back into his head as the men fastened him to the wooden cross. 'That hurts, doesn't it, James?' the captain asked, lighting another cigarette. He studied James as they fastened ropes to the crucifix and hauled it into the air above the church doors.

'After a few hours on the cross, you will know pain. You have no idea how much suffering your saviour endured but you will soon.' The captain inhaled deeply. He turned to one of his sergeants. 'Have the men patrol the bush. His people will be nearby, tired and hungry. Set up a perimeter to the north. If they run, they will head north. No one is leaving here. Not a single person.'

CHAPTER 8

B eb left the surgery first. The night was hot and sticky, smoke tainted the air making his eyes sting. He crouched near the back wall and waited for his family to catch up. The road was clear as far as he could see but he could hear trucks rumbling out of sight somewhere near. Gunfire was sporadic and coming from all directions. The rebels had been spread thin across the town by the escaping residents. Frightened screams came from the next street. He looked at his father.

'If we go left and head between the bakery and the market, we should pick up the path through the bush,' Kalu said. The girls nodded obedience.

'No father,' Beb whispered. 'There is a barbed-wire fence behind the market now and they built a drainage ditch between there and the bush. It is too dangerous that way. The girls will not get over it.'

'Are you sure?' Kalu asked, confused. It made sense. Since the foreign workers had been coming in, theft from the market had risen. He had heard that the town council were planning to improve security to the rear of the building.

'When did you last run around the alleyways, hiding and trying not to be seen?' Esse asked. 'He does it every day. If anyone knows the shortcuts through town, it's a ten-year old boy.' Beb smiled and nodded. 'Which way is it, Beb?'

'If we go right and then take the snicket behind the school, it will take us straight into the bush. The path to the right will take us to Marte, where father has the truck.'

'Okay, Beb,' Kalu said, looking up and down the road. 'Lead the way. Keep moving and don't stop until we are in the trees.' Beb nodded. 'Is everyone ready?'

Beb crouched low and stayed close to the walls as he headed towards a narrow snicket, like he had a thousand times before, playing wargames. Little did he know that he would be doing it for real one day. He disappeared into the shadows and didn't stop until his family were close behind him. They passed the school and reached a patch of open land between the village and the bush. The pathway through the trees was clearly visible, even in the darkness. Their eyes had become adjusted to the night and the lack of vegetation on the path made it easy to see. It was less than a hundred metres to the path. They crouched and waited for Beb to move out into the open but he didn't flinch. His eyes were focused to the left, where the drainage ditch had been dug near the market.

'What is it, Beb?' Kalu asked. Beb pointed a finger towards the ditch, which was two-hundred metres to their left. He could see a group of people hiding on the edge of the market. There were at least twenty or so people there. 'They are making their way into the bush too. What are you waiting for?' he whispered.

'They are waiting for something, father,' Beb answered. He had spent hours playing war on those paths, trying not to be seen by imaginary enemies. The market was not a good hiding place. It was too open with little cover but it did have a good view of the crossroads nearby. 'I think they can see something on the road that we can't see.'

Kalu was about to speak when the group broke cover. They made it over the barbed-wire fence halfway to the drainage ditch before gunfire erupted. The darkness was pierced by blinding gun-flashes and the silence was shattered by the cries of the injured. They watched as the group was mowed down. Two men dangled from the barbed-wire, their limbs still moving weakly. No one made it to the ditch. Beb and Kalu looked at each other and nodded.

'Now!' Beb whispered.

'Let's go, girls!' Kalu encouraged them. The soldiers would be partially blinded by the gun-flashes and their focus would be on the wounded.

They covered the ground quickly and were swallowed up in seconds by the trees and bushes. Beb weaved his way along the path with practiced ease as he had done a thousand times before. They walked quickly and in silence. Each one of them contemplated the events of the day, their reflections were deep and dark. The ramifications of the invasion were earth-shattering. Friends, family, school, routine and normality were gone in a flash. No one wanted to discuss what they had seen yet and the silence seemed to be cathartic.

An hour later, they had travelled over a kilometre. When he felt that the girls were tiring, he stopped and crouched. They caught up and were grateful for the rest. Their eyes twinkled in the darkness, reflecting the starlight. Beb loved them. He didn't tell them enough but he did. Nearly losing them had cemented that realisation into his mind. He made a mental note to tell them more often. Esse took a bottle of water from her bag and handed it around. Everyone drank thirstily from it and there was no more than a sip when it came back to her. Kalu opened another bottle so that she could drink. She nodded gratefully.

'Is anyone hungry?' Esse asked. Beb and Kalu smiled at each other. Mother had no idea on how to be anything else but mother. Always worried about everyone else. 'What are you smirking at? She scolded Beb.

'You want us to have a picnic in the bush,' Beb joked.

'No one mentioned a picnic, cheeky boy!' she tapped his cheek with her fingers, playfully.

'All the same, we don't have time for eating, Esse,' Kalu whispered. 'We're not safe yet.'

'I am checking that my family are not hungry. We are in the middle of the bush, Kalu!' Esse hissed.

'Mother!' Beb put his finger to his lips. Esse looked horrified that her son had shushed her. She was about to tell him so when he pointed to their right. Two sets of headlights pierced the darkness, swinging left to right through the trees. They were on the Monguno road about five-hundred metres away.

'What is it?' Kissie asked, moving closer to her mother.

'Trucks,' Kalu said. 'Boko trucks.'

'Can they see us, Kissie asked, frightened. She buried her head in her mother's chest.

'No. They are too far away. There is no way that the drivers can see us.' The sound of their engines drifted to them.

'Where are they?' Esse asked.

'On the road from Christown to Monguno.' Beb used the path sometimes when making deliveries for his father. They watched as the trucks slowed and stopped.

'They have been to Christown too?' Isime whispered.

'It looks like it,' Kalu said, watching the trucks. The headlights were switched off and they heard the engines revving as the vehicles manoeuvred a three-point turn. 'You hear that?' Kalu asked.

'What is it?' Isime asked.

'They have turned around. They are going back to Christown with no lights on,' Kalu explained.

'What are they playing at?' Esse whispered, as if the truck drivers could hear her.

'They want people to think that they have left Christown and gone back to Monguno but they haven't.' Kalu paused and thought about it. 'They are setting a trap.'

'Who for?' Isime asked.

'I don't know,' Kalu said, thoughtfully. 'Maybe reverend James and his people had time to hide in the bush. They may be hiding.'

'And Boko want them to think that they have gone?' Beb asked.

'Maybe.'

'We have to warn them,' Beb said, excitedly.

'Listen to me,' Kalu warned. 'If the Christians are hiding in the bush, then Boko will have patrols scouring for them, most likely to the north of Christown. We cannot go anywhere near there.'

'I thought we were heading north,' Esse said, worried.

'We are,' Kalu whispered. 'Beb. We need another path that will take us further away from Christown. Do you know one?'

'Do you remember the waterhole, father?' Beb asked. 'The one shaped like a wishbone.'

'Yes.' Kalu nodded. He did remember it from his boyhood; the images came from somewhere in the mists of his memory. He wouldn't have been much older than Beb the last time he had seen it. 'I remember it.'

'The path forks there. The right-hand path skirts the village. The other one goes up over the ridge and they meet on the road near Marte.' Beb explained. He paused. 'I haven't been over the ridge for a while but the path should be easy to follow. It is longer though.'

'How much longer?' Esse asked.

'Not much,' Kalu lied. He looked at Beb to support him.

Beb nodded. Esse frowned at her son. She knew when her son was lying.

'Don't lie to me, Beb!' she whispered. 'I am your mother. Ignore your father and do not lie to your mother. Is it much further?'

'A bit further,' Beb said, biting his lip. The image of the rocky ridge standing way above the tree canopy appeared in his mind. 'And it's a bit of a hill too.'

'You haven't answered my question. How much further is it?'

'A few hours.'

'A few hours!'

'It doesn't matter,' Kalu interjected. 'We have to avoid Boko. They are shooting to kill now. You saw what they did at the market.' Everyone nodded. It doesn't matter if it takes all night. We still have to get to Marte.' Nobody argued. 'I need all of you to keep your eyes open. If the Christians are hiding to the north, some of the men will be armed and they will be twitchy. We don't want to be shot by our friends by accident.'

'I don't want to be shot,' Kissie said, quietly.

'Will you be careful what you're saying, Kalu,' Esse said, curtly. 'Pick your words more carefully, please.'

'Sorry, Kissie.' Kalu sighed. He couldn't do right for doing wrong. If it hadn't been such a desperate situation, it would have been comical. 'No one is going to shoot you.'

'But you said our friends might shoot us by accident.'

'It is just a saying, Kissie,' Oke interjected. Kissie turned her face back into her mother's chest and hid from everything.

'Beb, let's go. Lead the way,' Kalu said, grateful for the bale out.

Beb headed off and kept a reasonable pace. He was quite impressed that the girls motored on through the bush without moaning or whining once. They followed the path until they reached the waterhole. Animals scurried in the undergrowth, their evening drinking routine disturbed by the clumsy humans. Wings fluttered above them, mammals squeaked and grunted beneath them. Beb stopped and searched the darkness. He could see the fork in the path. He took the ridge path. It was lightly used and the vegetation was advancing on all sides, narrowing the path and making it more difficult to see in the darkness. Progress was slow but steady. A slight gradient became a hill. A hill became a steep slope and the slope gave way to the ridge. Vegetation turned to rock beneath their feet and the climb became a steep one. Beb thought it was like climbing a staircase. He slowed down and kept looking back over his shoulder. The females were struggling, Kalu keeping up the rear. As they climbed the rocky outcrop, they rose above the tree canopy and were stopped in their tracks. The view below them stunned them into a terrified silence.

'What have they done?' Esse asked beneath her breath. She hugged her daughters to her. Kissie began to sniffle. Beb knew that she was crying again. That was okay though. She was only a little girl. Older than him but still a girl. That is what they did. He looked out over the trees as Monguno burned to the west, much more than an orange glow on the horizon now. It was an inferno against the backdrop of the night sky. Flames jumped and leapt into the air, towers of spiralling red and orange. To the east, Christown was burning. From the ridge, it looked like a burning apocalypse. They stared dumbstruck for a long time. 'We can't ever come back to this place,' she said, as if to herself. 'There will be nothing to come back to.'

'Let's keep moving,' Kalu broke the trance. Reluctantly, the family began to move once more, upwards to the peak of the ridge. Their eyes were transfixed on the devastation below, causing them to stumble occasionally. The smell of burning timber floated on the night breeze. There was something else there too, something sweet.

'It smells like barbeque,' Isime commented. Esse and Kalu knew that it was the sickly-sweet smell of human flesh burning. There was no need to part with that knowledge. They kept quiet and kept walking.

'Watch where you are walking,' Kalu warned, tripping over a rock. He cursed beneath his breath and received a black look from Esse for his trouble. They moved in silence for a while. The path seemed never ending, as if they would keep going upwards forever. Their resilience was being tested to the limit. Esse was tiring and her breathing was becoming laboured.

'This is the top,' Beb announced, proudly. 'It will get easier now.'

'I need a drink,' Esse said, relieved. She had felt like giving up. If it wasn't for her children, she would have. They sat for a few minutes while Esse shared another bottle of water. 'Pass it around,' she said, organising as usual. 'Are you okay, girls,' she asked, fussing. They nodded that they were, although their eyes said something different. 'I know that you're tired but we have to keep moving. We can sleep when we get to Marte.'

'Are we ready?' Kalu said, standing. 'It is all downhill from here, literally,' he joked. No one laughed. They were too weary to see the funny side of anything. 'Let's go, Beb.'

'Stay in the middle of the path all the way down,' Beb said. It is very steep on both sides.

Beb nodded and set off down the ridge. The path was narrow in places, the drop either side was steep and dangerous. He had seen an older boy topple and fall to his death from the ridge. It had taken three days to recover his body because the slope was so steep. By then, the animals had begun to dispose of his body. He could still remember the stench of his rotting corpse when they brought him back up. It was a good thing that it was so dark. At least the girls couldn't see the danger below them. He didn't think that they would be happy if they could. Oke could climb but Isime and Kissie were wimps when it came to climbing things. They were not even good at climbing buildings, never mind trees or rocks. Still, they were girls so it was to be expected. There were things they were better, like sewing and cooking. He loved his sisters but Beb was glad that he was a boy.

As they crested the peak and started to descend, machinegun fire exploded beneath them. Muzzle-flashes flared from the trees near Christown. They crouched and huddled together, too far away to be in danger but shocked nonetheless. Frightened screams reached them from the darkness. The flashes appeared as a semi-circle in the bush. The circle tightened until the gunfire stopped and the screaming was silenced. They all knew that some of the residents of Christown had walked into a trap. After a few minutes of quiet, Beb stood up and moved on without any prompting. There was nothing to say. They all knew what had happened. Each step, each gunshot, each death steeled the need to escape Monguno. His father had been right all along but then he was the cleverest man in their town. Beb didn't know how many clever people lived in Europe but he was sure that father would be just as respected there. He picked his footing carefully as they cleared the ridge and descended into the cover of the bush once more; each one of the family welcomed the foliage and the cover it provided them. The further down they went, the narrower and more difficult to navigate the path became. Beb looked up and spotted the north star. Father had taught him that it was the only star in the night sky that does not move. The path was heading towards north. They were heading in the right direction. Even if they lost it for a while, they would be moving in the right direction. Beb looked behind him and saw that the family was plodding on in his tracks. He felt proud to be leading the way through the bush, taking his family to safety. His confidence was growing with every mile they put between themselves and the rebels.

A noise to his right made him stop. He held up a hand and his family stopped behind him. He put his finger to his lips. The sound of twigs snapping and dry leaves crunching came from below them. Then they saw flashes of battery torchlight. At least half a dozen of them. The beams strobed the bush, moving steadily north on a parallel track to their path. Beb could hear the chatter of hushed voices drifting to them. They were female. The thought of making contact crossed Beb's mind. Reaching out to others who were fleeing their homes seemed like the most natural thing to do but something told him to be quiet. His father shook his head and wagged his forefinger in warning as if he had read his mind. They waited as the column of women weaved a snake-like path north, a few hundred metres down the slope from them. It would have been impossible to communicate with them without shouting at the top of his voice. They were nearly out of earshot when a gunshot cracked the night. A man's voice shouted but the words were lost on the wind. More gunshots followed, accompanied by the high-pitched wail of women in distress. Angry male voices shouted orders in foreign dialects.

'Boko has found the women from Christown,' Kalu whispered. 'We must wait until we are sure that they are gone. Settle down and rest a while.' They watched and listened as the convoy was overwhelmed. There was nothing that they could do to help them now. It was difficult to listen to women screaming and not being able to help, even when you are ten. He had seen enough to know that the Boko would have no mercy just because they were female. If anything, they seemed to demonise women. They certainly didn't treat them as equals. Esse took another two bottles of water and passed them around. Beb slurped greedily from one of them. He watched the torchlight change direction and head south, back towards Christown as Boko herded the women through the bush. It would be a long walk at the end of a machinegun and he wondered what would happen to them when they got there. Monguno had been lucky that a lone sniper had saved the townspeople from slavery or death. Beb didn't think that Christown would be so blessed. They drank and ate some dry biscuits while they watched the torches fade. Kalu yawned and sipped the water. He winked at Beb. That made Beb feel good. His father thought he was doing a good job. Kalu opened his mouth to speak when all hell broke loose on the path below.

'What is going on?' Esse asked, frightened by the incessant gunfire. The weapons were being fired in all directions. Women screamed and wailed and angry voices shouted a tirade of abuse. Their voices echoed through the bush. The torches were heading in different directions, the muzzle-flashes following them, like an explosion of light moving away from the epicentre. It was like a bizarre lightshow being played out below them.

'I think the women have made a break for it,' Kalu guessed. 'They're running away through the bush.'

'Good for them,' Esse said. 'Better to be shot running away than to be raped by those animals and put into a cage and sold like dogs.' Her daughters looked shocked by her language. 'You listen to me,' Esse said to her girls. 'If they catch us, you run. You hear me?' the girls nodded, fear in their eyes. 'You run as fast as you can and you don't stop until you can't run anymore. Better to be shot in the back than molested by that scum and sold into slavery. You would be better off dead, hear me?' Kissie clung to Oke and Isime held her hand.

'Enough, Esse,' Kalu said, calming her. 'I think the girls get the picture.'

'I think we should carry on, father,' Beb said, watching the chaos below. 'Boko will be distracted for a while.'

'I agree,' Kalu said. 'Lead on.'

The girls looked weary and frightened but more frightened than weary. That was a good thing, Beb thought. Being frightened would keep them going. He took one more glance at the dancing lights below them and moved into the bush. The path took a sharp turn to the left. From here on, they would not be able to see the paths leading to Christown. There had been times when Beb had wished that they had brought battery torches but now he was glad that they hadn't. It was a sure way to be seen in the bush. Torches gave the game away, he thought. A torch was not conducive with hiding in the dark. It was a beacon for predators to zero in on. The convoy of women could be spotted from miles around. It was like putting targets on their backs and talking through a loud-hailer to let Boko know exactly where they were. Beb couldn't understand their stupidity. Why were they using torches in the bush and talking at full volume as if everything was normal?

Then, he remembered the trucks turning around with their lights off. The Christians were not stupid people. He had met lots of them. They had been tricked into thinking that Boko had left Christown. When they had seen the trucks leaving, they probably felt safe and turned on their torches. Boko were sneaky men. Father had told him they were smart and cruel. Now, he had seen it for himself. He wondered if there were any traps up ahead for them. Was there a Boko patrol hiding in the darkness waiting for them to stumble into their midst? Beb started sweating. He couldn't let his sisters see his caution. His pace quickened slightly, more to prove to himself than to anyone else that he wasn't weak. Frightened yes, weak no. The further down the ridge they went, the gradient began to lessen but the bush became denser. There were a hundred shades of black surrounding them. Shadows merged into shadows, some darker than others, some shifting, some impossible to penetrate. The feeling of being watched from the inky blackness was disconcerting. He couldn't shake the feeling. Every tweet of a bat or croak of a toad was a heavily armed rebel hiding in the bushes. His shirt was soaked with perspiration as they reached the bottom of the ridge and the path levelled out and joined the main path in a clearing. It had taken them three and half hours to cross the ridge and join the path again but they had circumnavigated Christown without falling into Boko's traps. Beb felt a huge sigh of relief. All he wanted to do was go to sleep. He looked at his family behind him. They all did. He could see it on their faces. The adrenalin had worn off and sapped all their energy from their veins.

'We're back on the main path,' Beb said, pointing back towards Monguno. 'Monguno is that way, Marte this way.' The horizon still glowed orange.

'Well done, son,' Kalu said, rubbing his head. 'It isn't far to the truck from here. Another hour or so at the most. Then you can rest.'

'Well done, Beb,' Oke said, hugging him. Isime joined in the huddle. 'Not bad for a squirt,' she joked.

'I told you that eating your vegetables would help you to see in the dark,' Esse added.

'You eat lots of vegetables but you were struggling,' Beb said, frowning. 'Could you see properly, mother?'

'I couldn't see a thing,' Esse admitted. They laughed. 'But I am old. How far is this truck?'

Kalu was about to answer when the sound of something approaching drifted to them. They could hear twigs being snapped and branches twanging against tree trunks. Something was moving quickly in their direction.

'Quickly hide!' Kalu hissed. Beb grabbed his sisters and pulled them off the clearing into the bushes. They crawled as far as the thick undergrowth would allow them to. Kalu and Esse were five metres away, barely visible in the darkness.

They waited, frightened and exhausted as the noise grew louder. A woman came crashing through the undergrowth into the clearing. She was breathing heavily and soaked in sweat. Beb could tell from her clothing that she was from Christown. She looked right and left, unsure which way to run. The sound of a pursuer came to him. They weren't far behind.

'Hey!' Beb hissed. The woman looked in his direction. 'Over here, hide!'

'Beb!' Kalu whispered. 'What are you doing?'

'Quickly!' Beb moved to the edge of the clearing and pulled the woman into the bushes. He could hear someone running towards them. They were only fifty-meters behind. 'Hide in there,' he said pointing to where his sisters were crouched. They helped the woman to hide and tried to calm her breathing. She was panting like a wounded animal and would be easy to locate unless they could quieten her. Beb was about to return to his hiding place when he spotted a rucksack in the middle of the clearing. It was one of theirs. Someone had put it down when they stopped and hadn't picked it up. It was a dead giveaway that they were nearby. The pursuers would fall over it.

'Beb hide!' Oke whispered. 'They are coming!'

'The rucksack!' Beb said, pointing. He ran from the bushes and grabbed the bag, slipping it over his shoulder. The pursuer was only twenty-metres away now. There was no time to run back into the bushes. He ran to a big tree and shinned up to the lowest branches and hugged the trunk like it was a long-lost friend, trying to melt into the bark and disappear. His chest was heaving and the blood was pumping through his veins. A Boko soldier broke through the bush into the clearing and stopped, searching the bushes for his prey. He listened, turning his head slightly, left and right, trying to locate his fleeing prisoner. The bush was noisy, insects, birds, reptiles and mammals were all going about their business through the night, unaware of the dramas being performed by the humans. It was a cacophony of sound, exaggerated by the darkness. The soldier stepped into the clearing and walked around the perimeter slowly. He peered into the bushes, weapon pointing and ready to fire. Beb followed him with his eyes. The soldier had a torch hanging from his belt. His hand moved to it and hesitated over it. If he switched it on and pointed at where his family were hiding, they were done. Only the darkness protected them. A powerful torch would penetrate the night and show their clothes. The soldier decided against using it. Turning it on would allow his prey to know exactly where he was. He listened and stalked the perimeter again, passing close to where Kalu and Esse were hiding. As he reached the point where the girls had entered the bushes he stopped and knelt. The vegetation on the ground had been disturbed. He touched it with his fingers and followed it away from the bushes. Beb felt relieved until he realised that the Boko was following his footprints across the clearing towards the trees. The prints looked like dark smudges against the bush carpet of rotting vegetation. The rebel crept slowly, one step at a time across the clearing. In the middle was a dark patch where the rucksack had been. The soldier crouched and touched the ground, eyes following the tracks. He stood and walked towards the tree were Beb was hiding. The footprints stopped at the base. Reaching for his torch, he looked up into the branches, machinegun raised. Beb was frozen to the trunk, heart pounding in his chest, breath stuck in his lungs. The Boko had found him. He would switch the torch on and see him and then he would shoot him dead in the tree. All because he had grabbed the rucksack. The torch came on illuminating Beb in the branches, dazzling him; he held his breath and waited for the bullets to smash into his body. His eyes met the soldier's. They were cold and dark. There was no compassion in them. It didn't matter that the person up the tree was a boy. Beb heard the safety click and closed his eyes. The gunshot was deafening.

CHAPTER 9

When Beb opened his eyes, the soldier was face down in the undergrowth. The back of his head was a bloody mess. His father was standing over the body, the revolver still in his hand. His mother was at the edge of the clearing, shaking like a frightened dog. The girls were crawling out of their hiding place, helping the woman from Christown.

'Father!' Oke gasped. 'Help her. She has been shot.' Kalu looked up into the tree at Beb. He didn't look angry, he didn't look sad. There was a cool acceptance in his eyes, which Beb hadn't seen before. The choice had been between shooting the Boko or losing a child. It wasn't really any choice at all. Beb thought about climbing down but he couldn't let go of the tree. His limbs were locked with fear. 'Quickly, father, she's bleeding a lot.'

Kalu tucked the revolver into his belt and walked over to the injured woman. He knelt and looked at her, moving her hand from a bullet wound in her abdomen. The rent was wide and jagged and he knew it wasn't the entry wound. He reached around beneath her and felt around. The entry wound was below her shoulder blade. He looked at Oke and shook his head. The woman was covered in a sheen of cold perspiration. Kalu had seen it before. She was going into shock, lips trembling, eyes wide and staring. Her body began to shake and then suddenly, she was still. Kalu closed her eyes.

'Is she dead?' Kissie asked, her voice a whisper. Kalu nodded and touched her face. She held his hand and squeezed it tightly. 'The poor woman.'

'Get down from that tree, Beb,' Kalu said, standing. 'Get your things, everyone. We need to go now. There may be more of them coming this way.'

Beb peeled his limbs from the tree and jumped down. His knees felt weak. The dead Boko was already attracting the attention of insects. It made Beb feel queasy. He dumped the rucksack onto the ground and looked for the culprit.

'Who left their rucksack in the middle of the clearing? If the Boko had seen that, he would have known that we were here.' He pointed to the bushes where they had been hiding. 'Who left their bag behind?' Beb asked again. Everyone looked around at each other. The girls all had a rucksack on their back. Mother had hers but she felt it to make sure that it was on her back. Kalu patted his and looked Beb in the eye as realisation dawned.

'You did,' Kalu said, calmly. 'And you nearly died because of it.'

'What were you thinking, Beb?' Esse asked. She shook her head and hugged her son. 'Please do not do anything so stupid again. My old heart will not last the night.' She squeezed his cheeks. 'No more heroics, please!'

Beb was embarrassed. He felt like he had gone from hero to zero in sixty seconds flat.

'You made a decision with no time to think about it, Beb,' his father said, matter of factly. 'Don't beat yourself up. You are ten-years old.' Kalu rubbed his head. 'Can you lead us to Marte from here?'

Beb nodded, feeling better instantly. He slipped his arms into his rucksack. 'This path will take us there.' He looked at the bodies again. 'What about them?'

'The jungle will take care of them,' Kalu said. 'We don't have time. Let's go.'

Beb nodded and headed up the path. His knees were still weak and his palms were sweating. He rubbed them on his shirt as he walked. They walked for over an hour in silence. The path became wider as they neared Marte and the bush thinned out. The sun was beginning to rise as they reached the road. A thin blue line appeared on the horizon, chasing the stars across the sky. Beb felt relief and exhaustion as they stepped out of the bush. His family looked bedraggled.

'How far now?' Esse asked. Her face was drawn and tired. The sparkle in her eyes was not so bright.

'A kilometre north,' Kalu said. They all looked at the sky and turned left. Kalu smiled inside. He had taught them all how to read the stars. It was reassuring that his children were smart enough to listen. 'Keep to the side of the road,' Kalu warned. 'If you hear a vehicle coming, we'll hide in the bush.'

The road was deserted and they reached an old small holding that hadn't been worked for years. The wooden house had collapsed on one side and the roof was virtually non-existent. Trees grew through the rotting structure as mother nature claimed the land back for herself. Kalu turned off the road and walked towards it.

'Is this it?' Oke asked, confused. They followed their father behind the ruin to where an outbuilding stood. It was low and flat and was wide enough to fit two vehicles side-by-side. It had been repaired and the roof had been replaced with new sheets of corrugated iron. 'Who owns this place, Father?'

'No one, really. I'm just borrowing it.'

'You are borrowing a derelict farm?' Esse asked, sarcastically. 'Is that even legal? All this going on and we could be arrested too!' Beb smiled at his mother's sarcasm. 'I think an explanation is in order.'

'An old patient of mine left it to his son but he emigrated in a hurry and couldn't sell it before he left,' Kalu said, looking over his shoulder. Esse looked at him, open mouthed. 'Close your mouth, Esse. You look like you are catching flies.' Esse raised her eyebrows and frowned. 'I was going to buy it from him as a surprise for you but I'm glad that I didn't now. The old man was a patient of mine so I made his son an offer but I didn't hear from him again. I planned to renovate it and sell it on but never got that far. I'm sure that I mentioned it to you,' Kalu added, walking to the outbuilding.

'You mentioned borrowing a farm in Marte?' Esse wasn't letting him off the hook. 'I think I might have remembered that conversation.'

Kalu winked at Beb. He took a key from his pocket and reached for the lock. 'There is a well over there and the water is clean. It would make a decent farm for someone.' He paused and reflected on what he had said. 'Well, it would have yesterday, not so much anymore.'

'Father' look!' Beb said, pointing down the road, back the way they had come from. Kalu was focused on the lock. Esse and the girls looked and gasped. He was distracted and tired. 'Father. I think you should look now.' The urgency in his voice made Kalu stop what he was doing. He turned and looked down the road. People were streaming out of the bush onto the road. Dozens of them. 'They are the people of Christown,' Beb said as men, women and children gathered on the road. He could tell by their clothes. Some of them spotted Beb and his family. They waved and spoke to their friends and families as they emerged from the trees, helping those who were too exhausted to stand. A steady stream of people poured from the bush as far as the eye could see. Some of the people nearest walked towards the old farm to talk to Kalu and his family.

CHAPTER 10

One of the elders from Christown greeted him. 'Hello Esse, Beb, girls,' he raised a hand in a half wave. 'I am glad to see you're all okay.' The exhaustion was etched into every line of his wrinkled face. 'We didn't know for sure that it was you in the bush but I am glad it is.'

'I'm sorry?' Kalu didn't understand.

'We followed you through the bush. We found the dead Boko and knew that you were on our side so we followed you along the path to here. We were lost and disorientated and many of our people were ready to turn back.'

'How many of you made it?' Kalu asked, looking at the gathering crowd that was growing in numbers every minute. Many of them had collapsed onto the road, relief and exhaustion combining to demand rest.

'About half the families at a guess,' the elder said, looking at his people. 'Well over a hundred people. We tried to gather everyone together but some would not listen to reason. The elderly were hidden in the village. People wanted to believe that their parents were still alive. They thought that Boko had gone back to Monguno.'

'We saw them turning the trucks around and turning the lights off,' Kalu said, thoughtfully. 'They were well organised.'

'They were. We thought that we were but we underestimated them.'

'We all did, to be honest.'

'It could have been worse, much worse. We were lucky that we bumped into our womenfolk being herded back to the village. It was pure chance. They would be in chains now otherwise. We ambushed them. Some of our people are injured, Dr Kalu.' He gestured to the growing crowd. 'We could do with your help.'

Kalu looked at the key in his hand and then looked at the faces of his children. The wise thing to do would be to get into the truck and leave the area immediately but he couldn't do nothing. He nodded at Esse. She knew the conflict that was going on behind his eyes and she knew which side he would come down on.

'Bring the injured over here,' Esse said, making his decision easier. 'There is a well over there. The water is good. Let your people drink and rest.' The elder nodded and waved his people over.

'Thank you,' he said, gratefully.

'Beb,' Kalu said, throwing the keys to him. 'There are more supplies in the barn. Open it up and share out some of the food. There are some medical kits in there too. Bring them out for me, please.' Beb put the key in the lock and dragged one side of the double-doors open. A sliver Land Cruiser was parked inside. It was in good condition, clean and tidy. The tyres looked new. There were spare water and fuel containers strapped to the sides and a ladder ran to a roof-rack on top of the vehicle. A spare wheel was bolted to each rear door. It had been fitted out to cross the harshest terrain. Beb was impressed as he walked around it.

'Did reverend James escape?' Kalu asked. The elder shook his head, a grim expression on his face.

'He stayed behind with the elderly and sick. They killed them all and set fire to the building. We sent scouts back to check if they had gone. One of the men said that James had been crucified above the church doors.'

'Poor James,' Kalu said. 'He was a good man.'

'He was. Not that it matters to Boko. Crucifying any man takes a special kind of evil.'

Esse and the girls looked shocked by the news. Kalu could sense their fear growing. They had been brave on the journey through the bush, being on the move had given them a sense of hope; travelling gave them the sensation of escape. Now that they were static, their sense of vulnerability became acute. Boko could burst from the bush any second. He needed to get them to safety as soon as possible.

'You need to keep your people moving,' Kalu said, pointing to the north. 'Boko will follow you. They know that you will head north and they will fancy their chances of rounding you all up before you reach the border. They will wait for first light and then follow you. You won't have long.'

'I fear the same thing,' the elder said, nodding. 'But we can't move quickly with this many people. Add to that we have nowhere to go and we're faced with a real quandary.'

'Let's deal with the gunshot wounds first,' Kalu said, as the wounded were carried over. 'I can only patch them up so that you can keep moving. I will do the best that I can with what I have available.' He paused to think. 'I may have an idea.'

'We are very grateful for your help, Dr Kalu.'

Beb carried a cardboard box of wheat crackers from the outbuilding and put it down next to the girls. They opened it and began to distribute them amongst the stragglers. Water was pumped from the well and makeshift drinking vessels were crafted from all kinds of objects. Some of the Christians had water bottles with them from their spell hiding from Boko. Their food supplies had run dry overnight and the crackers were devoured quickly. Beb went back inside the outbuilding and came back with a large box of dried dates. The girls helped to hand them out while Esse and Kalu treated the injured. After an hour or so, the crowd was settled and resting. Many were sleeping, some were crying, mourning loved ones while some just stared into the sky, trying to make sense of what had happened. Beb opened the Land Cruiser and climbed into it. The girls followed suit and climbed into the back seat. Kalu walked over to the truck.

'Get comfortable and sleep for a while. We will leave soon.' He opened the glove box and checked inside. Their passports were there along with other identity documents, birth certificates and his driving license. He took out his mobile, switched it on and checked the signal. Nothing. Beb switched on the radio, but there was nothing but static. Boko had destroyed all communications networks. They made sure that the government had no idea what they were up to until it was too late. The true body count caused by their activities would never truly be known. Kalu walked around the truck and checked everything was ready to go.

When Kalu was happy that he couldn't do anymore, he walked over to where the Christown men were sitting. They appeared to be holding a council meeting. Their conversation stopped as Kalu approached. All eyes turned to him.

'Thank you for what you have done for our people, Dr Kalu,' one of them said. Kalu knew him as Joseph. 'We realise that we have eaten into your supplies.' He gestured towards the outbuilding. 'I see that you were well prepared for this?'

Kalu looked at the Land Cruiser. Beb was sleeping in the front seat, Esse and the girls were sleeping in the back. Everything that he loved was right there inside a fifteen-year old lump of scrap. He scanned the boxes piled up around it. There were tins of vegetables and fruit, dried biscuits and powdered milk. He had no idea how he had stockpiled so much. There was no way that he could carry it all. Every time a wholesale lot of non-perishables came along, he had bought it.

'I always dreaded Boko coming to Monguno. I hoped the government would smash them first but they are useless,' Kalu said, shaking his head. 'I made an escape plan in case they came. You need to make one too.'

'We had plans for Boko raiding too but they didn't include never going back to Christown. We thought they would come and go just as quickly. Wishful thinking on our part. Reverend James thought that they would see no value in an empty town and move on. It seems that they're not willing to leave emptyhanded. We were not prepared to leave our homes permanently.'

'Boko won't give up. They will chase you down.' Kalu shrugged. He was convinced that they were stalking their way through the bush as they spoke. 'You need to cross the border into Niger and take your chances from there.'

'Where are you heading for?' Joseph asked.

'Morocco,' Kalu answered. 'We'll try to fly from there to Europe.'

'You mean to cross the desert in Algeria?'

'We'll have to.'

'Be careful. The Tuareg tribes have become affiliated to Boko, Kalu.'

'I heard that,' Kalu said.

'They roam the Sahara like pirates. It is them who traffic people and drugs across the deserts for Boko. They are beyond being policed. You will need to be very careful using that route.'

'We will.'

'They have become a plague on North Africa.'

'Once we get to the Algerian border, I'll have to decide which way is the safest. Until then, I'm just guessing.' Kalu shrugged and rubbed his tired eyes. 'One way or the other, we need to get to Europe.'

'Sounds like a plan to me,' Joseph said, with a sigh. He looked around at his people and felt despair. What could he do with so many homeless people? They would look to him for answers and he didn't have any. 'I'm not sure what we will do.'

Kalu went to his bag and took out the map. He walked back to the council meeting and spread the map out on the floor.

'If you head north and stay on this road, you will come to the Niger border here at Diffa. I would head that way.'

'That is over a hundred miles.' One of the men complained. 'It is an impossible journey with so many.'

'You could walk it in four days, even with your wounded.' Kalu argued. 'There are two who need hospital care and won't be able to walk. I can strap them to the roof of our truck and carry them to the border. I will take them to the Red Cross camp. You can pick them up when you get there. It will lighten your burden. The rest are capable of walking.'

'We would still never make it all that way,' the man complained. 'If Boko come after us, we're sitting ducks.'

'What other choice do we have?' Joseph asked.

'There must be another way.'

'Think about it. What choice do we actually have?'

'We could sit here and wait for Boko to find us, you fool!' another man snapped, angrily. 'What are we arguing about?'

'We can't go back,' another agreed.

'There can be no discussion. Dozens of our people are dead or in chains. We must move or die. The doctor is right. Boko are not here for a daytrip, they're invading, taking over the district of Monguno.'

'Can they do that?' a man asked. 'I mean do they have that kind of force?'

'How many people are in the district?' someone asked.

'Over one-hundred thousand in the towns and the surrounding districts,' Kalu answered. 'Only time will tell how many of them have been displaced. We have no way of knowing what has happened in the other towns. All communications are down. Our mobile phones have no signal and the radio in the truck is dead.'

'Kalu is right. We must cross the border or we walk back and save them the job of finding us.'

'And what do you suggest we feed our people with?'

'We won't have to feed them if they're dead, you idiot.'

'You want to walk a hundred miles, and I'm the idiot?'

'Please stop arguing!' Kalu interrupted. The men looked at him. 'There is enough food in the barn there to get you to the Niger border. You can take as much water from the well as you need. I will stop in each village along the way and buy water and supplies and leave them for you to pick up when you arrive. You can make it from one town to another with supplies.'

'Thank you, Kalu,' Joseph said, gratefully. 'You don't need to buy it. We have money but you could order it for us. I would be grateful if you let them know that we will be passing through and will need to purchase bottled water. That would be a great help.'

'Maybe we can make it but what do we do when we get to Diffa?'

'We will have to see when we get there.' Joseph looked at his people. They nodded that it made sense.

'You can stop looking over your shoulder for one thing,' Kalu said, looking the man in the eye. The man didn't argue. 'I know that there are Christian communities in Diffa and in the next town, Basee. You can ask them for shelter. It isn't perfect but it is the best you can do for now. At least you will be safe. You need to get your people away from Boko and get across the border.'

'You are right. Thank you, Kalu,' Joseph said, nodding. He looked at the other elders. 'Unless anyone has a better idea, we are heading for the Niger border.' No one disagreed. 'We're grateful for your help. We couldn't make it to the border without your offer to carry our wounded. You're very kind.'

'Have your people strap the wounded to the roof rack and wrap them up well. The sun will be up soon, they'll burn if they're exposed. Hopefully, we'll be there before it gets too hot.'

'See to it,' Joseph ordered his men. They watched in silence as the wounded were carried to the Land Cruiser and made comfortable. 'I cannot thank you enough, Kalu. We would lose many more without your help.'

'You're welcome. Let's swap numbers. When the signal comes back on, I'll contact you and let you know where they are.' They exchanged numbers but the network was still down. 'Now I'm afraid that I must leave and I suggest that you do the same. Don't wait here too long.'

'How far is your journey, Kalu?' Joseph asked, standing to shake his hand.

'To Morocco, three-thousand miles. If we can't cross the border from Alegria then we will have to head for the Libyan coast. That is closer but more dangerous.'

Joseph nodded. 'It seems that we all have difficult journeys to make. Good luck, Kalu. God bless you and your family.'

'The same to you, Joseph.' They embraced and patted each other on the back, almost certain that they would never meet again.

Kalu picked his way through the sleeping throng to the outbuilding. His family were sleeping soundly in the vehicle. He looked into the back window and checked their supplies. Then he walked around the vehicle again and counted the fuel containers. There were six. He would have to fill up the tank three times and use the containers only when there were no petrol stations in reach. He looked at the boxes of food and thought about the people outside. They needed that food more than Kalu and his family did. Kalu had money and he had money in the bank. Once they had crossed the border into Niger and then Algeria, then it was a mere thousand miles to Morocco where things would be normal. Getting away from Boko was the priority. Satisfied that he had everything that they needed for the journey, he climbed into the driver's seat. Beb stirred from his slumber and opened his eyes.

'Is everything okay, father?' he asked, groggy from sleep.

'Everything is as okay as it can be, son,' Kalu answered. He turned the key in the ignition and the engine started first time. 'We are going to head for the border at Diffa. We should be there in a few hours. Close your eyes and go back to sleep, Beb.' Kalu engaged first gear and pulled the Land Cruiser out of the outbuilding. 'It has been a very long night.' Beb smiled and closed his eyes and was asleep in seconds.

The crowd of refugees from Christown parted as he crawled to the road. He opened the window as Joseph approached the vehicle. 'I've left the food for you. You're need is greater than ours. We'll be at the border in a few hours. When we get to Diffa, I will find the Christian leaders and tell them of your plight. Good luck.' Joseph shook his hand again and waved goodbye. Kalu pulled the cruiser onto the road and accelerated. His heart sank as he watched the crowd growing smaller in the rear-view mirror. It felt wrong to leave them there but he couldn't help everyone. His family was his priority and he had to get them out of the country.

CHAPTER 11

Kalu drove the cruiser as fast as he dared, considering the load it was carrying. He was concerned about the wounded on the roof. The containers of liquid strapped to the body made cornering difficult; the shifting weight made the vehicle lean and wobble, like driving a boat. All along the route, there were people pouring out of the bush from the south, all heading north towards the border. Most were strangers but he recognised some of the faces as neighbours and patients from Monguno. Passing them without stopping to offer help was contrary to everything he held precious but there were so many of them. He couldn't help them all and their supplies were limited. The closer to the border he drove, the more people there were. Dozens turned to hundreds, hundreds turned into thousands. It was a constant stream of human misery, pushing hand carts or trolleys with their entire lives piled on them. Others were carrying nothing more than water containers and small children. They all had the same look in their eyes; desperation and uncertainty were etched onto their faces.

When they reached a town called, Zari, he stopped next to a provisions store. Kalu had been there once before, as a child with his father. It stood alone on the corner of the main street and had a solid frontage with no glass in the windows. He didn't think it had changed appearance for forty years. The door was guarded by two men armed with shotguns. Kalu checked his mobile for a signal but it was still down. Refugees were drifting passed on foot, staring longingly inside the cruiser.

'Stay inside the truck,' Kalu told, Esse. 'There is a bad atmosphere here. People are desperate,' he said, looking at the armed men on the door. 'I don't like this one bit but I promised to organise water along the way. I'll be as quick as I can.'

'Be careful,' Esse said, yawning. She watched as Kalu climbed out and locked the doors before walking to the store. The gunmen stood in his path.

'Hello,' Kalu said, approaching them.

'What do you want?' one of the men grunted.

'I want to organise water and food for a group that will be travelling this way tomorrow.'

'Do you have cash?'

'Yes.'

'I need to see your cash before you enter,' one of them growled. Kalu took a wad of notes from his pocket and showed them. They moved aside and opened the door. Kalu walked in and nodded to the shopkeeper. The shelves in the small store were practically empty. He couldn't see any bottled water.

'Hello,' Kalu said, smiling.

'What do you want?' the shopkeeper snapped. There was no warmth in his tone.

'There is a group of people travelling this way. They should be here tomorrow and I promised to organise water and food for when they arrive.'

'How many people?'

'Over a hundred.'

'Christians or Muslims?'

'Why does that matter?' Kalu asked, calmly, although he didn't feel calm inside.

'It matters,' the shopkeeper said, abruptly.

'Why?'

'It affects the price.'

'Why does it affect the price?'

'Because some people have more money than others, so, the price goes up if they're Christians. Business is business.'

'I hope that you never have to leave your home in a hurry. It would change your outlook on things very quickly.' Kalu glared at the man. The man looked away, Kalu's size was intimidating.

'What do they need?' the shopkeeper asked, ignoring the barb.

'Bottled water and whatever dry food you have available.'

'Rice?'

'Rice will be fine.'

The shopkeeper opened a book and ran his finger down the page. He bit his bottom lip as he calculated things in his head.

'I can spare fifty bottles of water and two sacks of rice,' he said, without looking up.

'That isn't enough,' Kalu said, frustrated. 'They need water for the rest of the journey to the border.'

'Have you seen the road outside, friend?' the shopkeeper laughed dryly. 'There are hundreds of people out there who all want water and food. Did you see any supply trucks on your way here because I haven't seen any?' he asked sarcastically. 'All my goods come from Monguno. I drive half a day there, load up and then drive half a day back. Do you think Boko will let me pick up supplies in the next few days?' He paused for effect. 'I am a shopkeeper not a magician.'

Kalu shrugged and sighed. The shopkeeper had a point. He had what he had and when it ran out, that was that.

'Okay. If that is all you can spare, it will have to do,' Kalu agreed.

'Two hundred dollars, US obviously.'

'What?' Kalu asked, confused.

'Two hundred dollars for fifty bottles of water and two sacks of rice. I'll keep them to one side for your friends. I need the money up front.'

'That is madness,' Kalu said, shaking his head in disbelief. 'It is twenty-five dollars at a push. I expect to pay a little more but that is ridiculous. You can't charge that!'

'You could always shop around for a better price or you could get out of my store, stop wasting my time, and hope that there is something left when your friends reach here tomorrow.'

Kalu shook his head. He didn't want to be ripped off but he couldn't let Joseph and his people down either. If they reached Zari and there was no water, they would struggle to make the border. He was about to make the deal, however bad it was, when he had a thought.

'Okay, I'll pay it,' Kalu said.

'Good. I thought you would, given the options available,' the shopkeeper chuckled. 'Two-hundred dollars, please.'

'I will take it all now and drive it back to them,' Kalu said, counting the money.

'What?'

'I'll take it now,' Kalu said, raising his eyebrows. 'The water and the rice.'

'I don't have it here. It'll take me until tomorrow to have it brought over from the warehouse. The store is too small to keep all the stock in.'

'Your shelves are empty.'

'It's been busy.'

'You don't have a warehouse,' Kalu said, putting his money back into his pocket. 'And you don't have fifty bottles of water or any rice. You are a blood-sucking leech preying on the poor unfortunate people, who have lost their homes.'

'Get out of my store!'

'I will leave, no problem,' Kalu said, nodding. He remained calm despite boiling inside. 'I hope Boko come this far, I truly do. I hope that you have to walk alongside those people you have robbed when they were desperate. You will have to sleep with one eye open, friend,' Kalu warned. He opened the door and stepped out into the rising heat. A queue had formed on the steps of the store, held back by the gunmen. 'Do not give that man a penny unless you have your supplies in your hands.

He is a thief and a liar.' Some of the people waiting dropped out of the queue. Others asked him questions that he didn't hear and he didn't want to answer. He wanted to get back into the truck and drive away. There was a bad taste in his mouth and a knot in his stomach. He unlocked the truck and climbed in.

'Did you organise things for them?' Esse asked. Kalu started the engine and shook his head. 'No? What happened?'

'The snake behind the counter wanted me to give him two-hundred dollars for fifty bottles of water and two sacks of rice that he didn't have.' Kalu put the truck into first and pulled out through the line of refugees. 'He wanted me to pay him upfront but when I asked to see the goods, he said he didn't have it there. It was in his warehouse!'

'That is terrible!' Esse said, angrily. 'What is wrong with these people?'

'Opportunism at its most depraved, Esse. When there is no bottled water around, a fifty-cent bottle becomes worth a hundred times its value. Supplies will run out across Monguno province while Boko are here. It is no wonder all these people are heading north. Even if Boko don't raid their villages, there will be no supplies anywhere.'

'This is a disaster and no one can stop it, can they?' Esse sighed. Kalu shook his head and drove on in silence. Soon, Esse closed her eyes and drifted off again. The night's events had drained her. Kalu was struggling to keep his eyes open. They were gritty and tired. As they reached the outskirts of Zari, the road became wider and he pushed the cruiser a bit faster. The sooner they reached the border, the better, he thought.

The bush began to dwindle and greenery gave way to sand and rocks. The landscape became flat and Kalu could see for miles. Hundreds of people were converging on the road from both directions. After travelling for an hour, it became clear that Boko had caused havoc across the entire north east of the country, displacing tens of thousands of people, all, it seemed were heading north to the border rather than south towards the capital, Lagos. Broken down vehicles littered the side of the road and he wondered how many people had jumped into them wishing that they'd had a full tank of fuel when the rebels arrived. How many had planned an escape if Boko invaded? Not many by the looks of things, he thought.

As they neared the border, he slowed to a standstill behind a solid line of traffic and used the opportunity to check on the wounded. He gave them both water and reassured them that they were safe from the rebels now. As he climbed down from the running-boards, he looked around. Refugees streamed along each side of the road; some had nothing but what they were standing up in, making him feel guilty to be driving a vehicle packed with supplies. He wished that he had brought some of the food from the farm but where would he start to distribute it? Who would eat and who wouldn't? It was an impossible situation with no clear solutions. He could only hope that the government would react quickly and help those driven from their homes, although he doubted that they would.

The queue of vehicles edged forward slowly and eventually he could see that makeshift border controls had been erected. A barbed-wire fence stretched east and west as far as he could see and uniformed soldiers patrolled it at regular intervals. Tents and shelters had been erected on the Nigerian side of the fence, housing those who had not been allowed to cross, he assumed. Dozens of vehicles were abandoned on the dust plains to the west, buses, motorbikes, cars, trucks and lorries of all shapes and sizes were rusting in the baking sunshine. Most of them had been turned into temporary accommodation. The wave of human migrants trying to travel through Niger, had forced their government to impose a solid border, where for decades, there had been none. Kalu began to worry about the criteria being applied to people trying to enter Niger. Why were some refused entry while others could cross? He noticed a Red Cross camp about a mile away on the Niger side of the fence. The distinctive flag fluttered on the breeze. They would have to cross the border before he could unload the wounded from the roof rack. The sun was climbing towards the middle of the sky; temperatures were soaring. He figured on waiting another half an hour at the most before pulling over to check on them again. Two vehicles in front of them pulled out of the queue and stopped at the side of the road; steam poured from beneath the bonnet of the first one. Mechanical failure was top of Kalu's nightmare list. He had no mechanical prowess and most of their journey would take them across the remotest parts of the continent. Any kind of breakdown could be fatal, not only for the Land Cruiser but also for its passengers. Algeria would be the test. If anything went wrong in the desert, it could be a catastrophe.

Kalu overtook the broken-down vehicle and closed the gap between them and the vehicle in front. The queue had been split into two lanes by the soldiers. The left-hand lane was at a standstill while the right-hand lane was moving through the barriers across the border without being challenged. Two soldiers stopped Kalu, weapons hanging from their shoulders. He lowered the window and smiled, despite his tiredness.

'Where are you from?'

'Monguno Town.'

'Passports?' one of the soldiers asked, looking into the vehicle. Kalu leaned over and took them from the glove box. He handed them to the soldier, who gave the covers a cursory glance. 'Where are you heading?'

'Morocco,' Kalu replied. He didn't need to tell him that their destination was Europe. It would only indicate that they had cash.

'Are you going to cross the desert in Algeria?'

'Yes.'

'Be very careful. The Tuareg are hijacking convoys crossing the desert. You have women and children aboard. They are responsible for nearly all the trafficking nowadays. Don't try and cross alone. Try and join up with other travellers.' Kalu nodded that he understood. He was becoming more and more uncertain about the desert road with every conversation that he had about it. 'Do you want the slow lane or the fast-track lane?' the soldier asked, gesturing to the empty lane in front of them. He handed the passports back. Kalu noted that he hadn't opened any of them.

'What is the criteria for the fast lane?' Kalu asked, putting them back in the glove box. 'I would like to cross quickly.'

'One hundred US dollars per person,' the soldier said, shamelessly. He looked in the back seat. 'There are six of you in here and two on the roof, so, eight hundred.'

'Eight hundred dollars?' Kalu asked, reaching for a rucksack. 'The men on the roof have been shot. I am taking them to the Red Cross.'

'The Red Cross camp is across the border,' the soldier said, shrugging his shoulders. 'Eight people will cost eight hundred. Take it or leave it.'

Kalu wanted to tell the soldier that he was a thief but he had a rifle. No wonder so many weren't being allowed to cross. Eight hundred dollars was a lot of money. He took a roll of dollars and peeled off eight green notes, handing them through the window. 'That is a lot of money for these people,' he added, pointing to the crowds. 'Boko are only a hundred miles from here. These people cannot go home. What will you do if Boko decide to come out of the bush and attack your towns across the border?'

'Building fences and patrolling them is an expensive task. Someone needs to pay for it. Our president says it's a Nigerian problem and Nigerians need to pay for it.'

'It could be their problem sooner than they think.'

'If Boko come to Niger, we will crush them.' He gestured to half a dozen tanks, which were positioned on a knoll overlooking the border road. It was enough heavy armour to make a Boko raiding party think twice. 'Our government are not frightened of the rebels like yours,' the soldier said, winking. 'Drive on. Have a safe journey and I hope you make it to Morocco.' He added cheerfully, as he pocketed the dollars. Kalu drove passed two dozen vehicles parked in the slow lane. The drivers looked at them as if they had two heads. Once again, guilt gripped his insides and squeezed. Thousands of people would be in peril because they didn't have the money to cross the border or they had left their passports at home when they fled. There was no food and no water to feed the thousands in the makeshift camps. They would be left with the choice of climbing the fence and being shot or returning home to towns controlled by the extremists. He wished he had a magic wand to make it all go away but there was no such thing.

'Eight hundred dollars?' Esse said, sleepily shaking her head.

'What can we do?' Kalu scoffed. 'We had no choice. Pay it or get out of the queue!'

'One hundred dollars each? We don't even know the men on the roof,' Esse sighed. She looked at Kalu and immediately felt guilty. He smiled. She knew he understood. 'I didn't mean that how it sounded.'

'You did,' he teased.

'I did not!'

'We should have checked their pockets. They might have money of their own.'

'Stop it.'

'I could have left them on the side of the road,' Kalu joked.

'You would never do that.'

'Neither would you.'

'It is going to be like this all the way, isn't it?' Esse said, yawning. The girls were stirring now too, rubbing their eyes and stretching their arms. Esse passed water around. 'Why do people always try to make money from other people when they are in trouble?'

'Human nature, unfortunately,' Kalu said, shaking his head. 'Desperate people will pay anything to keep their families safe. We need to be very careful what we pay for our passage or we will run out of money quickly.'

'I didn't see any opportunity for bargaining with them,' Esse pointed out. 'He said, take it or leave it.'

'I'm beginning to think you're right. If you want something when you're fleeing, you either pay what they ask or don't have it.'

'It looks that way. I'm not sure that we should expect anything else, Kalu.'

'I expect to be charged for crossing borders but eight hundred dollars?' he laughed sourly. 'I didn't expect that. Luckily, we can pay this time but those other people are trapped between the devil and the deep blue sea. They have no way of finding the money to cross.'

'We would have been in their position if you hadn't prepared so well,' Esse said, touching his shoulder and squeezing it gently. 'If you hadn't stored the money and supplies at your surgery, we would have left Monguno with nothing.'

'I was thinking the same thing,' Oke said.

'What do you mean, Oke?' Esse asked.

'I mean, imagine if you had kept all the stuff at the house.'

'Exactly,' Esse said, as a shiver ran down her spine at the thought. 'We couldn't have gone home for anything.' She looked at the crowds of desperate refugees near the barriers. 'Having money in the bank would mean nothing. Some of these people will have money in the bank but how can they get to it?' she said, shaking her head. 'We were lucky that you hid cash. We were very lucky that you did what you did. I feel very sorry for them, Kalu. They have no way of getting to their money.'

'What money?' Beb said, waking.

'Don't you worry about it,' Kalu said, patting his head. 'Did you sleep well?'

'I'm okay. My head hurts.'

'You had a nasty bang to it,' Kalu said, looking into his eyes. 'There's some paracetamol in my bag, Esse.' Esse found the tablets and passed them to Beb with some water. He swallowed two and smiled.

'Okay?' Kalu asked.

Beb nodded and rubbed his eyes. 'Where are we?'

'We've just crossed the border into Niger.' Kalu pointed to the west. 'We need to take the wounded to that Red Cross camp there.' He indicated and steered the cruiser off the road towards a group of tents. 'Once we have done that, we can concentrate on our own journey.'

The approach was bumpy as the truck navigated rocks and boulders beneath the sand. He was conscious of the pain it would be causing the wounded. Ten minutes later, they were at the camp. Kalu parked the cruiser next to what looked like a triage tent. There was a queue of walking wounded stretching around it. Two dishevelled doctors, one male, one female, looked up from their work, noticing the wounded people strapped to the roof. It was obvious that they were a priority and they left what they were doing and walked towards the truck.

'I think that's a first for me,' the male doctor said, as they approached the cruiser. He had an accent of some kind. 'Can't remember ever seeing patients arriving on the roof of a Toyota.'

'I don't think I've seen it either.' The female agreed. Kalu knew she was English immediately.

'There is more room up there than inside,' Kalu said, climbing down from the truck. He stuck his head back inside the vehicle to speak to his family. 'Stretch your legs for ten minutes but don't go far. I want to be away from here as soon as possible.'

'Why, father?' Beb didn't understand the concern now they were across the border. 'I thought we would be safe now.'

'I'm not sure that we are, Beb.' Kalu looked at the growing crowds on the other side of the wire. 'If Boko decide to attack the refugees, a few strands of barbed-wire won't hold back thousands of people in a panic and there are not enough soldiers there to stop them or to defend them from Boko. We need to put some distance between us and the border.'

The doctors were listening to what he was saying. They looked at each other with concern and then looked at the crowds near the border crossing. It was beginning to look more like a humanitarian crisis with each passing hour.

'Do you think there are many more coming?' the female doctor asked.

'Yes,' Kalu said, nodding. 'Many more.'

'Where are you from?' the female doctor asked. She was white with blue eyes and pale skin. Her blond hair was scraped back into a ponytail.

'Monguno,' Kalu said, looking into the far distance towards home. 'The injured men are Christians from Christown. Boko shot them in the bush last night.'

'What happened?'

'Boko invaded both towns, rounded everyone up, shot anyone who argued, the usual.' He paused, thinking through the painful events of the previous day. 'We were lucky and got away, others weren't so lucky.'

'Were many injured?' she asked, gesturing to workers inside the tent. 'Give me a hand taking these patients down. Put them on trolleys and wheel them inside.' She instructed three large porters. 'Sorry. You were saying? Were many injured?'

'Hundreds, probably thousands,' Kalu said. 'They must have swamped the entire area surrounding Monguno town too. I saw thousands of people on the road heading this way. Most are two days walk away from here. You had better call in some backup or you won't be able to cope.'

'We are the backup,' the woman said. 'We were working in Mali last week when the emergency call for help came in. There is no one else coming.'

'What about the authorities here?' Kalu asked.

'Most of these people are Nigerian. They don't see it as their problem, yet. They will, eventually.'

'Let's hope so.'

'What about your government, will they send help?'

'From Lagos?' Kalu smiled, sadly and shook his head. 'They don't see anything in the north as their problem.' He shrugged. 'Boko have cut all communications to Monguno province. There are no mobiles, landlines or radios working. It could be days before they really know what has happened and to what extent.' Kalu shrugged again. 'They never send troops into an area if they think Boko are still around. I wouldn't count on them helping anytime soon.'

'We can't cope with many more patients. You can see how much pressure we are under already. A sudden influx now would be the straw that breaks the camel's back.'

'From what I've seen on the road here this morning, within two days, there will be tens of thousands trying to cross that border.' The wounded were taken down from the roof and wheeled away. Kalu watched as they were assessed.

'They've been patched up pretty well,' the woman said, looking at Kalu.

'I'm a doctor.'

'Where did you study?'

'London.'

'Me too,' she said. 'Different kettle of fish, eh?' she joked, looking at the crowds.

'Not as bad as A and E on a Saturday night,' Kalu smiled, remembering his time as a junior doctor. It seemed like a lifetime away. He looked at the wounded men as they were wheeled inside. 'I'll get word to their people that they are being treated here. I'm not sure how but I'll find a way.'

'They'll know to look for them here. The nearest hospital is five-hundred miles from here.'

'I hope so. Thank you for taking them.'

'You're welcome,' the female doctor said.

'Do you think Boko will come this far?' the other doctor asked. Kalu thought he might be French.

'No one thought that they would come to Monguno,' Kalu answered. The doctors nodded and half smiled. 'I wouldn't rule it out.'

'Where are you heading now?'

'North,' Kalu said, choosing not to mention crossing the desert again, in case his family overheard any warnings about the Tuareg. They would be frightened enough without that kind of information.

'Good luck.' The doctors shook hands with him and went back to their triage tent. Kalu didn't envy their position. He reckoned they would be overwhelmed in the next few days. He walked back to the cruiser and was surprised to see his family already in their seats.

'Did you have a walk around?' he asked. They nodded that they had. It was obvious that they didn't feel safe and wanted to leave.

'What's the plan from here?' Esse asked.

Kalu reached for the map and pointed to where they were.

'We're going to head up the N1 away from this crossing point. When we get to Bande, we will stop and get something to eat. If we can find somewhere that rents rooms, we'll stay overnight.' Everyone stayed quiet. He could see that they were numbed by the situation. 'Bande is far enough from the border to be sure that Boko cannot reach us.' He tried to reassure them. 'We all need a good meal and a decent night's sleep,' he said smiling. The girls smiled back. 'You all look tired and I could sleep for a week.' He was about to start the engine when the sound of automatic weapons drifted to them on the wind. They all looked across the plains towards Zari. In the distance, black smoke spiralled skyward. It looked like the town had been set alight. To the west, moving away from Zari, a plume of red dust towered above the horizon. There was a convoy of vehicles heading towards the border at speed. He figured that they were less than an hour away. Kalu put the cruiser into first gear and headed in the opposite direction.

CHAPTER 12

When they reached the main road, the traffic was heading north. Kalu waited for a break and then joined the line. He accelerated through the gears, reaching sixty without troubling the engine. He checked all the gauges and dials and looked at the smoke on the horizon in the rear-view mirror. His passengers were focused on the fast-moving plume of red dust. Beb was twisted in his seat, craning his neck to see what was approaching.

'It's Boko isn't it?' he asked. Kalu nodded and thought about Joseph and his people. They would have been caught in the open. He hoped that they had been captured and not killed. Maybe they'd had time to disappear back into the bush. He thought about the shopkeeper and what he had said to him. It seemed cruel now but he had meant it at the time.

'Why are they following us all this way?' Oke asked.

'Greed,' Kalu answered, looking at her in the mirror. The traffic was moving quickly and thinning out. 'Everyone on that road is carrying everything they own.'

'They want their money?'

'There were a lot of people on that road. That's a lot of money to steal,' Kalu said. Oke turned her head back to the east.

'There will be chaos at the border,' Esse said, thoughtfully. 'All those poor people will be in a panic.' She turned to Kalu. 'Do you think they will let them cross to get away from Boko?'

'There are thousands of people there,' Kalu speculated. 'I think they will overrun the fences. The soldiers can't shoot them all and they'll have their hands full with the Boko soldiers.'

'I can't believe they've come this far east,' Esse said, staring out of the window. They were quiet for a few minutes, all lost in their own thoughts. 'I still can't believe we're leaving our home.'

'It's been coming for years.'

'You saw it coming. Most people don't think that way.'

'Better that they came now than in five years,' Kalu said, thoughtfully. Esse looked confused. 'We're young enough and healthy enough to take our family out of the country and relocate. Some of our older friends will struggle.'

'It doesn't bear thinking about. Families will be scattered all over the place. I don't even know where my sister and her family are or if she's alive or dead.'

'Once the phones go back on, we'll track her down.' Kalu reassured her although he didn't feel confident that the phones would be on soon or that the family had made it out of Monguno alive. He had no idea whether they had been captured or had managed to flee into the bush. There was no way of knowing. There wasn't time to worry about others yet.

The road to Bande was wide and flat and apart from the odd broken-down vehicle, there was no sign of mass migration. There were other vehicles driving north but the journey was unhindered. Less than two hours later, they entered the town of Bande and a sense of normality returned. People were going about their business peacefully. Their experiences since the invasion now seemed surreal. It was like stepping through a time-warp from madness to normality. Kalu saw a sign for food and accommodation and he pulled the cruiser over and parked outside a row of shops. He rubbed his eyes and turned off the engine. His family opened the doors and climbed out. They were scruffy and dirty and their dishevelled appearance was attracting attention from the locals. Esse noticed that people were staring and began brushing dirt and dust from her dress. The girls did the same, helping each other. Beb watched them, totally unimpressed by their efforts.

'I'm hungry,' Beb said, trying to speed things up. He looked at Kalu for backup.

'Me too,' Kalu said. He understood how embarrassed the females were but trying to look like they hadn't been running through the bush all night was futile. They had been running through the bush all night. 'There's no need to be embarrassed. People will have heard what has happened across the border. They will expect people fleeing to look a little rough around the edges.' He smiled. The girls blushed a little. They needed clean clothes and a bathroom and soap and water but he needed food and sleep first. 'Let's get inside and see if they have some rooms free. Then we can eat and get cleaned up.'

Esse looked around at the shops. It had suddenly dawned on her that they had nothing. No clean clothes, fresh underwear, toiletries, nothing. Not even a comb or a brush. She was hoping that they could buy some essentials from somewhere nearby. Beb and Kalu walked into the café. The tables were empty and there was no one behind the counter but the smells of food cooking filled the air. They paused, not knowing if the establishment was open. A large woman in a bright green dress appeared from the kitchen, her apron was white and pristine. She eyed the family and beckoned them in.

'Come in, come in,' she said, a look of concern on her face. 'You people look tired and hungry. Sit down, sit down.'

'Thank you,' Kalu said.

'I am Alice,' she introduced herself. 'Welcome to my place!'

'We would like to eat and stay for one night,' Kalu said. 'Do you have any rooms free?'

'Of course, I do,' Alice said, ushering them to a table which had benches on each side. The tables were covered with yellow cloth with a chequered pattern. 'I can give you three rooms so that you can have a bed each. How does that sound?'

'That sounds perfect.'

'There are two bathrooms upstairs, so you can bathe or shower if you prefer,' Alice fussed. 'All the bedding and towels are fresh. You look tired, young man,' she said, rubbing her hand over Beb's head. 'Sit down. Make yourselves comfortable.'

'Thank you,' Kalu said.

'Are you from across the border?' Alice asked, putting a jug of water and six glasses on the table. Her arms were thick and strong and her hair was scraped into a bun on top of her head. 'Of course, you are,' she answered herself.

'Yes,' Esse answered. 'We're from Monguno.'

'There were some people in here earlier. They were from Zari. It is terrible what has happened,' Alice said, putting her hands on her hips. 'The government should be ashamed of themselves letting those animals run riot anywhere they choose.' She looked at their faces and shook her head, sympathetically. 'You have such pretty girls. They are beautiful.'

'Thank you,' the girls said, in unison.

'And you are a handsome young man,' she said, turning to Beb. Beb grinned shyly. 'What on earth happened to your head?' she asked, touching his forehead gently. The gash was scabbing over but was swollen and angry looking. 'Do you want some ice for that?'

'Boko beat me,' Beb answered, quietly. The woman put her hand over her mouth, shocked.

'Let me get some ice before we do anything else,' Alice said, disappearing into the kitchen. Kalu smiled at Beb.

'Is ice good for it, father?' Beb asked.

'It won't do it any harm,' Kalu said, winking. Alice came back with ice wrapped in a clean white cloth. She put it onto Beb's forehead gently.

'Thank you,' Beb said.

'The animals did this to a boy?' she asked Esse.

'They did much worse to others,' Esse said, nodding. There was an uncomfortable silence which followed. The family didn't want to discuss the details. It was all too raw. They were tired and hungry.

'Would you like some chicken stew and dumplings? It was freshly made today.' Alice added, excitedly. She sensed their reluctance to talk and moved away before they had answered. 'Of course, you do,' she said for them. 'And I have freshly baked bread. We'll have your bellies full in no time and then I'll show you to your rooms.'

'That would be great, thank you,' Esse called after her.

The sound of plates clinking and pots and pans being rattled drifted to them from the kitchen. The family was exhausted. Kalu didn't think that anyone would have trouble sleeping. He stood up and walked to the counter. The kitchen was open so that he could see, Alice working.

'Could you point me to the toilets, please?'

'Down the corridor on the left.' Alice was spooning stew into bowls with a ladle.

'May I ask you a question?' Kalu lowered his voice. 'Where are your customers?' Kalu saw her expression change. 'No offence, Alice but there are no locals here.'

'And you think that they are all packing up their things and running away?' she said, chuckling. 'There's no need to worry. Boko won't come here. Our town council is holding a meeting about the refugees. They are concerned that we could be overwhelmed unless they are prepared.'

'I see,' Kalu said, nodding. 'Please excuse me. I meant no offence.'

'None taken,' she said smiling. 'You are protecting your family. Hurry now. You need to eat this while it is hot.'

Kalu found the toilet and was pleased that it was clean and in good order. It was clear that Alice was a good innkeeper. He filled the sink with hot water and splashed his face, patting it dry with a fluffy brown towel. His reflection showed a tired looking man, ten years older than his actual age. He had a bad feeling about their escape, something that he couldn't put his finger on. It had been a traumatic twenty-four hours, he couldn't expect to feel normal. He made his way back to the dining room and sat down. There was a bowl of steaming hot stew in front of him and a big chunk of bread. The dumplings were the size of tennis balls and the smell made his mouth water. His family were unusually quiet, looking at him for permission to eat. He felt guilty for making them wait.

'Eat, eat,' he said, smiling. He picked up his spoon and tasted the stew, before breaking a piece from the bread and soaking up the gravy. It was as good as it looked. Alice was waiting for their approval. 'The stew is very good, Alice. Just what we needed.'

'Good. I'll leave you in peace to eat. If you need anything, give me a shout,' Alice said, walking towards the kitchen. 'I'll go and turn your beds down. You'll want to sleep once you've eaten, I'm sure.'

'Alice,' Esse called after her. 'Do any of the shops nearby sell clothing? We only have what we're wearing.'

'No,' Alice said, shaking her head. 'But I have fresh clothing for you all. My family are all grown up and gone and I can't throw anything away. I could open a market with the clothes I have upstairs.'

'Oh no!' Esse said. 'We couldn't impose like that. We can buy new, can't we, Kalu?' Kalu nodded and chewed on a dumpling. 'We don't want to be any trouble.'

'It is no trouble at all and there are no clothing shops here. We have a market but that is on Sundays. You are welcome to them. It will make room. I've got enough clothing to dress an army upstairs. Your journey is going to be an expensive one. You're going to need all the help that you can get. I have clothes that will fit you and the girls and my boys don't' fit into anything anymore. They don't stop growing.' She looked at Kalu. 'My husband is about your size. We can't leave you out, can we?'

'Much appreciated, Alice,' Kalu said, chewing. 'You're very kind.'

'I'll put some in your room and you can pick whatever fits. There are bottles of soap and shampoo in the bathrooms and you can buy toothbrushes from the hardware store next door. Let me know if you need anything else.' She wandered off, smiling and waving her hands. 'Enjoy your dumplings. They are my specialty.'

'What a lovely woman,' Isime said, when she had disappeared into the kitchen.

'It restores my faith in people,' Esse agreed. 'She's the first person who hasn't tried to rip us off. Quite the opposite, she wants to help.'   'I can't wait to have a shower,' Oke said, shovelling a mouthful of stew into her mouth. 'I'm not sure about wearing someone's old clothes though.' Her sisters laughed and nudged each other.

'Listen to you,' Isime laughed.

'What are you laughing at?' Oke asked, confused.

'We wear your old clothes all the time. We always get your old clothes,' Isime said, chuckling. Oke grimaced, realising what she had said. She flushed, a little embarrassed. 'It will be nice to have something that you haven't worn,' Isime added.

'I agree,' Kissie said, chewing. 'Oke's old clothes smell.'

'They do not smell,' Esse said, trying not to laugh. 'I wash them.'

'It doesn't matter how much they are washed, the smell never goes away,' Isime argued.

'What smell?' Oke asked, offended.

'Your smell,' Kissie said, holding her nose.

'It's like cat pee.'

'Isime!' Esse said, smothering a laugh. Beb giggled with Kissie. Kalu hid a smile behind his bread. Oke looked at them all, one at a time, to let them know that it wasn't funny.

The front door opened and four soldiers walked in, dressed in camouflage uniforms and cloth peaked caps. Their weapons were hung from their shoulders. They eyed Kalu and his family suspiciously. The family stopped smiling immediately, avoiding eye contact with them. One of the soldiers approached the table.

'Hello.'

'Hello.' Kalu replied, nervously.

'Where are you from?' he asked.

'Monguno,' Kalu answered, politely.

'We're you attacked by Boko yesterday?'

'Yes.'

'We heard about it. They have been attacking towns all over the north for days.'

'It appears so. There are thousands heading for the border.'

'It has been getting steadily worse for months,' the soldier said, smiling at the girls. 'Where are you heading?'

'North.'

'North to where?'

'Morocco.'

'How are you crossing the desert?'

'I'm going to drive up the N1. We have a truck, an old Land Cruiser,' Kalu explained. He put his spoon down in his bowl, showing the soldier as much respect as he could. His family followed his lead and stopped eating 'It should get us across.'

'Are you travelling alone?' the soldier said, looking at the girls. 'I mean just you and your family?'

'Yes.'

'You won't make it across the desert alive,' the soldier said, matter of factly. 'Do you mind if I have some water?'

'Of course not,' Kalu said, handing him a glass. 'Help yourself.'

'Thank you.' The soldier drank thirstily from the glass. He wiped his mouth with the back of his hand. 'The desert is virtually a no-go area. The Tuareg have aligned themselves with al-Qaeda. They have been attacking anyone crossing the desert and selling off their women and children to traffickers.' Esse looked at Kalu, startled. The girls looked at each other, frightened. Beb was fascinated by the soldier's machinegun.

'Oh, my word!' Esse gasped.

'I don't mean to frighten you, ma'am,' the soldier said, tapping his cap in respect. 'But I wouldn't risk taking my family across the desert to Morocco by road.'

'Is it that bad?' Esse asked.

'Yes. The Tuareg are attacking anything and anyone, even armed convoys. You might be lucky and not see them but if you encounter one of their camel trains, you will have no chance.'

'The entire route north is crazy lately,' another soldier added.

'We may have to rethink our journey,' Kalu sighed. His heart sank inside, disappointment and despair gripped him again. The feeling of helplessness returned with a vengeance.

'I would forget that plan. Even the border road into Algeria has become dangerous. There are pirates everywhere,' another soldier said, listening in to the conversation. 'There are so many people heading north nowadays, it's rich pickings for the criminals.'

'Thank you for the warning,' Kalu said, relaxing a little. Despite the disappointing news, he realised that the soldiers meant them no harm. 'Which way is safe?'

'East into Chad is the only truly safe route,' the first soldier said. 'Do you have a map?' Kalu nodded and took the map from his rucksack. He laid it out on the table. 'Can you afford to fly?' the soldier asked. Kalu nodded reluctantly. 'Then drive across the border into Chad here and head for N'Djamena.'

'And fly to Marrakesh direct from there?' Kalu anticipated his thinking.

'You can fly direct to Europe if you have the money and the right papers.'

'How far is it,' Kalu asked.

'About six hundred miles. But the roads are safe.'

'That makes sense. Thanks for the advice,' Kalu thanked him with a handshake.

'Enjoy your food and good luck to you,' the soldier mock saluted Beb. Beb saluted in return, his back straight, chin raised. The soldiers laughed at him and then sat down at a table near the kitchen.

'We cannot risk driving north, Kalu,' Esse said, shaking her head. 'Not now I've heard that. We cannot take the children that way.'

'It doesn't sound good, does it?' Kalu said, thoughtfully. 'It sounds like things have become lawless.' He ate another spoonful of stew. 'I think that we should take their advice and fly from Chad direct to Europe.'

'It seems to be the safest option.'

'It does.'

'Kalu.'

'What?'

'Why didn't we do that in the first place?' Esse asked.

'Two reasons,' Kalu said, eating.

'Go on.'

'We couldn't cross the border from Monguno into Chad. The border road is patrolled and its closed and the bush paths are mined. They are paranoid about Boko crossing their borders and they are shooting people first and asking questions later.'

'That is a good reason,' Esse said, nodding. She was still uncomfortable that Kalu had made plans without consulting her. She had to analyse his thought process. 'What is the second reason?'

'Money.'

'Money?'

'Yes. The flights from Chad to anywhere have tripled in the last twelve months. I couldn't understand why but what the soldiers said explains everything. The route north is so dangerous that more people are flying from Chad. I thought we could make it north to Morocco safely in the truck and fly from there. It's a quarter of the price. I was wrong.'

'You were wrong, Kalu, but I can see what you were thinking.' She took another mouthful of stew. 'I don't think the cost matters anymore,' Esse said, looking at her children.

'I agree.'

'It is safer to go to Chad.'

'Then that is what we'll do.' Kalu stopped talking and stared at Beb. His mouth opened but no words came out.

'What's the matter?' Esse asked, confused. Kalu stood up and walked around the table quickly, crouching next to his son. Blood was running from his right ear. Beb was staring into space, a vacant expression on his face. Kalu waved his hand in front of his eyes. 'What is the matter with him?' Esse stood up, panic in her voice.

'Beb?' Kalu said, remaining calm. There was no reaction and no recognition in his eyes. 'Beb, can you hear me?'

Beb's eyes rolled back into his head and his body began to convulse violently. Kalu picked him up and laid him gently on the floor. The soldiers looked on, concerned and the girls looked terrified.

'What is happening to him?' Esse asked, tears rolled down her cheeks. Beb was fitting violently.

'He's having a seizure,' Kalu said, looking into her eyes. 'This can happen after a head injury, Esse. Don't panic.'

'Don't panic?' she muttered. 'Don't panic?' she said louder. 'Do something, Kalu!'

'There's nothing we can do until the seizure stops,' Kalu said, calmly.

'What on earth is wrong?' Alice came running from the kitchen. She looked at Beb, hands covering her mouth. 'I'll go and get the doctor.'

'I am a doctor,' Kalu said.

'I didn't realise,' Alice apologised.

'Do something, Kalu,' Esse repeated.

'There's nothing that we can do except make sure he doesn't hurt himself or swallow his tongue.' Esse shook her head. She touched Beb as if to stop the seizure.

'What is wrong with him?' one of the soldiers asked.

'He had a blow to the head yesterday. There may be some damage there that I can't see.'

'Is there anything we can do?' one of the soldiers asked.

'No. but thank you for asking,' Kalu said. Beb began to settle. The fitting was subsiding. Kalu felt his pulse. It was racing. His eyelids flickered and his lips were parted, making him look like he was snarling. 'It's passing,' Kalu said to Esse. She squeezed her son's hand and touched his face with her fingers.

'There's blood coming from his ear.'

'I know.'

'Where's it coming from?' she asked.

'Inside his head.'

'From his brain?'

'Possibly,' Kalu said, nodding. 'He may have a skull fracture. Without an x-ray and a scan, I can't see what is going on inside there.'

'We need to get him to a hospital, quickly, Kalu,' Esse said, her voice breaking. 'What are you waiting for?'

'There is nothing that a hospital can do for him,' Kalu said, shaking his head. 'When the seizure stops, we'll see how he is when he comes around.'

'What do you mean, we'll see how he is?'

'We'll see if he is lucid or not.'

'So, we do nothing?'

'Waiting and observation is not doing nothing,'

'Well, it feels like nothing,' Esse panicked.

'We have to wait.'

'We cannot do nothing, Kalu!'

'I'm not doing nothing, Esse.' Kalu remained calm and kept his voice level. 'I am waiting. You need to wait too.' His tone had hardened. Esse looked like she was going to speak but she decided not to. Kalu watched his son twitching and writhing, the movement becoming less violent, easing slowly with every second that went by. Eventually, he stopped twitching and became still, looking like he was sleeping.

'Is he dead?' Kissie asked Isime.

'Don't be ridiculous!' Esse snapped. 'Do not talk like that!'

'Sorry,' Kissie said, starting to cry. Esse reached out and held her, feeling guilty for shouting.

'He's coming around, Kissie,' Kalu reassured her. He checked Beb's pulse again and took a deep breath. 'Don't worry. He'll be fine. It looks much worse than it is.'

'It looked terrible,' Oke said, her voice a whisper.

Kalu squeezed her hand and nodded that he understood. The group watched Beb in silence. The atmosphere was tense.

'I'm going to take Beb upstairs and put him in bed,' Kalu said. Esse looked concerned. 'I'll keep my eye on him while he comes around. Don't worry.'

'Don't tell me not to worry,' Esse mumbled. 'He's my child, of course I'm going to worry!'

'Why don't you take the girls upstairs and get them washed and ready for bed?'

'How can you think about sleeping?' Esse moaned.

'Everyone is exhausted. Let's get him upstairs while he recovers and we'll see how he is when he comes around. He will need to rest. Trust me. All we can do is wait.'

Esse didn't look convinced but she stood up and gathered the girls. Kalu picked up Beb, taking care to keep his head and neck stable. Alice led them upstairs and opened doors along the way. She showed Kalu into a bedroom that had twin beds separated by a bamboo table. He put Beb onto the nearest one and supported his head with a pillow. His eyes flickered for a moment and then opened. Kalu watched the pupils contract, a good sign. A slight smile touched Beb's lips. Kalu knew that he had recognised him. Another good sign. He touched his forehead and looked at the bump. He had checked for depressed fractures in the skull and found nothing detectable by hand. Beb closed his eyes again. Kalu sat on the bed next to him and looked at the anxious faces in the doorway. He gave them a thin smile.

'Go and get cleaned up,' Kalu said, gently. The girls looked at each other. Esse nodded to them to do as their father asked. 'Come and see how he's doing when you're are washed and changed. I'll be here with him.'

'Come along now, girls,' Alice said, cheerfully. Although her eyes were full of concern. 'Let's get you comfortable, shall we?'

Kalu and Esse stayed with Beb, holding hands with him, their eyes focused, looking for any sign of improvement. They heard water running and the sound of a shower being turned on and off. Alice was managing the distribution of clothing; the sound of her voice rising and falling, drifted down the corridor.

'This, changes everything again,' Kalu said, thoughtfully. He looked Esse in the eye. She tilted her head in question. 'Beb could have a skull fracture somewhere. Even if we could find it, there's nothing to do but allow it to heal.'

'I don't follow.'

'The air pressure on a plane,' Kalu said, vaguely.

'You're not making any sense,' Esse sighed. 'What are you talking about?'

'He has an unstable head injury,' Kalu explained. 'Even if he comes around and is lucid, there's no way that Beb can step foot on an airplane for a while.'

CHAPTER 13

Hours later, Kalu sat bolt upright, tired and confused and not quite sure where he was. It was dark outside and he wasn't sure what had woken him. He looked around the room. Beb was sleeping soundly; his chest was rising and falling gently. The tension on his face had gone. Esse was asleep on the other bed, wearing some of Alice's old clothes. Earlier, she had taken the time to have a quick shower after much persuasion from Kalu. Convincing her to leave Beb for any length of time had been difficult. A loud knocking noise made him stand up. It was coming from downstairs. Kalu walked to the window and looked outside. He recognised the soldiers that he had seen earlier. They looked worried and agitated. A jeep was parked in the middle of the road, the engine running, dust swirling in the headlights. The driver waved his hand at Kalu as the front door was opened. He heard Alice talking to the soldiers. There was a brief exchange of words and then they ran to the jeep, waved up at Kalu and then drove away at speed. Kalu opened the bedroom door and stepped into the hallway. Oke opened the door opposite. She looked tired and confused.

'What's going on, father?'

'I don't know,' Kalu answered, rubbing the sleep from his eyes. They heard footsteps running up the stairs and turned to see Alice coming towards them, a panicked expression on her face; her dressing gown was wrapped around her ample frame. 'Alice, is everything okay?'

'The soldiers came here!' she panted, as she reached the top of the stairs. 'Just now. They were at the front door!'

'I saw them, Alice. Try to stay calm,' Kalu said. 'What did they want?'

'They have been sent to the border,' Alice said, pointing to the west. 'Boko has overrun the border. They said that they have an army. The soldiers said there's a rebel convoy heading north towards Bande!'

'I don't believe it!' Esse gasped, hands covering her mouth again. 'How can they have crossed the border?'

'The soldiers said there are many men, more than anyone thought.'

'We need to get out of here!' Esse panicked, grabbing Kalu's arm.

'We need to stay calm,' Kalu said. He looked at Oke and touched her hand. 'Wake your sisters and pack your stuff as quickly as you can. Meet me downstairs.'

'Okay, father.'

'What will we do?' Esse had her hands over her ears.

'We will stay calm, Esse,' Kalu said. He walked back to the bed where Beb was sleeping. 'We have a few hours before Boko can reach here, and that is if they can make it through the government troops.' He sat on the bed next to Beb and took his hand. Beb's eyes flickered and opened. He smiled at his father and looked around. 'How do you feel?' Kalu asked, taking his pulse.

'Hungry,' Beb said, trying to sit up. His father touched his shoulders.

'Stay where you are. If you are hungry, that's a good sign,' Kalu said, turning to Esse, who was rushing to her son.

'Say something. Talk to me!' she said, excitedly.

'What do you want me to say?'

'That will do,' Esse rolled her eyes and sighed with relief. 'We were so worried about you.' She smothered him with a hug and then looked into his eyes. 'Do you have a headache?'

'No,' Beb shook his head. He looked at his father, confused. 'I don't remember much after arriving here. What happened?'

'You had a seizure,' Kalu said. 'It's nothing to worry about but you need to rest.'

'I feel okay,' Beb said, wobbling his head.

'Don't do that,' Kalu said, smiling.

'What is going on?'

'We need to leave here and head for the border to Chad.'

Beb looked out of the window, seeing it was the middle of night.

'Why?'

'Boko have attacked the border crossing and are heading north. We need to leave,' Kalu explained. 'They are hours away but as a precaution, we must go.' Beb nodded that he understood. Esse rubbed his shoulders. 'Do you think that you can walk?'

'Of course, I can,' Beb answered, sharply.

'Pack up our things,' Kalu said to Esse. 'I'm going to make room in the back of the cruiser so that Beb can lie down, while we travel.'

'Take the mattress and the bedding,' Alice said, fussing.

'Thank you,' Kalu said. 'I'll make room in the truck, hurry and pack.'

'I don't need to lie down!' Beb objected, his pride hurt.

'You need to rest,' Esse said. 'Listen to your father. He's a doctor.'

'Your mother is right,' Alice agreed. 'Your father is a doctor.'

'I know he's a doctor,' Beb said, looking at Kalu, confused. He shook his head slowly in disbelief. Kalu winked at him and scurried out of the bedroom, heading down the stairs, through the dining room and out to the truck.

The night air was dry but hot. Kalu looked down the street towards the border. Lights flashed on the horizon. Muzzle-flashes, he thought. Boko had attacked a position protected by an armoured column. That was ballsy, to say the least, unless they had called on reinforcements to come from the west, which would have flanked the Niger troops and caught them in a pincer movement. Kalu was beginning to think that there was more to Boko Haram than met the eye. He had a theory that the troops they had encountered were a small cog in a much bigger wheel. Their military prowess had been underreported. The press made them out to be an unruly mob armed with automatic weapons. The last twenty-four hours had demonstrated them to be able to attack an entire province with stealth and planning. It also appeared that their true objective was to infiltrate further into surrounding nations. They were not content with being confined to Nigeria. That made leaving imperative. Whatever doubts people had about leaving their homes, their options were disappearing by the day.

Kalu opened the rear door and pulled out some of the fuel tanks. He used two to fill up the tank. Their journey into Chad would be much shorter than his planned trip to Morocco, but in the back of his mind, he knew that their situation had become more complicated. The family would not be able to remain as one unit. Beb wouldn't be able to safely fly for weeks. They didn't have weeks to wait. There was only one option. He would have to stand up to Esse because she wouldn't be happy but he couldn't see any other solution. He lifted some of the water containers out of the back and put them next to the petrol cannisters. There was room for a makeshift bed now. The sound of diesel engines approaching from the north drifted to him. He walked to the front of the truck and watched as army lorries appeared around the bend in the road. They were Niger military vehicles, lots of them. Troop carriers, armoured trucks and tanks trundled by, spewing diesel fumes and dust behind them. It looked like an entire division had been mobilised against Boko. Part of him was relieved that they would slow down their progress but another part was seriously concerned that Boko wasn't just making a surgical incursion into Monguno and that it was a full-blown attempt to invade south Niger with a considerable exploratory force. From there they could spill over the borders into Chad. If so, things could escalate very quickly. Their possible exit routes could be swallowed up by a major conflict in the region. Borders would be sealed and travelling made impossible. His angst was at an epic level. He was beginning to feel claustrophobic, as their world closed in on them.

Esse and Alice were the first ones to follow him out. Alice had a bundle of bedding in her arms. Esse had the thin mattress under one arm and she held Beb steady as he walked with the other. The girls followed, looking bewildered, carrying all the rucksacks. Their faces looked older somehow, haunted and traumatised. It was as if a whirlwind had blown into their lives and shattered their reality and continued to chase them down relentlessly, never letting up so that they could rest.

'Put the mattress down in there, please,' Kalu said to Alice. She spread it out and put the bedding on top. 'Thank you.'

'There we are, that will be comfortable,' Alice said, patting the bed.

'I don't want to lie there,' Beb protested. 'I'm not sick.'

'You need to rest. Get in, please,' Kalu said, guiding him gently. 'You've had a seizure. Now you need to rest and sleep and when you wake up, you can come back into the front seat, okay?' Beb sighed like a petulant child but did as he was asked. He climbed into the bed and put his head on the pillow. Kalu closed the door and made a thumbs-up sign through the glass. Beb frowned and closed his eyes, sulking. 'We need to get going.' Kalu touched the petrol canisters. 'Alice, I need another favour from you.'

'What can I do?'

'Can you keep these cannisters safe for me?'

'Of course,' she said, confused. 'What is in them?'

'Water and fuel.' Esse looked baffled. The girls looked on, unaware of what was happening. They were dazed. 'I'll pick them up on the way back.'

'What are you talking about, Kalu?' Esse asked, a look of concern on her face. 'When are we likely to come back this way?'

'You won't,' Kalu said. 'Beb and me will have to.'

'What?'

'Beb can't fly.'

'What on earth are you talking about?'

'Beb can't fly for a while.'

'You're not making sense to me.'

'He has a head injury,' Kalu said, calmly. 'If his skull is fractured, then it would be dangerous for him to fly.'

'What can we do?'

'You and the girls are going to fly from N'Djamena,' Kalu explained. 'Myself and Beb will drive back here, pick up the supplies and head north.'

'Are you mad?'

'We don't have many options, Esse.'

'You have lost your mind.'

'A man and boy are not worth anything to the traffickers. They want females. We can avoid the Tuareg by going north-east into Libya.'

'And then what?'

'We can get a boat from the coast to Europe. Then we can take a train to meet up with you.'

'You are talking nonsense. I will not leave him behind.'

'You're not leaving him behind, Esse. He will be with me.'

'I'm not leaving my son and I'm not leaving you,' Esse said, folding her arms defiantly. 'We'll stay together. There must be another way.'

'Okay. You can think about it,' Kalu said, looking at his watch. 'We can talk about it on the way but right now, unless you have a better plan, I'm taking you and my daughters across the border into Chad and I'm going to get you out of harm's way. Beb and I will be fine and we can be with you in less than a week.'

'I'm not moving.'

'Don't be ridiculous.'

'I'm not being ridiculous.'

'Esse, you are.'

'I am not being ridiculous. Your idea is ridiculous. Leaving my son behind is ridiculous. Do not tell me that I'm being ridiculous, Kalu!' Esse wagged her finger at him. 'Your plan is what I would call ridiculous.'

'Of course, it is but it is the only one that I have.' Kalu raised his hands in the air, seeking help from above. None came. 'Can't you see that this is a ridiculous situation, Esse?' Kalu pleaded. 'But it is also a very dangerous one. Look at them.' He pointed at the girls, who were huddled together, frightened by what was being said. Kissie was crying again. 'Getting them out of this hellhole is our responsibility as parents. You will be with them, so I know they will be safe. I will be with Beb. Nothing will happen to him while I am breathing. Trust me, this is the only way.'

'Why is this happening to us, Kalu?' Esse buckled. She began to sob into her dress. Kalu held her around the waist. 'We're good people. I don't understand why this is happening.' She buried her head into his shoulder and tried to compose herself. 'I'm sorry,' she whispered. 'I know that you're trying your best.'

'There's no need to be sorry,' Kalu whispered back to her. He looked at the girls. 'Get into the truck, girls,' he said, gesturing with his head. 'Oke, you get in the front seat. Mother will need to keep an eye on Beb in the back.'

'I'll look after these for you,' Alice said. 'And I'll keep a room for you for when you return, as long as Boko don't reach here.'

'Are you going to stay here?' Esse asked, concerned.

'I am an old woman. This is my home. Where else would I go?'

'Take care of yourself, Alice. I'll be back in few days,' Kalu said. There was nothing else to say. The decision to run or stay was an individual one. 'Thank you for everything, Alice.'

'You're very welcome.'

'How much do I owe you?'

'Pay me on your way back,' Alice said smiling. She hugged Kalu and helped him putting Esse into the back seat. 'Good luck to all of you. Look after them, Kalu.'

Kalu nodded and walked to the driver's door. He opened it and turned on the interior light. His map was in one of the bags and he checked two before he found the right one. He spread it out over the steering wheel and traced their route with his forefinger. They had to drive ten miles back towards the border, then it was a simple left turn and then they had to follow one road, into N'Djamena. He folded the map and put it between the seats. Kalu waved through the window to Alice, engaged first gear and guided the truck through a three-point turn.

'Everyone okay?' he asked, looking in the rear-view mirror. Esse, Kissie and Isime nodded silently. He wasn't convinced that they were okay at all but there wasn't time to have an in-depth debate about the decision. A huge explosion in the near distance lit up the night sky with an orange plume that climbed hundreds of feet into the air. Kalu reckoned only an ammunition dump being hit could make that kind of explosion. Ammunition dumps were heavily guarded. If Boko had hit that, then they were there in huge numbers. He was becoming more convinced by the minute that everyone had underestimated the size of Boko's army.

The ten miles drive to the turn off was like driving towards hell. They were heading towards the violence instead of away from it. Explosions and muzzle-flashes lit up the horizon like an impromptu firework display. The urge to turn around and hightail it north was overwhelming. He breathed a sigh of relief when the signpost to Chad appeared and they turned off the road and headed in the direction of N'Djamena.

CHAPTER 14

The road to the border was busy. All the traffic was heading in the same direction. Esse and the girls dozed and Beb was quiet in the back. It was a few hours later when Kalu noticed that traffic was going in the opposite direction too. Lots of traffic. In front of him, he could see a line of red taillights stretching for miles and it had slowed to a stop. It didn't look good. He spotted a small convoy of military jeeps heading their way, stopping every few hundred yards to talk to the drivers of the vehicles queueing to cross into Chad. He could see angry exchanges going on and guns were raised and pointed at drivers. Dozens of vehicles pulled out of the queue and turned around, heading back towards Bande. He wasn't sure what the soldiers were doing but some kind of selection process was taking place. When the soldiers reached them, Kalu lowered the window to speak to them.

'Where are you heading?' a soldier asked.

'N'Djamena,' Kalu answered.

'To the airport?'

'Yes.'

'Do you have flights booked?'

'No, not yet. Why?'

'Thousands are trying to leave by the airport. The flights are filling up quickly. Unless you have flights booked already and you can show your confirmation at the border, you will not be allowed into Chad. They are sealing the border.'

'We have money to buy tickets when we get there,' Kalu said.

'That doesn't matter.'

'Why not?'

'By the time you get to the airport, there won't be any tickets to buy.' The soldier raised his eyebrows, waiting for an argument. Kalu thought better of it. 'If you don't have tickets, you won't cross the border. Understand?'

'I'm sure that we could get a flight to somewhere if we could get to the airport,' Kalu said, holding a rolled up hundred dollar note. The soldier looked around to see if they were being watched. He gestured to the note and shook his head slowly. Kalu took another one from his pocket, reluctantly and placed it with the other. The soldier snatched the notes and stuffed them away quickly. 'Shall I drive on?' Kalu asked, smiling.

'You don't have flights booked, do you?'

'Not yet, but?' Kalu stammered, confused.

'But what?' the soldier said, shouldering his weapon.

'I thought we had an agreement.'

'What are you talking about?' the soldier shouted. Other soldiers were watching now. His raised voice was attracting attention. 'Do you have flights booked or not?'

'No,' Kalu mumbled. 'We don't.'

'Then you need to turn around and go back to where you came from,' the soldier shouted, angrily. Kalu could see his hands shaking. He couldn't risk the gun being fired by accident. The shouting had woken Esse and the girls.

'Okay, I understand, thank you,' Kalu said, pulling the cruiser to the side of the road. He felt angry that he had been robbed so easily. There was nothing that he could do about it. 'I'll check my map and turn around.'

'What was that about?' Esse asked, dozily. The girls stirred, disturbed from their sleep. 'Why was he shouting like that?'

'Because he can,' Kalu sighed.

'Why have you pulled over?'

'They have closed the border unless we can show a booking confirmation. All the flights are filling up with people trying to get out of the country.'

'Can't we buy them when we get there?'

'There won't be any flights left when we get there,' Kalu said, sighing. He wanted to bang his fists on the steering wheel but he couldn't let his family see him cracking. They were at breaking point. He had to be the calm in the storm.

'If we can get a signal, we could buy them online,' Oke said, reaching into her rucksack.

'Good idea, Oke. Try it.'

She took out her mobile and switched it on. The screen powered up and lit the inside of the truck with a blue glow. Icons appeared at the top of the screen. 'Come on signal, come on, come one,' she said to the phone. 'Give us a break and be there.' The Airtel logo appeared alongside three bars of coverage. 'We've got a signal.'

'Search for flights to Europe from N'Djamena today,' Kalu said, reaching for his wallet. 'There must be something.'

'Where shall I try first?'

'London, then Paris, then Amsterdam,' Kalu said, shrugging. 'I'll pay for them on my card. They'll send an email confirmation and we'll be allowed to cross.'

'What is going on?' Beb asked from the back.

'We're trying to book flights to Europe,' Isime answered him.

'Cool,' Beb said.

'It's not cool for you,' Kissie mumbled.

'Kissie!' Esse snapped.

'Sorry, mother.'

'What is she talking about?' Beb asked, rubbing his eyes, completely unaware what she meant.

'Take no notice of her,' Esse said. 'How do you feel?'

'Hungry,' Beb said.

Esse reached into her rucksack and took out some nuts. She opened the packet and handed them around.

'Is anything coming up?' Kalu asked Oke.

'It's still loading.'

'If we have a signal, I want to call my sister,' Esse said, searching in her bag for her phone. 'I need to know if she made it out.'

'Try her,' Kalu said, nodding. 'Any joy?' he asked Oke, who was scrolling through flights. She was shaking her head.

'There's nothing, father. Everything I've looked at is full.'

'Keep trying. There must be something.'

'Here,' Oke said, staring at the screen. 'Ethiopian airlines have a flight to Paris in the morning for one thousand, eight-hundred euros.'

'That is madness,' Esse said, shaking her head.

'They can charge what they like today, Esse,' Kalu said, shaking his head.

'They are no better than thieves.'

'There's a lot of them about. Book it,' Kalu said. 'We don't have a choice.'

'When I said they have a flight, I mean one seat. There is nothing else available.'

'They only have one seat?' Kalu asked, amazed.

'Yes.'

'That is no use,' Esse said. 'Try other destinations.'

Oke tapped the screen. She held it up higher.

'The signal has gone,' she said, looking at Kalu. 'There was nothing available anyway, father.' Kalu nodded and stared at the never-ending line of traffic in front of them. 'Looks like we'll be staying together after all.'

Kalu waited for a gap in the oncoming traffic and turned the truck around.

'What are you thinking?' Esse asked.

'We're back to square one,' Kalu said. 'We have the truck and we have fuel. We can't cross the Sahara to Morocco, so we head north-east into Libya and try to cross the Mediterranean.'

'Will we get a boat, father?' Beb asked.

'We will, Beb,' Kalu said, trying to sound confident. 'We'll get a big ship that we can drive onto and drive off on the other side.' His eyes met Esse's in the mirror. She looked at him, a shake of her head almost imperceptible. Kalu wished that he hadn't told her as much as he had about the migrant crisis trying to cross the sea to Europe. Millions were trying and thousands were dying. He had hoped to avoid the issue by flying. Crossing the sea had never been a serious option but he had underestimated how far Boko would push and the knock-on effect on the borders and airports. The logistics of travelling had changed completely. 'One way or the other, we'll get there.'

'What are these fools doing?' Esse said, pointing ahead.

Kalu looked and saw two sets of headlights heading in their direction at speed. They appeared to be racing side by side. He slowed, trying to gauge their line. They were on his side of the road, neither adjusting their line to avoid him.

'What are those mad men doing?' Esse said, watching the speeding vehicles closing. 'Be careful, Kalu!'

'I've seen them,' Kalu said, steering the cruiser off the road and onto the rocky plain that stretched as far they could see.

He drove the truck away from the oncoming vehicles. They didn't veer from their path. As they neared, Kalu realised that one of the vehicles was a military jeep, the other a Ford van. The van was heading towards the back of the stationary line of traffic and the soldiers were trying to stop it. Gun flashes lit up the interior of the jeep and the van's passenger window exploded. The van swerved violently and rammed the jeep, trying to knock it off the road. Another volley of shots hit the van as it hurtled towards the line of traffic. Kalu was level with the end of the line when the van hit the rear vehicle without slowing. The impact was devastating, crushing the stationary vehicle to half its original size. The van driver and his passenger were launched through the windscreen and landed broken and lacerated on the boot of a Mercedes, three vehicles in front. Kalu could see the rear vehicle clearly in the headlights of the jeep. It was overloaded with passengers. None of them could escape, the doors were crushed and jammed. Smoke drifted from the wreck. Flames began to flicker between the vehicles, spreading and climbing quickly. He looked at the driver as he tried desperately to climb out of the window, but his legs were trapped between the steering wheel and the seat. There was a desperate look in his eyes when the vehicles exploded into a ball of flame.

'Those poor people,' Kissie said.

'What just happened?' Oke asked, shocked. 'Why were they chasing them, father?'

'Someone desperate to cross the border,' Kalu said, guessing. 'It looks like they panicked and tried to outrun the soldiers.'

'Can't you help them, Kalu?' Esse gasped.

'No one can help them now, Esse.' Kalu put the cruiser in gear and crawled back to the road. He picked up speed and the truck travelled smoothly, leaving the chaos of the border traffic behind.

No one spoke as they headed back to Bande. The distant horizon to the south was still ablaze, plumes of flame climbed skyward before falling back to the earth. At least the journey north would put some distance between them and the advancing rebels. It was the only positive that Kalu could think of.

CHAPTER 15

It was daylight when they arrived back in Bande. Esse and the children had slept most of the way; Kalu was exhausted. There was no sign of Boko forces having reached the town although the streets were deserted. He slowed down and pulled the truck into a space in front of Alice's. Alice was looking out of the window, a worried expression on her face. She saw the truck arriving and her face lit up, a smile reaching from ear to ear. Kalu turned the engine off and rubbed his eyes. His head felt like it was stuffed with cotton-wool. He needed sleep before they attempted to drive north.

'We're here,' Kalu said, waking everyone.

'I need the toilet,' Oke said, opening the passenger door. She climbed out and closed the door behind her.

'Me too,' Isime said, following her.

'Are we going to eat here again?' Beb asked. Esse reached over the back seat, rubbed his stomach and laughed. 'I'm sure your legs are hollow. How are you feeling?'

'I'm okay.'

'No headache?'

'No headache. I'm fine.'

They climbed out of the truck and Kalu locked it before heading towards the dining room. Alice opened the door and smiled, although Kalu could see she was troubled.

'You couldn't get there?' Alice asked, shaking her head. 'Thank heavens. I was so worried.'

'No. They closed the border to anyone who didn't have flights booked.' Kalu thought it odd that she was pleased they hadn't made it to N'Djamena. He frowned.

'You haven't heard the news, have you?'

'I didn't have the radio on; everyone was sleeping,' Kalu said. 'What's happened?' he looked at the television in the corner of the dining room. It was on but the volume was turned down.

'It's been all over the television. Boko broke across the border from Monguno into Chad,' Alice said. She stopped and took a deep breath. 'They stormed N'Djamena airport an hour ago.'

'They captured the airport?' Kalu asked, astounded.

'Yes. Can you believe it?'

'No, not really.'

'When I heard the news, I thought you would be there, waiting for a flight. Thank heavens they didn't let you cross.'

'If we had, we would have been caught up in the attack,' Esse said, shaking her head. 'Some things happen for a reason. I believe that.'

'I believe that too,' Alice agreed. 'At least you're all safe and sound.'

'For now,' Kalu cautioned.

'Are they any closer to here?' Esse asked.

'No. Our troops are holding them near the border. The news is full of it. Boko are attacking all over the place. You should definitely head north; It might be a dangerous route but it must be safer than waiting for Boko to overrun the place.' Alice put clean glasses and a jug of water onto a table. Kalu took a glass and filled it, passing it to Esse. She took a long drink and handed it back to him. He emptied the glass and refilled it. 'I'll warm up some stew so that you can eat. You must be hungry.'

'Can I have some dumplings too?' Beb asked, excited.

'Sounds like you're feeling better,' Alice said, smiling. 'Your fuel and water cannisters are around the back of the kitchen. I didn't leave it outside. People are starting to panic.' She leaned closer to Kalu's ear. 'Four people have been shot and killed trying to steal fuel from parked cars,' she whispered to him. 'Looting has begun already.'

'That will get worse before it gets better,' Kalu said, looking through the window at their truck. The spare fuel and water tanks that were strapped to the sides were suddenly very valuable. He touched the handle of his gun through the material of his shirt. It was an involuntary reflex. Self-preservation was going to be the order of the day, every day. 'We'll eat and leave this afternoon.'

'You look tired. Why don't you lie down while I heat up the stew?' Alice suggested. 'I'll keep my eyes on the truck.'

'My mind is too busy to sleep but thank you. I'll load up the truck.' Esse looked at him and touched his hand.

'I'll drive for a few hours while you get some sleep,' Esse said. 'You must be shattered.'

'You'll drive?'

'Yes.'

'I could sleep for a week. Are you sure?'

'I'll be fine. I can't get lost, can I?' she said, shrugging. 'There's only one road north, right?'

'Right, even you can't get lost,' Kalu kissed her cheek. 'I'll load up. We need to keep, moving. If Boko have overrun N'Djamena, they can circle behind the government troops and reach here in a day or two.'

'I'll help Alice with the food,' Esse said.

Kalu walked into the kitchen and found the cannisters. He picked up one in each hand and carried them through the dining room. Beb saw him coming and opened the door to the street.

'Do you need any help?' Beb asked.

'I don't want you carrying anything heavy but you can help me strap them to the truck.'

'Okay. Under normal circumstances, I am good at lifting heavy things.'

'I know that, son.'

'Last week, Omar tried to lift a tree branch but he couldn't. I lifted it.'

'Good for you,' Kalu said, looking at the expression on Beb's face. Mentioning Omar had given his brain a jolt. His friend was dead and wouldn't be lifting branches again. 'Come one, let's strap these to the truck and then we can eat.'

'Good. I'm hungry.'

They walked outside and Kalu put the cannisters down on the road. It was hot and dry and he was parched. A vehicle passed them, slowed down and then stopped fifty yards away. It was a Renault. Kalu thought it might be a Laguna. A very old Laguna; rust had eaten most of the wheel arches away. The reversing lights came on and the car rolled backwards towards them. It stopped and two men climbed out of the front seats, leaving the engine running. They looked nervous and edgy. Kalu felt sweat trickling down his back.

'Hello friend,' the driver said, smiling. There was no warmth in it. The passenger didn't look friendly either. He was stooped at the neck, like a hyena; his eyes were dark and piercing. Kalu felt threatened immediately. 'Where are you from, friend?'

'Monguno,' Kalu answered, flatly.

'Are you running from Boko?'

'Yes.'

'Where are you heading?' the driver said, walking towards the truck. He was talking to Kalu but his eyes were all over the Land Cruiser.

'North.'

'We're heading north too.'

'Good luck.'

'Nice truck,' the driver said, looking inside. His eyes focused on the cannisters inside. Then he looked at the cannisters that Kalu had carried. 'It looks like you have plenty of supplies.'

'We have just enough.'

'We don't have enough.'

'Look. We have enough to get to where we want to go and no more,' Kalu said, flatly. He tried to keep aggression from his voice. The atmosphere was tense. He could sense menace from them. It wasn't safe. 'Go inside, Beb.'

'What?'

'I said, go inside.'

'Why?'

'I won't ask you again, go inside,' Kalu said, firmly. Beb skulked away, glancing behind him every few steps. He could sense something was wrong. He didn't want to leave his father alone. Kalu waited until he was safely inside. 'I am taking my family north and we don't have anything to spare,' he said, calmly.

'I haven't asked you for anything,' the driver said. The passenger leaned on the bonnet and stared at Kalu. 'Did I ask him for anything?' he asked his friend.

'Nope. Nobody has asked you for anything,' the passenger said, staring at Kalu.

'I was just being friendly.'

'I don't need any new friends today,' Kalu said, standing his ground.

'You can't have enough friends at a time like this. We all need to help each other.'

'I can't help you and I don't need your help, thanks.'

'You're not a very nice man, are you?' the driver said, shaking his head. He eyed Kalu, trying to size him up. Kalu could almost hear the cogs inside his mind turning, deciding whether fight or flight was the correct option.

'You're running from Boko, just like us. We're all in the same situation.'

'I understand that but I've already told you that I don't have anything spare.'

'Come on, friend. It would be a big help if you could spare one of those cannisters of fuel.' He gestured to the fuel tanks near Kalu. 'The petrol station in town has run dry already. People are panicking. I only have a quarter of a tank and that won't get me to the next petrol station. It would be a big help.'

'I don't have any to spare, in fact, I'll need to fill up at least three times before we get to where we're going.' Kalu shook his head.

'If you could lend me a tank full, I can return it to you at the next petrol station.'

'How much money do you have?' Kalu asked, considering his request.

'What?' the driver said, eyes narrowing to slits.

'It's a fair question; How much money do you have?'

'I have enough to fill up my car.'

'How much does it normally cost to fill it?' the driver looked at his friend. 'From what I have seen so far since the invasion, everything has gone up tenfold. The petrol stations will put their prices up because people are desperate; If you're struggling to fill it at normal prices, you won't have a chance.' The men remained silent. It was obvious to Kalu that they had no money and no means of paying for petrol. 'I'm sorry but I may not be able to buy any more so I need what we have. It's going to be the same story everywhere. The chances of me finding petrol stations with supplies on the way are going to be slim. I can't help you.'

'You could help us but you won't.'

'My family come first.'

'What about our families?'

'I can't be responsible for them,' Kalu said, feeling a twinge of guilt. Despite their menace, he could empathise with their plight.

'We could take it all,' the driver said. He reached into his pocket and pulled out knife. The blade flicked out with a loud click. 'I only wanted one but now I think we'll take it all, your truck too.'

Kalu pulled out the revolver and pointed it at the man's head. His hand was trembling. The passenger stood up quickly and backed away towards the Renault.

'Leave it, man,' he said to the driver. 'We'll find fuel somewhere else.'

'Listen to your friend,' Kalu said, gesturing with the gun. 'Get back in your car and be on your way. I mean you no harm but you won't take anything from me.'

'We'll see you along the way somewhere,' the driver said, waving the knife in a slashing motion. 'I'll be looking out for you!'

'Good luck,' Kalu said, holding the gun steady until the men were in the Laguna and driving away. When they had disappeared around the bend, Kalu tucked the revolver into his belt and leaned his back against the truck. He looked up at the sky and sighed with relief. The door opened and Esse rushed out, followed closely by Beb and the girls. She ran to him and threw her arms around him. 'Don't make a fuss. I'm fine.'

'I cannot believe that man pulled a knife. What on earth is wrong with people? It as if they have all gone mad overnight.'

'It is every man for himself, I'm afraid,' Kalu sighed. 'It is going to be the same story all the way. We will need our wits about us.'

'I'm frightened,' Kissie said. Oke hugged her.

'We'll be fine,' Esse reassured her. She glanced at Kalu and he nodded.

'We'll be safer when we're moving. I'll strap the supplies on, then we'll eat and get on our way. The truck is like a goldmine sitting here.'

'Bring it around the back,' Alice said from the doorway. 'It will be safer in the yard. No one will see it there.'

'Thank you,' Kalu said. 'Go and eat while I move the truck. Beb give me a hand.'

The girls went inside while Kalu and Beb strapped the water and fuel to the truck. Two army trucks appeared from the south and for a terrifying moment, Kalu thought Boko had broken through the lines. He pulled Beb behind him. As they neared, the markings became visible and he relaxed a little. They watched as the troop carriers rolled by, loaded with government soldiers.

'Are they going to fight Boko, father?'

'No.' Kalu shook his head. He had a sinking feeling inside. 'They are going in the wrong direction.'

'Why are they going in the wrong direction?'

'I don't know for sure. I just hope they are not running away.'

CHAPTER 16

Two hours later, they said goodbye to Alice. Saying goodbye took the best part of twenty minutes. Kalu put the children into the truck, kissed her on the left cheek and climbed into the passenger seat. The children were in the back, Beb and Kissie by the windows, Isime and Oke in the middle. Esse climbed into the driver's seat and adjusted it before putting on her seatbelt. She started the engine and waved at Alice through the window. The alleyway behind Alice's was narrow and she guided the truck slowly to the main road. Kalu kept his eyes peeled, looking for the men in the old Laguna. The streets were quiet. One or two vehicles trundled down the main road, heading in the opposite direction.

'Turn left and keep on going,' Kalu said. Esse nodded and drove the Land Cruiser slowly towards the edge of town. 'One road, all the way north.'

'Until we see the sea, mother,' Beb joked.

'Will we see it today?' Kissie asked.

'Not today, stupid,' Beb said, pointing to his head, suggesting she was thick.

'Beb!' Esse snapped. She gave him that stare in the mirror; the stare only mothers can do. 'Don't call her stupid.'

'Well, if she thinks we're going to see the sea today, she is stupid,' Beb defended himself.

'Why is he saying that?' Kissie asked, sulking.

'Because it's a long way,' Oke said, hugging her. 'Take no notice of him.'

'How far is it?' Kissie asked.

'Two thousand miles,' Kalu said, turning around.

'Two thousand miles,' Kissie repeated.

'So, if we average fifty miles an hour, how many hours will we have to drive?' Kalu asked, turning to look at her.

'Forty,' Kissie answered, smiling. She looked at Beb, who was still thinking of the answer and stuck out her tongue.

'Not so stupid, eh Beb?' Kalu said, looking at his son.

Beb shrugged, unimpressed and looked out of the window. He was impressed with her maths but he wasn't going to admit that. She couldn't kick a football to save her life, so he wasn't too concerned.

'Forty hours is less than two days,' Oke said. 'That's not long.'

'It's not if we keep driving and don't stop for food or to use the toilet.' Kalu said, stretching. 'And we need to sleep.'

'We can drive in shifts. That way we could keep moving,' Esse suggested.

'What if we need the toilet?' Isime asked, frowning. 'We can't not stop for two days.'

'Of course, we'll stop,' Kalu said. 'It's not a race. Once we put some distance between us and Boko, we can take it easy.'

The road north was quiet, which was a relief. Kalu was struggling to keep his eyes open. He didn't want to close them and not be aware of what was going on. Protecting his family was his most utmost concern. Eventually, the gentle vibration from the engine and his exhaustion got the better of him. He rested his head on the back of his seat and closed his eyes. 'I'm going to close my eyes for half an hour. If you see anything at all untoward, wake me immediately, okay?'

'I'll be fine,' Esse said, glancing at him. 'Sleep.' Kalu didn't need to be told twice. He had drifted off within seconds. Esse looked at the children in the mirror. They were quiet, looking out of the windows. Everything was new to them. New and frightening. They were still very tired and she knew that they would be asleep before long. Sleep would do them good. She had never experienced the sheer dread that they had encountered, traumatising enough for an adult to process but for children, a thousand times worse. How could she explain to them? There was no way. Protecting her children against life had been hard enough. Oke had malaria as an infant. The doctor at the hospital told them that she would die so Kalu argued with him. He took her home and nursed her back to health. Isime was a breech-birth and Esse had needed a caesarean. Once again, she was told that she might lose her child and once again, they were wrong. Kissie had been a sickly child, always poorly. She had suffered with mumps, measles and whooping cough. Then she was hit by a car and knocked unconscious and they were told that she might not make it through the night. Her brain had swollen and it was touch and go. It was a week before they got the all-clear. Then there was Beb. Beb had been a walking accident since he was old enough to move. He had needed more stitches over the years than anyone she had ever met and he was only ten-years old. Kalu said that he was held together by scar tissue. It had been a real roller-coaster ride but at no point had she ever felt the terror and unadulterated fear of her children dying; not to the same extent as the last few days. The dread of someone taking her children from them was like an ice-cold fist grabbing her insides and pulling them around. It was debilitating. The helplessness was smothering.

She glanced at Kalu as she reflected on things. Had he not prepared for the invasion, where would they be? Captured or killed, no doubt. Whatever happened in the future, she would never be able to thank him enough for saving her children. The road ahead stretched into the far distance, dusty plains flanked the asphalt. There were half a dozen cars in front of them, the nearest half a mile away. She saw a vehicle approaching from behind; dust spewed from the wheels. It was closing the gap quickly. When it was a few hundred yards away, it slowed and kept its distance. Esse didn't think much of it, in fact, having company was reassuring. She decided not to wake Kalu, who was snoring gently.

The kids were asleep too. Beb had his mouth wide open. He always slept like that. When he was younger, she used to close his mouth but he would open it a few seconds later. Kalu said that he had a problem with his sinuses and so she left him alone. Kissie looked like a fairy when she was sleeping. She didn't make a sound. Esse had bent close to her face every night, trying to feel her breathing on her skin. Just to make sure she was alive. Isime was the opposite, breathing through her nose when she slept, she snored like a pig. Oke was a fidget. She couldn't keep still for more than a few minutes and would wake up entwined in her bedding, unable to move. They were all so different in their own way. She couldn't think about losing them, not for a second. Almost unconsciously, she pushed her foot down on the accelerator. The quicker they reached safety, the better. Oke had her head on Isime's shoulder. How she was sleeping while Isime snored in her ear, she didn't know. Esse reflected on what had happened. Tears filled her eyes. She wasn't sure why. Was it relief? She couldn't explain how thankful she was that her children were safely sleeping in the back of the truck. The stress of fleeing from their home had taken its toll on her nervous system. There had been times when she felt she would implode, collapse and scream. Only her children and Kalu's calmness had kept her sane. She glanced at him. He was in a deep sleep.

She checked the mirror again; the vehicle was still following at a distance. There was a minibus and another car behind it now. Up ahead she could see a cluster of camouflaged vehicles parked on either side of the road. There was a jeep, a few trucks and two tanks. They had stopped all the vehicles in front of them. She slowed down, allowing the tailing vehicles to catch up and indicated left, pulling over to the side of the road. The three vehicles overtook them. Their occupants all had the same confused expression on their faces. Were the soldiers friendly or not? She didn't want to make that decision on her own. She felt bad waking Kalu but it was the right thing to do. She tapped his knee and he jerked awake.

'What's happening?' Kalu asked, groggily. He sat upright and looked around.

'There are soldiers up ahead,' Esse said, pointing.

'It's probably just a checkpoint,' Kalu said, looking at the vehicles in front of them. He spotted a rusty, gold coloured Renault Laguna in front of a minibus. Were they behind us?' he asked.

'Yes. All of them were,' Esse asked, confused. 'Why?'

'See the old Laguna,' he gestured. She nodded. 'That is the men who pulled a knife earlier.'

'Are you sure?' Esse said, her hand to her mouth. 'They have been behind us for over an hour. I wondered why they didn't overtake. What are they doing?'

'Stalking us, I bet,' Kalu said, rubbing his eyes.

'What do you mean?'

'They're waiting to see if there's an opportunity to steal fuel from the truck. They're heading north anyway. The best thing to do is follow a vehicle with supplies in it and hope it breaks down, crashes or is left unattended.'

'I didn't think, sorry.'

'How would you know it was them?' Kalu touched her hand. 'You weren't to know. I'll drive for a while, if you like.'

'Have you slept enough?'

'I'm okay,' he said. 'I'm awake now. Swap seats.' Kalu jumped out of the truck and walked around to the driver's side. Esse slid over into the passenger seat. He touched the revolver as he climbed in and made sure that he could remove it quickly. Esse watched but didn't say anything, not wanting to frighten the children. She hated guns with a passion, despite their situation. They had been through enough trauma. Kalu read her expression and nodded. 'It'll be fine.'

He climbed in and adjusted the seat and then pulled the truck onto the road. There was nothing behind them. He drove slowly towards the checkpoint, watching what was happening to the vehicles being stopped. The car at the front was being searched. Troops looked in the boot and under the wheel arches. The occupants were lined up, hands on the roof, legs spread apart while they were patted down.

'What are they looking for?' Esse asked.

'I don't know,' Kalu replied, shaking his head. He took the revolver from his belt and slipped it beneath his seat. It wasn't illegal to own a weapon but it was better to be safe than sorry. 'We're in the middle of nowhere.'

The first vehicle was passed and waved on. Kalu slowed to a crawl as the Renault was stopped. There was an army truck next to the checkpoint, parked on the right of the road. Four soldiers were in the back, weapons trained on the vehicle being searched. A jeep was parked on the left, two officers sitting in the front seats, smoking cigarettes. The tank crews were a little further back, to the left; their gun turrets were pointing south. Kalu thought it was overkill for a checkpoint. They were positioning brake points in case Boko broke through the lines. The men in the Laguna were ordered out of the vehicle and searched. Their vehicle was searched thoroughly. The driver looked around and saw the truck. He waved and smiled at Kalu. The soldiers looked at the truck too and then barked orders at the men. One of the soldiers found the knife in the driver's pocket. There was an exchange of words and the driver argued angrily. The driver was slapped repeatedly around the back of the head with a truncheon and he cowered against the car until the soldier stopped beating him. He wasn't smiling anymore.

'Why are they beating him?' Esse asked, shocked.

'Who knows, probably because they can,' Kalu said.

The beating stopped and the men were forced back into the Laguna. The soldiers had a conversation with the officers in the jeep but they didn't seem to be concerned. It was waved on after a few minutes. Kalu watched the rusty Laguna drive away, leaving a dust trail behind it. The minibus pulled up next and the car behind it followed. One of the soldiers gestured to Kalu to close the gap. He put the truck in gear and crawled slowly towards them. The minibus and the car behind it reached the checkpoint. The government soldiers stopped them both and surrounded them. There was a brief exchange with the driver of the minibus and voices were raised. Kalu was only a few hundred yards away when the minibus exploded.

CHAPTER 17

When the initial blast wave had settled, only the twisted wrecks of the minibus, the army truck and the officers' jeep remained. The jeep was burning fiercely; the officers mutilated to unrecognisable cinders. There was no sign of any human survivors in the army truck; its tyres were burning, thick black smoke spiralled skywards. A deep crater had appeared near to the wrecked minibus. Bodies were strewn across the ground. Soldiers rushed to help their comrades at the checkpoint. Some tried to extinguish the flames while others checked if their colleagues were alive. More soldiers ran from the trucks and the tanks to help. As they rushed around, trying to deal with the devastation, the car exploded. Most of the remaining troops were obliterated in the blast. Kalu put the truck into reverse and floored the accelerator. The cruiser raced backwards.

'What on earth?' Esse gasped.

'What's going on, father?' Oke shouted.

'Hold on,' Kalu said, slamming the cruiser into low gear. He took the truck off the road and headed out into the rocky land to the right. He steered a line that would circumnavigate the burning checkpoint, passing it by five-hundred yards to the east. He looked at the scene of devastation. There was little to no movement there. He could see one man crawling away from his legs. His clothes were ablaze and Kalu knew there was nothing that he could do for him. Within seconds, he was still. He drove as far away from the checkpoint as he could, trying to limit his family's view of the carnage. They were shocked into silence for a while. The terrain was bumpy and it was all he could do to keep the steering wheel straight.

'What happened, father?' Beb asked, staring at the burning vehicles.

'I'm not sure but I think it was Boko suicide bombers,' Kalu said, navigating the bigger rocks. The last thing he needed now was a shredded wheel.

'Why on earth would they do that?' Esse asked, her voice almost a whisper.

'I think they've sent them north to soften up the troops.'

'Soften them up?' Esse said, staring at the inferno. 'That's an understatement.'

'I bet they did the same at the border at Diffa and the airport in Chad. It explains how they did it.' Kalu surmised. It was a genius strategy. Suicide bombers were invisible until it was too late.

'What do you mean?' Esse asked, shell-shocked by the savagery of the attack.

'There were troops and tanks at Diffa. The troops can see enemy soldiers coming but they can't see civilians with bombs hidden on them,' Kalu explained. 'They were hidden in plain sight, especially in a crowd. Remember all those people and vehicles at Diffa. There's no way they could spot a bomber until it was too late.' He gestured toward the checkpoint. Black smoke towered above the scene. 'No wonder they've overrun the military in Chad and Niger. They infiltrated the crossings, mingled with the soldiers and then blew themselves up.'

'I'm frightened,' Kissie said, burying her face into Oke's dress.

'Sorry, Kissie,' Kalu said. 'Don't be scared. We'll be miles away in no time.'

'I can't believe they are this far north,' Esse said. 'If I hadn't woken you up, we could have been right there at the checkpoint.'

'We could have been but we weren't.'

'Do you think they'll go further?'

'They must think they are going to get this far at least, or why bother?' Kalu asked himself. 'Every time I think we're putting distance between us, they prove me wrong. Let's hope we can drive unhindered for a few days.' He steered the truck around in a big semi-circle, avoiding the ditches and dry riverbeds that had been carved out by last years' rains. As he drove the cruiser onto the asphalt, he peered into the distance. He could see the gold Laguna on the horizon. It was moving at speed away from the area. Behind them, traffic was building up about mile before the inferno. He put the truck through the gears and picked up speed, taking it as fast as he dared. Boko were driving north at terrifying speed and they needed to push on and stay one step ahead of them.

CHAPTER 18

The next eleven hours went by in a blur. They travelled six-hundred miles through the Tamanrasset region, towards the Algerian border town of In-Guezzam. Kalu and Esse took turns to drive, while the others slept. They stopped to use the toilet and to buy water and fuel and the journey was uneventful. Uneventful was very welcome inside the Land Cruiser. The children were patient and they chattered while they were awake and they slept for long periods. The landscape was increasingly desert-like. Abandoned vehicles littered the sides of the highway and the wrecks of destroyed military vehicles, the result of decades of border skirmishes, were scattered across the desert. Burnt out helicopters were dotted in the sand. The remnants of war were everywhere. Kalu kept his eyes on the gauges. It was an inhospitable place to breakdown or run out of fuel. Military convoys were moving south, some fifty vehicles long and as they neared In-Guezzam, Algerian troops became more apparent. As did their Airforce. Aging fighter planes roared overhead, rolling and climbing into the blue sky. There were soldiers parked randomly every hundred yards or so and they stared suspiciously at every vehicle that passed. Kalu had managed to relax a little on the way north but the presence of so many armed soldiers, set the nerves jangling again. The impending feeling of doom settled over him again. He couldn't shake it off. Everything about their journey was a risk that he wouldn't take under normal circumstances however, circumstances were far from normal. It was dark when they reached the town. Jets screamed overhead breaking the sound barrier. The sonic boom was deafening.

'Look, father,' Beb said. 'War planes.'

'I can see them,' Kalu said.

'There must be an airport.'

'It's a military base,' Kalu said. 'We can't fly from there.'

They spotted the border crossing about a mile away to their left. Headlights and taillights stretched for miles. The queue to cross into Algeria was a long one. Once across, they would have to travel fourteen hundred miles through the Algerian desert into Libya. There would be nowhere to restock and they would need to keep moving. Kalu felt relieved to have reached the border but there was trepidation about the next leg of their journey. It was a massive undertaking. His family was a fragile unit with a thousand weak spots. Keeping it intact was a daunting task. His exterior had remained cool, calm and collected; inside was a cauldron of uncertainty.

'We need to find somewhere to rest overnight,' Kalu said, turning towards the town. The roads south, were busy with haulage trucks. Military vehicles were parked on every corner; soldiers stood in groups talking and smoking. Their presence, meant to give a sense of security to the town's residents and visitors, had the opposite effect. The atmosphere was oppressive. The buildings were one-storey boxes with flat roofs and white render. They passed a night market that sold everything from coconuts to camels. It was illuminated by spotlights mounted on poles.

'I can buy food for the journey from there,' Esse said, craning her neck to inspect the produce. 'The vegetables look a little old,' she commented as if everything was normal. Kalu smiled. Some things didn't change no matter what the situation. Mother will always be mother.

He noticed a white building with a row of flagpoles outside. Floodlights lit up the front of the building. It was small but it was the only hotel he had seen so far. The truck trundled into the car park but Kalu had to drive around to the back of the hotel to find a space. There were military vehicles and commercial vans in most of the parking bays. The rear car park was unlit; the only light filtered from the streetlights nearby.

'Do you want to stretch your legs while I see if they have any rooms?' Kalu asked, pulling on the handbrake. Two soldiers eyed them from the corner of the street. One of them tossed his cigarette onto the road, unzipped his fly and started to urinate into the gutter. The family looked on in silence. Kalu coughed, a little embarrassed. 'Don't look, girls. That isn't pleasant.'

'It isn't. Talking of which, I need the toilet,' Esse said, shaking her head. 'I'm bursting but I will wait to use a real toilet.'

'Me too,' Oke agreed.

'Me too,' Isime added.

'And me,' Kissie piped in.

Beb shook his head in despair. He wondered where all their wee came from. It was as if they always needed a wee at the same time. Must be a girl thing, he decided.

'I'll stay with the truck, father,' Beb offered. 'We can't leave it unguarded, can we?'

'No, we can't,' Kalu said, turning the engine off. He twisted in his seat and looked at Beb. 'I'm sure we'll be fine. There are soldiers everywhere.'

'Leave your gun under the seat, father,' Beb said, seriously. He made a gun with his fingers. 'If anyone tries to steal anything, I'll shoot the bastard in the face.'

'Beb!' Esse said, astounded. 'I cannot believe those words came out of your mouth!' she twisted in her seat. 'I am flabbergasted!'

'Esse,' Kalu said, raising his hand. 'Don't overreact.'

'Do not Esse me. This is your fault. I told you that I don't like guns,' she turned on Kalu. 'I don't want them anywhere near guns. This is what happens when children see guns as normality.'

'We wouldn't be here if I didn't have a gun,' Kalu argued. He was exhausted and didn't need the blame pointed in his direction. She looked like he had slapped her. Her eyes bored into his soul.

'I cannot believe you are defending him after he said those words.'

'He's tired and in shock and he has a head injury.'

'Do not try to defend him when I am annoyed with him!'

'I don't want an argument,' Kalu said, calmly.

'Now you've started an argument. Nice one, idiot,' Kissie said, seeing an opportunity for a dig.

'And you can be quiet too, young madam!' Esse turned to Kissie. 'I do not want to hear you saying anything like that ever again, young man,' she said, pointing her index finger at Beb. He could see the disappointment in her eyes. 'I am lost for words. I am ashamed of you!'

That hurt Beb. Tears filled his eyes but he wouldn't let them see him cry. No way. He hadn't meant to upset anyone. It was meant to help his family, it just came out wrong, as if he was playing war with his friends. He climbed over the back seats into the boot and sulked amongst the cannisters.

'You take the girls to the toilet, I'll be in shortly,' Kalu said. 'I'll speak to him.'

'Don't you be letting him off, Kalu,' Esse said, angrily. 'I do not want my children talking like that. I am disgusted that came from the mouth of my child.'

'He doesn't normally say things like that, does he?' Kalu reasoned. 'They have been through a lot. It will have an effect. Once we get back to normality, he'll be fine.'

'He had better be,' Esse said, opening the door.

She climbed out and slammed the door too hard. Kalu jumped. The girls climbed out, grateful to escape the tension in the truck. They walked towards the rear entrance of the hotel and Beb watched as they opened the door and went inside. He felt sick that he had upset his mother. There was a moment of uncomfortable silence. Kalu looked out of the window and then looked at Beb. 'That wasn't the smartest thing you've ever said,' Kalu said.

'I'm sorry,' Beb mumbled. 'I didn't mean it. It just came out.'

'I know,' Kalu said. 'Your mother is exhausted and very stressed, son. She didn't mean to shout. The last few days have knocked her sideways. She'll come around after a good sleep in a proper bed.'

'I shouldn't have said that in front of mother and the girls. I'm very sorry, father.'

'Apology accepted.'

'Are you ashamed of me too, father?' Beb said, his voice breaking a little.

It was the first time that he had looked ten-years old for a long time, Kalu thought. He was so busy growing up, trying to become a man, that it was easy to forget he was just a boy.

'I am not ashamed of you and neither is your mother, Beb,' Kalu said.

'She said she was.'

'Sometimes, grownups say the opposite of how they really feel. Your mother loves you and she's very proud of you and so am I.' Kalu felt his bowels cramp. His stomach had been gurgling for hours but he hadn't wanted to stop on the highway where there was no cover. Squatting at the side of the road in front of his family was not good. His insides felt like a washing machine on spin. Whatever was in there, needed to come out. 'I'm going to go inside and book us some rooms. I won't be long.' Kalu took the gun from beneath the seat and tucked it into his belt.

'Okay, father. I'll stay and guard the truck,' Beb said, saluting.

'I'll lock the doors, okay?'

'Okay, father.'

Kalu climbed out of the truck and closed the door behind him. He locked it and knocked on the window and waved at Beb. Then he jogged to the rear entrance and went inside. Beb watched his father go into the hotel. He felt awful; he hadn't wanted to upset his mother. He hoped his father was right, that she would come around after sleeping. She was exhausted, he said. He was the cleverest man in Monguno, so he must be right. Beb lay down and looked up at the stars through the back window. His eyes filled with tears and he choked a sob. Disappointing his mother had hurt him. He let a few tears run and then dried his eyes with the back of his hands. Enough was enough. No more crying, he thought. He focused on something else. Looking at the stars, he tried to recall the constellations of the Northern Hemisphere but his head was foggy. His brain didn't feel as sharp as normal. The pain had been worsening for the last few hours but he didn't want to complain in front of the girls. He would tell his father later, when they weren't listening. He felt weary, suddenly. His eyes flickered and closed and he slipped away into a warm, silky darkness.

CHAPTER 19

Kalu walked into the hotel and headed towards the toilets. Esse and the girls were still in the ladies. He could hear them chattering. There was no time to wait for them to come out, he needed the toilet, urgently. He pushed open the door to the gents and walked in. The single cubicle was empty and he dashed to it, locking the door behind him. He managed to take his trousers down and sit, just in time. It was a painful ten minutes later when he emerged. Esse and the girls were exiting the ladies at the same time.

'There is only one cubicle in there; it takes forever with children,' Esse said. 'Have you booked a room yet?'

'No Esse,' Kalu answered, deciding not to explain the delay. 'I'm going to reception now.'

'Where's Beb?' Esse asked, searching the foyer with her eyes.

'Guarding the truck.'

'Is he okay?' Esse said, biting her bottom lip. She felt guilty for shouting at him. 'I shouldn't have shouted at him like that.'

'He was upset but he said he was sorry,' Kalu held her. She put her head on his chest. 'Don't worry, he'll be fine. He didn't mean to upset you.'

'I know. Give me the keys.' Esse smiled and kissed his cheek. 'I'll go and see him now.'

'Okay. Take it easy on him.'

'I will. I'll leave the girls with you,' Esse said. 'Stay with your father.' They nodded and walked with Kalu to the reception desk. The foyer was oval shaped with five large settees forming a square at the centre. Its ceiling was high and painted white, the walls a muddy brown.

'Good evening and welcome to the Algiers Hotel,' the pretty receptionist said. 'How can we help you tonight?'

'I need some rooms please,' Kalu said. 'There's my son and I, my wife and three daughters.'

'I'm afraid we only have one room available,' the receptionist said, smiling. She had the kind of smile that made everything okay. 'It's a family room with a double bed, two singles and a pull-out bed in the sofa.' She grinned. 'With a little imagination, you'll squeeze in. It's the best we can do, I'm afraid. Everywhere in town is full. So many people are heading for the border and the army has commissioned half our rooms.' She lowered her voice. 'Between me and you, they're a nightmare.' She grimaced. 'They're so rude and very badly behaved.' Kalu heard shouting. He was trying to be polite but it was distracting him. It was coming from outside. 'How will you be paying?' she asked.

'Mastercard, please,' Kalu said, turning away. He heard Esse screaming but it was muffled. She was outside. He didn't know how he could be sure that it was her, but he was. 'That's Esse,' he said, under his breath. 'Two minutes!' he said, walking quickly away from reception. The rear entrance door opened and Esse screamed again. This time it was full volume. It was a gut-wrenching wail.

'Kalu, Kalu!' she shouted. He reached the corridor; Esse was halfway down it, stumbling towards him. Blood was running down her forehead, trickling into her eyes. There was a gash running into her hairline. 'Kalu!' she wailed like a banshee. She collapsed a few yards in front of him. Soldiers came running from their rooms, alerted by the screaming. The receptionist ran to help. 'Kalu!' her voice was thick with phlegm and distant now. Her eyes closed.

'Does she need a doctor?' the receptionist asked.

'I am a doctor,' Kalu said, cradling her head. 'Esse, can you hear me?' Esse didn't respond. 'Could you get me some water and some tissue, please.' He looked at the girls. 'Go and see if Beb is okay, Oke.'

'Is everything okay?' an officer asked, approaching. The receptionist shook her head. 'What is wrong?' he asked, kneeling next to Kalu.

'I don't know yet,' Kalu replied. A bottle of water was handed to him. He twisted the top off and poured water onto the tissue. He put it over the gash in her head, applying pressure gently. She moaned. He put the bottle to her lips. Her eyes flickered open and she tried to sit up. 'Esse, what happened?'

'Beb!' Esse stammered. 'Beb!'

'What happened, Esse?' Kalu asked.

'Father,' Oke said, running in. Kalu turned to her. The three girls looked close to tears. 'The truck has gone!'

'What?' he gasped.

'They hit me and took the keys, Kalu,' Esse rambled. Her eyes were darting around the gathering crowd. 'There was nothing I could do; they were so strong.'

'Where is Beb?' Kalu asked but he already knew the answer. She was hysterical. 'Esse. Where is Beb?'

'He's in the truck!'

CHAPTER 20

Esse and the girls were sitting on a settee in the hotel foyer. The receptionist was fussing around them, bringing water and sweet tea. Esse was hysterical. She would cry and wail until she couldn't breathe anymore and then there would be respite for a few minutes, while she sobbed her heart out quietly. Kalu had sprinted to the rear car park with the officer and soldiers from the hotel. They ran quickly but the truck was long gone. The roads were quiet. Kalu ran to the street and looked up and down. There was no sign of any witnesses. The road left, led to the border crossing, the road right, led to the town and the desert beyond. Kalu could see soldiers stationed on the corner, two hundred yards to his right. He made to run towards them.

'Wait!' the officer shouted, holding him back. Soldiers were close behind him. 'What are you doing?'

'I'm going to ask them if they saw my truck driving by,' Kalu said, trying to get passed. 'Get out of my way!'

'Calm down,' the officer said. 'What is your name?'

'Kalu.' He tried to remain calm. 'Dr Kalu Adaku.'

'I am Colonel Biko,' he said, proudly, offering his hand. Kalu shook it, frantic to look for Beb.

'Look, colonel. I need to look for my son!'

'Where will you look?' the colonel asked. He looked around and shrugged. Kalu put his hands on his knees, thinking he might vomit. 'We'll ask those men if they saw anything, okay. Bring those soldiers to me,' the colonel ordered. One of the soldiers set off to the street. 'It will be quicker if I speak to them.' Kalu nodded and tried to control his breathing. 'It is dark and we are surrounded by three and a half million miles of desert. We need to search but we need to narrow it down, okay?' Kalu nodded and looked at the starlit sky. He was numb. Beb was gone, abducted, kidnapped, whatever the name was, he was gone. His son. His ten-year old boy was in the back of a truck in the middle of nine million kilometres of wilderness. The feeling of dread that had been hovering over him descended now, saturating his soul, weighing him down like concrete being pumped into his veins. Helplessness surrounded him like a sea of treacle. He couldn't move freely and breathing was difficult. The colonel was talking but he could barely follow a word he was saying. 'How long was your son alone in the truck?'

'Just a few minutes,' Kalu stammered, trying to work out how long it had been. What had he been thinking leaving him? 'There were soldiers across the street. I wouldn't have left him otherwise.' A tear rolled down his cheek. How could he have been so stupid leaving a ten-year old in a vehicle packed with supplies? 'It wasn't long. Ten minutes at the most.'

'Then your wife came out to see him and she was attacked?'

'Yes.'

'Was it locked?'

'Yes,' Kalu said, looking at him. Did he think he would have left his truck unlocked with his son in it? Did the colonel think he was stupid or irresponsible or both? 'Of course, it was locked.' He shook his head and tried to compose himself. The colonel was helping but interrogating too. 'I locked it before going into the hotel.'

'My wife took the keys to go and sit with Beb. I gave them to her.'

'She had the keys on her?'

'Yes.'

'Hence the bang on the head?'

'I think so.'

'She put up a fight, good for her,' the colonel said, nodding.

'Her son was in the truck,' Kalu said, biting his lip.

'What type of vehicle is it?' the colonel asked. His black face was creased by a lifetime in the sun.

'A Toyota Land Cruiser, nineteen nineties model. It's silver coloured. There are two spare wheels on the rear doors and fuel tanks strapped to the outside.'

'Get the description communicated to our troops,' the colonel ordered another one of his men. 'Running around the street like a headless chicken will not find your son. Stay calm and we'll do everything we can to help.'

'Thank you,' Kalu sighed.

'Let's see what your wife can tell us about her attackers,' the colonel said, gesturing that Kalu should lead the way inside. Kalu felt like he was being escorted. His legs were shaking and sweat was pouring down his back. The sensation of gagging, feeling like he was going to vomit was becoming more intense. No matter where he tried to take his mind, he couldn't escape the agonising pain of loss. 'Did she say anything about them?'

'No. she didn't have the chance to.'

'Your son is how old?' the colonel asked, frowning.

'He's ten,' Kalu choked. He had to stop walking. It broke. All the tension, fear and pain had built up to boiling point and now it spilled out. He leaned against the wall and sobbed. The colonel walked on to give him some space but two soldiers remained nearby. Tears blurred his vision. Pain blurred his mind. If only he hadn't left him alone. If only he had taken him with him. If only they hadn't come this way. If only they had gone straight to Chad. If only he had booked flights sooner. A million ifs rattled around his mind. He had let Beb down when he most needed his father there to protect him and he couldn't cope with the guilt. Long minutes ticked by before he could function. He rubbed his eyes on his shirt and took a deep breath. The soldiers looked away while he composed himself. Eventually he stood tall and took a deep breath. He walked down the corridor, his head in a spin. When he reached the foyer, he could hear Esse sobbing. The girls were being comforted by the receptionist. It reminded Kalu of a wake. They were as distraught about Beb as he was. Esse was devastated. He would have to shoulder their anguish too. It was time to be stoic once again. He sat next to Esse and she threw herself around his neck. She could hardly breath. Her sobs came from deep within her chest.

'I'm so sorry, Kalu,' she wailed. 'I couldn't stop them!'

'This is not your fault,' Kalu whispered. 'You did nothing wrong.'

'I shouted at him,' she said, pulling away and wiping her nose. Her face was etched with pain. 'I told him I was ashamed of him!'

'You told your child off for using bad language, nothing more,' he tried to reassure her.

The colonel and his soldiers approached. She looked at the colonel with contempt.

'Why is he here?' she snapped. Kalu held her. Everything was such a mess. Nothing made sense anymore.

'I know you're all upset,' the colonel said, coughing to get their attention. 'We need to ask some questions so we can look for the truck and bring your little boy back.'

'Are you looking for him?' Esse broke away from Kalu and stared at the officer. 'What is it, guilty conscience?'

'Esse,' Kalu whispered. 'It is not his fault.'

'You are looking for my son?' she relented.

'Yes.' He nodded and sat opposite her. 'We've distributed a description of the truck and our men are looking for it but we need to narrow the search.'

'How can we narrow it?' Esse asked.

'First of all, tell me what happened?'

'What can I tell you?' Esse said, shaking her head. 'I walked to the truck,' she paused to look at Kalu. Tears trickled from her eyes again. 'I can't believe that I shouted at him.' She closed her eyes and more tears spilled out. 'I walked around to the driver's door and put the key in the door,' she said, trying not to lose control. He must have heard me because he sat up. His little face lit up when he saw me.' She broke down again, her body racked with sobs. It was the most painful thing Kalu had ever witnessed. He had seen bereaved parents a hundred times but listening to his wife recounting the abduction of their son was like torture. He didn't want to listen. It was too much. Minutes went by until she recovered. 'The soldiers came,' she said. 'Beb was smiling and saluting as he does.' She stopped again. Her breathing uncontrollable.

'My soldiers came to help?' the colonel asked, his head tilted in question.

'What?' Esse asked, her voice a mere gasp.

'The soldiers, my men,' he said. 'They came to help you and then what?'

'They didn't come to help me,' Esse said. She had a horrified expression on her face.

'I don't understand,' the colonel, said frowning.

'They hit me over the head with a gun,' Esse said. Kalu sat with his jaw wide open. He couldn't take it in. 'It was the soldiers who took Beb.' She pointed her finger. 'Your soldiers took our son.'

The colonel's face turned to thunder. He coughed to clear his throat. The vein at his temple pulsed visibly.

'You're absolutely sure they were soldiers?' he asked, standing.

'Absolutely positive.'

'Then I will do everything within my power to find your son safely and return your truck to you.' He was about to walk away but Esse wasn't done.

'How, colonel,' she asked. 'How will you find him?'

He checked his watch. 'I will have more patrols at the crossable sections of the border within an hour and I will have a helicopter up at daybreak. You have my word that we won't stop looking for these men until we find them.' He looked at Kalu and Esse in the eye. Kalu believed he meant what he had said. Esse nodded and began sobbing again. There was nothing else that they could do. Once more the feeling of hopelessness was overwhelming. 'May I speak to you for a minute?' he said to Kalu.

They walked across the foyer, the colonel, gesturing his sergeant with them.

'I am embarrassed and horrified by these men's actions.' He paused. 'Sergeant, I want immediate roll calls in every unit within the hour,' he ordered.

'Sir.'

'I want to know who is missing and where they are from. At least we'll know which direction to search. It will narrow down the search considerably.'

'Yes, sir.'

'And double the number of units on the soft border for another twenty miles in each direction.'

'Sir?' the sergeant said, shaking his head as if it couldn't be done. 'We're stretched as it is.'

'I didn't ask for a debate on the subject, sergeant,' the colonel snapped. 'Get it done or I'll find a corporal who wants another stripe to do it.' The sergeant flushed red.

'Why are you still here?' the colonel barked. The sergeant scurried off, leaving Kalu and the colonel alone. 'There has been disquiet amongst the ranks since the Boko attacks in the south.' The colonel explained. 'I think that the men who took your son have requested leave to return home, its been refused and they have resorted to desertion.' Kalu listened and nodded. It made sense in theory, not that it mattered. Beb was out there somewhere in the dark, with strange men, who were probably armed and desperate to return home. Desperate men make rash decisions. A ten-year old boy was a witness. He could identify them. He was baggage. His guts felt like a giant hand was squeezing them. 'I'm not making excuses, you understand?' Kalu nodded. A gaggle of military men walked into reception. Kalu could see that they were junior officers. The colonel gestured to them to wait. 'I'll speak to my men and keep you posted if anything happens, Kalu.' Kalu nodded again. 'I'll let you get back to your family. They'll need you.' They shook hands and the colonel walked to reception. He summoned his junior officers around him.

Kalu walked to his family. It was agony to see them so distressed. His eyes filled up again and he had to wait a few seconds to speak.

'What's happening?' Esse asked.

'The colonel is going to keep us updated. I think we should go to the room. At least we'll have some privacy,' Kalu said. Esse nodded. 'I'll go and get the key,' he said, turning and walking to the reception. The receptionist smiled, concern on her face. 'I didn't get the key earlier.'

'Here it is,' she said, placing the key on the desk. 'Room twenty-two. Top of the stairs to the right.'

'Thank you,' Kalu said, flatly. He couldn't even pretend to be nice. Inside was numb. He turned to walk away.

'The colonel is paying the bill,' she added. Kalu thought about it for a second and nodded. He didn't have it in him to reply. What could he say? My son was kidnapped but we got a free room, bargain of the century. Soldiers took him but the army compensated us with a family room. There's a gesture you won't forget. He felt like telling him to shove it, but he needed his help. There was no way Kalu could look for Beb and the truck on his own. He had no transport anyway. The military were the only people with any chance of bringing him home. Once again, they had a bad choice or no choice. It was emasculating. 'If you need anything, anything at all, just let me know.' Kalu smiled thinly. He glanced at the officers across the foyer. They eyed him sympathetically. They had a three-minute conflab in a huddle and then they were gone. The colonel too.

CHAPTER 21

E sse was sitting next to the window with Kissie on her knee, her face buried into her neck; she was staring blankly over the main road. The other girls huddled on the double bed, looking like two peas in a pod, their faces streaked with tears. Kalu paced the room, waiting for news from the colonel. Time seemed to warp. Night was slowly turning to day; a thin line of silver appeared on the horizon. He checked his watch for the third time that minute. No one had thought about sleep. The longer they waited, the further away Beb would be. Kalu felt like his heart was being ripped from his chest. He knew the geography of their position. The sheer size of the desert would hinder the search. The Sahara was bigger than continental America and then some. There are three hundred and twenty-three million people in America but in comparison, only two-million in the Sahara. It is a vast empty sandbox where people vanish forever. The odds of finding someone, who doesn't want to be found were a million to one. The stark reality of the situation wasn't lost on Kalu. The chances of finding Beb were virtually zero. He looked at his family and felt detached from them. They had become a group of individuals grieving alone.

Esse was falling apart. She was beating herself up inside. Her last words to her son were that she was ashamed of him. Disgusted with him. What if she never saw him again? He could be dead already. She wasn't stupid. Kidnapped children in Africa seldom go home. Not alive. Would he spend his last moments on the earth thinking that his mother was ashamed of him? Would he think that she didn't love him? Probably, she thought. He would die frightened and alone, ripped from his family and taken into a sand covered wilderness. She wished she hadn't lost her temper. The feelings of loss and guilt were suffocating her.

A knock on the door broke the silence. Kalu opened it. There was a soldier there; Kalu didn't recognise him.

'Doctor Adaku,' the soldier said. 'Colonel Biko wants me to take you to him.'

'Why?' Esse said, excited. 'Has he found my son?'

'I don't have any information,' the soldier said, shaking his head. 'My orders are to take Doctor Adaku to the airport.'

'The airport?' Esse asked, confused. 'What is going on?' she moved Kissie from her knee. 'What has happened?'

'I don't have any information,' the soldier repeated. 'You need to accompany me, doctor.'

Kalu nodded and moved for the door.

'What are you doing, Kalu?' she asked, angrily.

'The colonel is helping us.' Kalu kissed her cheek. 'If he says he needs me to go to the airport, then that's what I'm going to do.'

'Be careful,' she said, defeated.

'I'll be fine,' Kalu said. He kissed the girls one at a time. 'I'll be with the army.' He walked out of the room and closed the door.

Outside, a jeep was parked, lights on and engine running.

'Sit in the front, doctor Adaku.' The driver didn't look at Kalu as he climbed into the front seat. The other soldier climbed into the back.

'Can you tell me what the colonel wants me for?' the soldiers shook their heads. 'Is there news of my son?'

'We don't know anything, doctor.'

The drive to the airport took twenty-five minutes. It was a long twenty-five minutes. His head was full of a thousand scenarios. Some were good, some were terrible. He was anxious yet excited. When they arrived at the airport, the jeep was waved through three sets of barriers. Tall floodlights lit up the runways. Military planes were parked in neat lines, ready for action. The jeep headed for the far side of the airport, where a helicopter was waiting to take off. He could see the colonel sitting inside. He gestured to him to get in. Kalu climbed out of the jeep and ran, head down to the helicopter. The downdraft was powerful and took his breath away. A second helicopter was warming up and soldiers were climbing aboard.

'Get in, get in,' the colonel shouted. Kalu climbed in and fastened his seatbelt. He looked to the colonel for information but he was busy pointing to a position on a map, chatting with the pilot.

'What is going on colonel?' Kalu asked. 'Have you found him?'

'We don't know yet,' he shouted over the engines.

'What do you mean?'

'We identified two men missing from roll call,' the colonel said, turning around. The helicopter climbed rapidly and banked left. 'They live to the north east of here.' Kalu nodded. It sounded like positive news. 'One of our helicopters was on a routine flight when they spotted a vehicle about a hundred miles north that fits the description of your Land Cruiser.' Kalu smiled inside. It was positive news. 'We're going to find it.'

'They didn't stop it?' Kalu asked.

'It was part of a military operation, Kalu.'

'Was it moving?' Kalu asked. He couldn't help but feel a little disappointed. His son might be in that truck.

'No, it's stationary.' The colonel turned around again. 'Don't get your hopes up. There are thousands of those trucks in Africa, that's why I asked you here.' He paused. 'I need you to identify the vehicle when we get there.'

Kalu felt his heart beating in his chest. Maybe the thieves were sleeping, thinking that they had travelled far enough from the town to be safe. Maybe Beb was safe and sound in the back, frightened but unharmed. On the other hand, he could be dead in the desert somewhere, killed and dumped in the sand. They might have thrown him out of the truck alive. He could be wandering, thirsty, hungry and alone, lost in the never-ending dunes. His brain tortured him with different horrific possibilities. They outnumbered the positive outcomes by ten to one.

The sky turned blue as they travelled quickly over the desert. Rusted vehicle skeletons littered the sand either side of the roads, a testament to the harsh conditions on the ground. The main highway north was to their right; they followed it until a barely visible track veered off to the west. The helicopter banked and followed it. Ten minutes later, they were circling a silver cruiser. The closer they got to it, the worse Kalu felt. His eyes filled up as he analysed the scene. The helicopter landed, spraying sand hundreds of yards into the air. The second helicopter landed next to them and six soldiers jumped out and surrounded the vehicle. They looked inside and gestured to the colonel that the area was safe.

'Let's go,' the colonel signalled. Kalu undid his seatbelt and climbed out. Sand filled his ears, nose and throat as he ran towards the cruiser. As they neared it, Kalu could see the windscreen had been shot through. The driver was sitting upright; the passenger slumped against the side window, both riddled with bullet holes. Kalu felt sick. He ran towards the truck; the soldiers stepped aside. The fuel cannisters that had been strapped to the sides were gone. Kalu wanted it to be another truck but it was his. There were bullet holes in the wing but the tyres were intact. He looked inside the truck. The soldiers who had stolen it had been dead for hours. He could tell by the congealing blood. The back seats were empty. He walked to the back of the vehicle where Beb had been lying on his makeshift bed. The rear door was ajar. Kalu opened it, his heart in his mouth.

Beb was gone.

'Is it your truck?' the colonel asked. Kalu collapsed to his knees and screamed at the sky.

The colonel left him for a few minutes and then approached him. 'Listen to me,' the colonel shouted over the noise of the rotor blades. Kalu looked at him through bloodshot eyes. 'Is it your vehicle?' Kalu nodded and vomited onto the sand. 'Your son is not here. That's a good sign,' the colonel shouted. 'If he was dead, his body would be here.'

'Where is he?' Kalu asked, sobbing. 'Where is my son?'

'I don't know, Kalu but we'll keep looking for him. I promise you that.' Kalu looked around. There was nothing to see but sand. He vomited again. 'Get this truck back to town,' the colonel ordered. He grabbed Kalu by the arm and lifted him to his feet. 'Come on,' he encouraged him. 'We'll take a look around from the air.'

Kalu felt like his legs were jelly as they bundled him into the helicopter. The colonel was talking to his troops but Kalu didn't compute what was being said. He watched as the bodies were dragged from the truck and dumped unceremoniously onto the sand. A soldier draped a waterproof cape over the driver's seat to stop the blood staining his uniform. He started the engine and turned the cruiser around. The helicopter climbed above the scene, making it surreal. Kalu could see it from directly above. The truck, the dead bodies and the sand. Nothing but sand as far as the eye could see.

'Why are there no tracks?' Kalu shouted. 'Surely there should be tracks?'

'The wind covers everything in minutes,' the colonel explained. 'I've been out here in tanks and you can't see the tracks for more than a few minutes. The sands shift so quickly.' Kalu felt dizzy as the helicopter climbed steeply and circled the area. Even from that height, he couldn't see anything but sand. Kalu rested his head against the window and studied the sands below. His mind played tricks on him, making him think he had seen movement from the corner of his eye, but when he looked there was nothing. It was a desolate landscape for thousands of miles in every direction.

Two hours later, the colonel said they were low on fuel and the pilot needed to return to base. He looked apologetic as he spoke. Kalu felt heartbroken as they headed back to the airport. The desert was so vast, it was an impossible task. Beb was gone, all the helicopters in Africa wouldn't be able to find him.

CHAPTER 22

The next five days went by in a nightmare haze. Esse and the girls spent the daylight hours trudging the streets of In Guezzam in a hopeless search for Beb. She was adamant that he may have been thrown out of the truck before they reached the desert and that he may be wandering the streets lost and alone. Kalu couldn't tell her anything different. A small part of him, the wildly optimistic part, hoped she might find him kicking a football around on a piece of waste ground, complaining that he was hungry. The nights were grim. The family would eat, mostly in silence and then Esse and the girls would spend hours on Oke's Facebook, looking at pictures of Beb. They posted pictures of him on internet sites that Kalu had never heard of. Keeping active took her mind away from the pain for a while. Searching for him helped. Then they would try to sleep, listening to their mother sob in the dark. That was the worst of it for Kalu. Not being able to say or do anything to stop her hurting was torturous. He had cured thousands of people but he couldn't cure this.

At first light, every morning, she would be up, dressing the girls for another long day searching the streets again. How could he tell her to stop, that her son was gone and that she had to accept that? Hope was all that she had. She was clinging to the hope for dear life. He couldn't take that one thing away from her. Not until she saw the reality herself. It was an impossible conundrum.

Kalu spent hours on the phone to his brother trying to come up with a plan to get them to Europe. Boko Haram were making slow progress pushing north into Chad and Niger. They couldn't stay on the border indefinitely. All the options were dangerous, some more dangerous than others. The colonel had been a shining light of human decency. He had ordered all routine flights to dedicate some time during their missions to search in ever increasing circles, looking for a Tuareg caravan, which may have taken Beb. If it hadn't been for him, there wouldn't have been any kind of search at all. His force was depleted by the battles in the south, yet he wouldn't give up. He had the Land Cruiser brought back to In-Guezzam and repaired. The windscreen was replaced and the bloodstained seats were cleaned. He promised Kalu that when they were ready to leave, the truck would be fuelled and strapped with enough petrol to get them into Libya and on to the coast. It was the only silver lining in this storm cloud.

At least they could continue north despite the tragic loss of their son. The truth was, that the danger hadn't passed. It was still there, following them. Esse seemed to have forgotten why they were fleeing north in the first place. Her coping mechanism was fixed firmly on searching for her son every day. Kalu understood perfectly but he knew that he would have to break the cycle at some point and he was dreading it. He looked out of the hotel room window as the world went on turning. Their life had been put on hold by the loss of Beb but still the world spun on its axis. Cars and buses went by, people walked to work, babies would be born, old people would pass away, wars would be won and wars would be lost. Time didn't stop for anyone or anything. The clocks kept ticking. Beb was gone but the danger wasn't.

Across town, Sunbola climbed out of a minibus. She had been taken from a small village on the edge of the Borno province of Nigeria, two years earlier when she was thirteen. The Boko soldiers who took her had offered her a choice, marry and conform or be sold. It was the choice offered to hundreds of missing girls. Sunbola conformed and now her husband had told her that it was her time. Leaving her children to make the journey had been heart breaking but she would see them later. She hitched up her black abaya dress and fixed her hijab across her face. The sun was intense and she was sweating. Her pulse was racing as she entered the diner. Brass fans turned lazily, trying to cool the room but failing miserably. The tables were packed with men in uniform, who patronised the place. Some of them looked up when she walked in, most didn't. The air was thick with cigarette smoke and grease. A fat cook looked over the counter at her. Women didn't frequent the diner often. She had nice eyes, he thought, although they looked a little sad. The ash fell from the cigarette that dangled from his mouth into a goat stew; he stirred it in, no one would know.

Sunbola looked around and spotted a table full of officers. She walked towards it. One of the men looked up and frowned. As she approached, her lips moved in silent prayer and then she detonated the bomb around her abdomen.

Kalu watched in horror as a series of explosions rocked In-Guezzam. Black smoke drifted upwards from four sites, nearby. He turned from the window and ran from the hotel room.

CHAPTER 23

Esse and the girls were near the market when the first explosion went off. She felt the vibrations through her feet. People began to panic and run in all directions, knocking each other to the ground, trampling on the fallen. She grabbed the girls and ushered them to a low stone wall. Crouching down, they watched as explosions shook the town. Esse looked on in terror as another suicide bomber hit the market. It was crowded with people trying to get out. The explosion was devastating. When the smoke cleared, there were bodies everywhere. There was a moment of stillness as if time stood still and then the frantic effort to escape began. Chaos reigned.

Esse looked around to fix her position. She had been wandering around the town for days, never really knowing where she was. Her mind was preoccupied with thoughts of Beb and where he was. She knew he wasn't dead. She would have known if he was dead. She would be able to feel him gone from this place. Her eyes focused on the flagpoles sticking up above the buildings. The hotel was a few streets away.

'Come on, we need to go,' Esse said, pushing the girls in the right direction. They stayed low as they ran across the road. Severed limbs littered the pavements. Kissie tripped over a crash helmet and fell. The motorcyclist's head was still inside it, the eyes staring at her, accusingly. She screamed as her mother dragged her to her feet and pulled her away. 'Run!' Esse shouted.

The streets emptied as people took cover inside. It didn't take Esse long to navigate their way past a bombed-out diner to the hotel. Kalu was outside talking to a soldier, who was helping him to strap petrol cannisters to the side of the truck. The girls ran to their father and hugged him.

Esse stopped in her tracks and began shaking her head. She knew what this meant. It hit her like a ton of bricks. Kalu was preparing to leave.

'No, Kalu,' she shouted. She shook her head, vehemently. 'I will not leave!' Kalu walked over to her and tried to hold her but she stepped back and brushed him off. 'How can you think about leaving? He's your son and he's out there somewhere!'

'Esse,' he said, calmly. 'Look at the smoke. Boko are here, Esse.'

'I will not leave my son, Kalu. Not for you, not for Boko, not for anyone,' she said, angrily. 'I cannot believe you would consider leaving your son!'

'Do you see those three girls there, shaking they're so frightened?' Kalu raised his voice. Grief was not a monopoly. He was grieving too. 'Do you see them, Esse?'

'Of course, I do!' she snapped.

'Good. because they're your children too. Look around, Esse,' he said turning and pointing at the towers of black smoke. 'Look around you!' he said, louder this time. 'Boko are here, Esse and they want our daughters!'

'I can't leave my son, Kalu,' she said, trembling.

'Beb has gone,' Kalu said. Tears spilled from his eyes as he said it aloud. He hadn't said it before. He had thought it, but saying those words cracked something inside. 'We have tried everything to find him, Esse. Even the army can't find him. They've searched the desert for days with helicopters and they can't find him. What chance do we have?' his lip quivered as he spoke. His voice was thick. 'Beb has gone, Esse.' He shook his head and wiped tears from his eyes. 'Beb has gone and we have to protect our other children. We have to get the girls out of here.'

'How can you say you'll leave him here?' she sobbed. 'He's here somewhere.'

'He has gone, Esse.' Kalu opened the back door of the truck. 'Get inside, girls,' he said, gently. 'We need to go.' The girls looked at their mother. She nodded, almost imperceptibly. Beb was gone. She knew it but her heart wouldn't let her accept it. Beb was gone. It echoed around her mind. Her son was gone.

'I promise you that when the girls are safe in Europe, I will come back here and search every inch of that desert until I find him.' He put his hand on his heart. 'I promise that I will come back and find him, Esse. If he's still alive, I'll find him.' Kalu felt twisted inside. He was making a promise that he couldn't keep. He knew it and so did Esse. She sank to her knees and put her head on the floor. He could see it in her eyes. Beb was gone and no one could bring him back. Not even the cleverest man in Monguno.

CHAPTER 24

When the cruiser was loaded, Kalu helped Esse into the passenger seat. She was weak, fragile and confused. The grief was so intense that she couldn't think straight. Kalu was about to get into the driver's seat when the colonel pulled up in a camouflage jeep. Kalu walked over to his vehicle.

'Boko have bombed the border crossing,' the colonel said, shaking his head. 'You'll never get across there. The tailback is miles long.'

'What shall I do?' Kalu asked.

'Head east for about ten miles,' the colonel pointed. 'You'll come to a wrecked tank on the right-hand side of the road. You'll see a track heading north. Follow that for about fifty kilometres and you'll meet the main road north.' He offered his hand. 'I have your number, Kalu. If we see anything of your son, I'll contact you.'

'Thank you, colonel and thank you for everything that you've done.'

'Good luck.'

'And to you,' Kalu said. The jeep pulled away and slid into the traffic.

Kalu walked back to the truck and checked the straps were tight. The canisters hid the bullet holes, which was a blessing. He didn't want Esse and the girls seeing them. They were unsettled enough as it was. He checked the back door and opened it. The mattress was still there. He rolled it up and pushed it to one side. The carpet over the wheel well was curled at one corner. He pulled at it and it came away. His stomach turned when he looked into the well where a spare wheel could be stored. There was Beb's rucksack. He took it out and looked inside. The money was still there, so was his phone. There was no sign of the gold coin. He thought about telling Esse but decided against it. She was a mess. There was no need to add more confusion to the mix. Kalu knew that Beb had hidden the bag purposely. He must have feared that it would be stolen from him. That indicated that he had been thinking clearly when the soldiers stole the truck. He wasn't sure what that told him or if it changed anything. The soldiers had been ambushed. An ambush in the desert pointed to the Tuareg tribes, that roamed the dunes. He had to assume that Beb had been taken by the Tuareg. However difficult it was to come to terms with that fact, it meant he could be alive somewhere.

Kalu put the rucksack back into the wheel well and closed the door. He climbed into the driver's seat and started the engine. Esse was staring into space, her mind in turmoil. He reached for her hand but she snatched it away. There was anger in her eyes when she looked at him. Real anger. What could he do? She felt that he was giving up on Beb, dragging her away from her son. He looked at the girls in the mirror and put the truck into gear. Their frightened faces were enough to confirm that he was doing the right thing. He had to get them to safety.

They headed east and left In-Guezzam behind. The sun blazed down and baked the earth. It was becoming almost unbearable in the truck. The girls passed water around, usually Esse's role but she was transfixed by the sand, searching it in the hope of seeing Beb somewhere out there. When they reached the remnants of a tank, he turned north and followed a narrow track, just as the colonel had said. Fifty kilometres on, he could see the main road running parallel to them. He followed the track to the point where it met the road and then pulled into the heavy traffic that was heading north. The line of slow moving vehicles stretched as far as he could see, in front and behind. They stayed on that road until they were north of Tamanrasset, then they took the right fork and headed for the Libyan border. They had just over a thousand miles to go to reach the coast near Tripoli. Esse was mute, almost catatonic and he couldn't ask her to share the driving. She didn't know what day it was. Despite his tiredness, he trundled on following the RN53, heading north-east to the Libyan border town of Ghadamis. The traffic was minimal, most people choosing to continue north and drive to Algiers. At the border, they were waved through without being searched or questioned. The Libyan border guards were playing cards and chatting and looked disinterested as they passed.

Kalu was surprised at how easy it had been to cross until they came to a checkpoint a few miles on. He joined a queue of a dozen vehicles and waited for his turn to be robbed. Libyan soldiers moved along the line, taking money from the drivers before waving them on. Kalu lowered his window as the soldiers approached.

'One hundred US per person,' the soldier said, holding out a grubby hand. Kalu peeled the notes from a roll of dollars.

'That's six hundred,' Esse snapped.

'What?' Kalu asked, confused.

'You've counted six hundred dollars,' Esse said, glaring at him. 'There are five of us now, remember. We left our son in In-Guezzam.'

It was a knife through the heart. Kalu took a note back and handed the five hundred to the soldier. He couldn't find the words to defend himself. There were no words. Esse was hurting so much that she couldn't see that he was broken too. He waited for the traffic to move on and then continued driving deeper into Libya.

An hour into Ghadamis, Kalu spotted a petrol station. It was a single pump outside of a brick-built hut. Next to it was a café with a toilet block fashioned from wooden pallets. There were piles of tyres dotted about, most of them worn and shiny. An engine block had been turned into a seat next to the entrance. The owner was stooped and toothless, his skin like leather from sitting in the sun. A sandy coloured dog was scavenging through a discarded binbag, its ribs clearly visible beneath his fur. Kalu had been driving on autopilot for hours. It was time to stop, eat and relieve themselves.

'Where are we?' Esse asked. Her eyes were deep and bloodshot. She looked around at the girls. They smiled at her. She hadn't looked at them since they'd left In-Guezzam. 'Are you okay, girls?'

'We're okay,' Oke answered. She didn't ask how her mother was feeling. It would be a stupid question. The pain was etched into her face. Her eyes, the windows to the soul, were haunted. Seeing her mother in such pain was difficult. She wanted to say something to ease her suffering but the words just wouldn't come.

'I need the toilet,' Kissie said, crossing her legs.

'Me too,' Isime agreed.

'We'll all go together,' Esse said opening the door. 'Don't leave anything in the truck. Take your rucksacks with you.'

'I'll fill the tank up and follow you in. We need to eat,' Kalu said. Esse looked at him, her eyes piercing. He could feel the anger in them. Her pain was being focused on him. He sensed it, however misplaced it was. It was there. It was tangible. She closed the door without answering him. Kalu felt a sinking feeling in his guts. It was like a kick in the teeth. He had lost Beb and Esse simultaneously. Misery and despair were becoming familiar friends.

Kalu watched Esse and the girls walking to the toilet block. There was a small queue outside. He climbed out of the truck and stretched his arms and legs. His bones felt weary. He unstrapped one of the petrol canisters and opened the cap. Emptying it, he was trying to gauge if he needed to refill the canister at the pump. He decided that he should, just in case. It took two canisters to fill the truck and he took them to the pump and asked the owner to fill them. He said he would pick them up when they were ready to leave. The dog trotted over to him, searching for food and Kalu skirted around him. Stray dogs carried rabies and he didn't need that to add to his troubles.

As he walked back towards the café, he saw a rusty Renault Laguna parked near the road. He couldn't be sure if it was the same one but it made him uneasy. The truck was locked, the fuel tanks emptied and Esse had made sure that the girls had their rucksacks. It was parked in clear view of the café. He tried to relax but it was difficult; Beb was very much on his mind.

Raised voices snapped him back to reality. He stopped to see which direction they were coming from. A woman's voice was panicked and angry; a male voice was deep and aggressive. They were coming from the toilet block. He ran around the truck towards it, trying to decipher what was being said. When he turned the corner, he stopped. Esse and the girls were backed up against the toilet block. Three other women were next to them. They were cowering in fear. Two men stood in front of them, brandishing knives. Kalu recognised them as the men from Bande. The Laguna driver and his mate. It appeared that robbery was still their bag but this time, the driver had acquired a gun. He was waving it around, the weapon horizontal to the floor, like a gangster in a movie. The men were shouting, demanding that Esse and the girls hand over their rucksacks. Esse looked at Kalu, eyes accusing him. *This is all your fault, they said.* Kalu snapped.

CHAPTER 25

A lice watched through the window as the first Boku Haram militiamen roared
through Bande. It was a sad day. The Niger forces had been outflanked and
overrun. She had watched them retreating for hours through the night; the
lucky ones were onboard trucks, the unlucky ones on foot. They looked beaten and
frightened as they trudged by. The soldiers who had helped Kalu had stopped and
asked for food and water. Of course, Alice had fed and watered them but they didn't
hang around. They told Alice that Boko were on their tail and that she should leave.
They left in such a rush, one of them left some of his belongings. She hoped he would
pick them up on their way back when they were driving Boko from their country.
Convoy after convoy retreated north, where they hoped to regroup and make a
counterattack. Most of the residents of Bande had fled, in the hope that they could
return when the rebels were defeated and driven back to border regions. The Niger
government hadn't seen Boko as a serious military threat but no one had told Boko
Haram that. Some, like Alice had remained. She clothed herself in traditional dress,
hiding her face with a hijab. Boko were strict and they were brutal. Angering them was
easy. As she watched, some of the Boko vehicles were stopping to deploy troops. They
began to sweep the town looking for enemy forces who might be hiding there.

She watched from an upstairs window as they approached. A bang on the door
made her jump with fright. Her husband and sons had left to stay in the next village
where her in-laws lived. Men were rounded up and killed if they resisted. It was better
that they weren't there. She tiptoed down the stairs when another rap on the door
came. It sounded like they were going to break through it. She switched on the light
and walked through the kitchen, into the dining room. Shadows loomed at the door.
She opened it and rebels barged in and swept her aside.

'Who is here with you?' one of them growled.

'I'm alone,' Alice answered. She placed some clean glasses on the table and filled a
jug. 'It is hot tonight. Would you like some water?'

Two of the men eyed her suspiciously. Two more thumped up the stairs to search the living quarters. She could hear them clomping about, going from room to room. It was difficult listening to strangers ransacking her home but she could put things straight when they had gone. It was better to bite her lip than to provoke their anger. They looked angry without any help from her. She tried to behave as normal as possible, despite her fear.

'Are you hungry?' Alice asked. 'I could heat up some stew and dumplings.' She put the cooking pot on the stove without waiting for an answer. 'Of course, you're hungry, silly question. You men are always hungry. You must have been travelling all night?' Cutting some bread, she put It on to a plate and took into the dining room. 'Sit, sit, sit,' she ushered the men. She placed the bread on the table and filled up the water jug. The men snatched the bread and stuffed it into their mouths. The other men came downstairs noisily. They entered the kitchen and smelled the food. The sergeant frowned and looked around.

'There are men's clothes upstairs,' he shouted. 'You said you were alone.'

'I'm alone. There's no one else here.'

'I don't believe you, woman. Where are they hiding?' he said, walking through the kitchen. He stopped dead when he saw the men in the dining room, sitting around the table eating bread. 'What are you doing?' he asked.

'The woman is making stew and dumplings,' one answered. 'She brought us this bread to eat.'

'Stew and dumplings?' the sergeant said, his temperature rising.

'Yes. It smells good,' the man said, smiling. 'We might as well eat. We don't know when we will eat again.'

'Stew and dumplings,' he repeated.

'Is something wrong?' the man asked, confused.

'Get up!' his superior shouted. 'Get up and do your duty!' spittle flew from his mouth as he spoke.

'What's the problem?' the man said, standing quickly. He was frightened of the sergeant. He was brutal, no matter whose side you were on but the soldier's patience was wearing thin. Hunger was making him braver than he would normally be. He stood face to face with the sergeant.

'What is the problem?' the sergeant repeated.

'Yes. What is the problem?' he said, insolently. He was pushing his luck.

'We're here to sweep the town for enemy soldiers and you think that you have time for stew and dumplings?' the sergeant said, putting his forehead against the soldier's face, incensed by his attitude.

'I didn't think it was a problem, sergeant; I was hungry.' He stepped back, putting some space between them.

'Shut up and search the back yard,' the sergeant shouted. He slapped the soldier across the cheek with his right hand. The soldier glared angrily at him but didn't dare retaliate. 'You will eat when I tell you that you can eat!'

'There's no need to shout,' Alice said, trying to calm the situation.

'Shut up woman!' the sergeant turned on Alice. 'Whose clothes are upstairs?' the sergeant snapped.

'They're my husband's,' Alice answered.

'Where is he hiding?'

'He's gone to a funeral in the next village. His father is dead,' Alice lied. 'He died two days ago.' She filled a glass of water and handed it to the sergeant. He took it from her and emptied it in one long gulp. As he put the glass down, something caught his eye. A camouflage cap and a rifle stood leaning against the wall. Alice turned to see what he was looking at. 'Did your husband leave his hat and rifle here when he went to the funeral?'

The sergeant pulled out his pistol and shot Alice between the eyes. She was dead before she hit the floor.

****

Colonel Biko inspected the aftermath of the bombings with some of his junior officers. The souk, a Sunni mosque, a diner and the border crossing had been attacked, almost simultaneously with devastating results. The timing of the attacks was impressive. No one expected Boko to move through Niger with the speed and ferocity that they had, least of all, the Algerian army. Boko had sent a wave of attacks as a precursor to their military following up. It appeared that they weren't going to stop until someone stopped them. The suicide bombers were an invisible foe. He couldn't see them coming, no one could. Their effect was devastating, not just physically, but the emotional impact that they had on the population was immeasurable. The relentless flow of humans migrating from the south was testament to the effects. People were leaving their homes in the thousands and heading north. Fear stalked the continent.

The colonel watched as engineers worked on the damaged border crossing. A car bomb had left a crater, six-feet deep and ten-feet wide. A guard hut had been reduced to splinters; the metal barriers were buckled and twisted beyond repair. Eight border troops and thirty civilians had been killed by the device. Across the town, the death-toll was in the hundreds. The damage meant that the crossing was down to one lane, traffic was horrendous and the colonel was worried that so many vehicles in close proximity to each other was inviting another bomber to take his trip to paradise. He ordered the crossing to be opened with minimal checks until the backlog was cleared. Things were moving and the engineers were estimating the crater would be filled and covered within twenty-four hours. Repairing the damage from the attacks was farcical. The suicide bombers were just the breeze warning of the tornado to come. It felt like putting an Elastoplast on an amputation. The patient was going to die no matter what he did.

'Colonel Biko,' one of his officers called him. 'There's a phone call for you,' he said, handing him a Samsung.

'Colonel Biko,' he answered.

'Colonel. One of our patrols has encountered a Bedouin caravan about a hundred miles west.'

'And what?'

'They were questioned about the Nigerian boy. They said that they found two bodies in the desert north of where they are now. Not far away from where we recovered that Toyota. One of them was a young black boy, could have been Nigerian, the other an Algerian soldier.' The colonel closed his eyes and rocked his head backwards. 'Colonel?'

'Yes. I heard you,' the colonel said. 'What did they do with them?'

'They said they buried them, sir.'

'Did they have any ID on them?'

'Not according to the tribesmen, sir. They said they had been shot.'

'Did they mark the graves?'

'No, sir.'

'Okay, thank you,' the colonel said, hanging up. He checked his watch. Kalu and his family would be well into Libya by now, all being well. Telling him that a body had been found not far away from where the truck was found would not help them right now. Crossing the Mediterranean was going to be difficult enough without being told that their son had been shot dead and buried in the sand. The colonel decided that it was in their interest not to tell them. If Kalu contacted him when they had reached their destination, then he would tell him. Telling them now wouldn't bring their son back. For now, they all had to focus on surviving.

CHAPTER 26

Kalu picked up a rock. He aimed it at the Laguna's passenger and threw it as hard as he could. The rock struck him on the back of his head, knocking him forward. He collapsed to his knees, cursing in pain. The driver turned quickly, recognition and fear in his eyes. He aimed the gun at Kalu but it didn't slow his advance. Kalu wasn't for stopping. He pulled out his gun and aimed it at the driver's chest. The driver waved the gun and grinned like a madman.

'Hello, friend,' he said, shaking his head, 'We meet again!'

'We do,' Kalu said, walking towards him. Inside him was ice. There was no fear in there, only pain. 'Drop the gun.'

'I don't think so, my friend!' the driver fired a shot. Kalu heard it whistle passed his right ear. The driver looked disappointed. He fired again but the gun clicked, empty.

Kalu pulled the trigger and shot him in the chest. He looked surprised as he clutched at the wound. Blood pumped through his fingers. He staggered backwards and fell; Kalu put another bullet into him. His body jerked like it had been hit with an electric shock. The passenger scrambled across the sand on his hands and knees. Blood was running from the wound on the back of his skull. He turned to face Kalu as he approached.

'Don't kill me!' he begged.

Kalu raised the gun and aimed at his head. He heard Beb's voice in his head.

'If anyone tries to steal anything, I'll shoot the bastard in the face.'

He pulled the trigger and the man toppled backwards onto the sand, eyes wide and staring at the sky, frightened and confused.

'No, Kalu!' Esse shouted.

Kalu fired again; the bullet struck the dirt an inch away from his left ear.

'Kalu, stop!'

A third bullet struck the ground an inch from his right ear. Kalu fired a fourth that barely missed his head.

'Kalu!'

Kalu kept firing until the revolver was empty. When he stopped firing, the passenger opened his eyes and wondered why he wasn't dead. He looked up at Kalu and put his hands together in prayer.

'Please don't kill me!'

'You've got the time it takes me to reload to get out of here,' Kalu said, reloading. The man scrambled to his feet and staggered off as fast as his legs would carry him. He ran to the road and sprinted back towards the border. Kalu finished loading the gun and put it back into his belt. He turned to look at his family. The girls were shocked, looking at the dead body. Esse didn't take her eyes from him. She shook her head in disbelief. Kalu could feel the contempt in her eyes but the way he felt, it just hardened his resolve. He needed to get the girls out of the madhouse to safety.

CHAPTER 27

Kalu strapped the petrol canisters to the truck, while Esse bought food from the café. They decided that eating on the move was the wise thing to do. The petrol station owner had some of his workers take the body across the road and into the desert before it started to stink. He moved the Laguna around the back and started the engine up, lifting the bonnet, he stood watching the engine turn, very impressed with his knew accusation. A man had been shot and no one fluttered an eyelid. Chaos reigned across Africa. Life was always cheap but the price had dropped to rock bottom. Kalu felt remarkably well. In fact, it was the best he had felt since Boko had arrived in Monguno. The girls were looking at him a little differently but one day, they would realise that the situation was extreme. Extreme measures had to be taken sometimes. The man had taken a shot and missed. Eventually those two men would use their gun and knives, if they hadn't already. Others would lose their lives. Some may think Kalu had done the world a favour. He didn't know how he felt about much, if he was honest with himself. His entire being was numb.

Esse eyed him coldly as she returned with the food. She opened the passenger door and climbed in, sharing the food with the girls. Kalu got into the truck and she passed him, soup and bread and bottled water. He drank and ate greedily. Hunger and thirst had taken a backseat for a while. When he was done, he turned and smiled at the girls. They looked at him and half smiled. He still looked like their father despite him acting differently.

'All ready to go?' he said, smiling. They nodded that they were and fastened their seatbelts. 'Esse?'

'What?' she asked, as if he was mad.

'Are you ready to go?'

'Am I ready to go?' she asked, sarcastically. 'Are you ready to go or would you like to shoot somebody else before we go?'

'No,' Kalu said, starting the engine. 'I'm all done shooting people for today. I should have shot them the first time around in Bande,' he added, sarcastically. Esse was going to speak but decided not to. There was no fight left in her. 'They were trying to rob a group of women at gunpoint,' Kalu added. 'He tried to kill me, unfortunately, he missed and now he's dead. I can live with that, so should you.' Esse didn't reply. She stared the other way at the desert. He drove the truck onto the road and headed for Tripoli. Half an hour went by in silence.

'I don't think you had much choice, father,' Oke said. Contradicting her mother was a rare occurrence. 'There were two of them, mother,' she reasoned. 'And they had a gun and knives. That man shot at father.'

'Be quiet, Oke! One of them dropped his knife and held his hands up,' Esse said, turning in her seat. 'The other was trying to get away. He pleaded for his life.' She turned back to Kalu. 'You shot at him anyway.'

'Two less bad people in the world,' Kalu said.

The atmosphere in the truck was tense as they drove the three-hundred miles to the Gharyan Road, which led into the city. The girls sat forward, amazed by the skyline. Tripoli is an eclectic mix of modern high-rise tower blocks and terraced slums. The Medina tower dominated the skyline. Ancient and new put together in a cultural melting pot, seasoned by war and revolutions. The country was still reeling since the fall of Colonel Gadaffi. As he neared the suburbs, he realised the scale of the migrant crisis. There were thousands of black Africans lining the streets, many sitting on the floor in large groups. Impromptu market stalls had been set up, selling toiletries, cigarettes and lighters but the most common article that they could see were life-jackets. Every colour of the spectrum. There were hundreds, if not thousands of life-jackets for sale.

'Why are there so many life-jackets?' Oke asked.

'A lot of people here have boats,' Esse answered, before Kalu could. She shot him a look that said, don't frighten them. 'What is the plan?' she asked Kalu.

'I want to get to the coast road,' Kalu said. He turned at a signpost that depicted a yacht and assumed it would take them to the harbour. A mile on, the road dipped and they could see Tripoli port. Huge container ships were docked next to small fishing boats and big trawlers. Giant cranes straddled the dockside loading and unloading containers. To the left was a marina, where millionaire yachts were once moored. They were long gone, stolen during the fall of their dictator. There were a few burnt out wrecks remaining. 'My brother said most of the transport across the sea is going from the east of the city,' Kalu said. 'We'll head east and find somewhere to stay. Once we're settled, we can organise passage on a boat.'

'I can't believe we're here,' Esse said, staring at the sea. 'Beb so wanted to see the sea.' No one answered her. They could see that she was crying again.

'I think it's beautiful,' Kissie said, watching the sun reflect from the blue water.

'It is beautiful,' Kalu agreed.

'We are going to get to Europe, aren't we?' Isime said, almost surprised.

'We are,' Kalu said.

'I didn't think we were going to make it,' Oke said.

'Me too,' Kissie agreed.

'Me too,' Isime added.

'It's not your fault,' Esse said, looking out of the window. Kalu looked at her confused.

'What?' Kalu asked.

'I said, it isn't your fault.' Kalu looked at her. Her eyes were still watery and red. 'Beb being taken, those thieves trying to rob us, being here in Tripoli thousands of miles away from our home,' she said with a shrug. 'None of it is you fault.' She squeezed his hand. Kalu nodded silently. 'We've got this far. Let's get the girls somewhere safe.'

Kalu drove the truck east, keeping the sea on his left. Eventually the giant container port gave way to smaller harbours and natural rock coves. The buildings had a more middle-eastern flavour. A huge red castle rose above the terraced hillside. The roads were narrow and busy. They reached the walls of the old town and Kalu parked the truck on a car park.

'Take everything,' he said. The girls and Esse grabbed their bags and climbed out. Kalu went to the back of the truck. He opened the door and uncovered Beb's rucksack, taking the money and the phone without Esse seeing, he put it back into the wheel well. They walked through an ancient archway and into the old town, unwelcome glances followed them. Kalu noted that there were not as many black faces in this part of the city. The black people that he did see, looked to be working there.

'Hey,' a voice called to them. Kalu turned to see an elderly man, dressed in traditional clothing, and sandals. His beard was grey, white in places. He smiled to reveal tobacco stained teeth. 'Are you looking for somewhere to stay?'

'Yes,' Kalu said. The man gestured for them to follow.

'Follow me. I'll give you the best price.'

'How far is it?' Kalu asked.

'Not far,' the man said, gesturing them to follow. They hesitated but tiredness and exhaustion meant the first offer was the best one. They followed the old man, who was spritely for his age. They weaved through a maze of streets and alleyways, Esse and the girls chatting as they walked. Esse seemed to be returning to somewhere near her normal self with them. The girls were young and resilient and the loss hadn't hit them with the same ferocity. Once everything had settled down and they had time to reflect, things might catch up with them. Thirty-minutes later, they were there. It was a small guesthouse; the signs written in Arabic. 'I have a large room with two beds. They're big enough for you all to sleep. Or you can have two rooms, it's up to you.' He opened the door and they walked into a square room with low ceilings. Tables and chairs were laid out for people to eat.

'How much are the rooms?' Esse asked.

'How long are you staying?' he grinned. 'The longer you stay, the better the deal.'

'We're not sure,' Kalu said, cautiously.

'Shall we say a week while you organise your transport?' he said winking at the girls. 'You are trying to get a boat, aren't you?' If it's any less, you can have some money back.'

'How much are the rooms?' Kalu asked, flatly. He was beginning to become suspicious of the old man.

'Five hundred US for the room for a week or eight hundred for both,' the man said, offering Kalu his hand. Kalu didn't shake it. 'I'll need another hundred as a deposit for any damages of course, and I'll need to hold your passports until you leave.'

'Forget it. We're leaving,' Kalu said, walking towards the door. 'Come on, girls.'

'Come on, friend,' the man said, smiling like a snake. 'What is your best offer? We can come to a deal, surely.' He stepped in front of the doorway. 'Make me an offer.'

'Move out of my way,' Kalu said, staring into his eyes. 'I won't ask you a second time.' Fear flickered in them and he stepped aside. They walked outside and headed down the street.

'You won't get a better price, anywhere else!' the man shouted after them. 'You're migrants. If the police find out you are migrants, they'll detain you in a camp. You won't like it there, I can tell you! They'll arrest you as soon as they look at you.'

'Why is he saying that?' Oke asked.

'Why will the police arrest us?' Kissie asked.

'Ignore him,' Kalu said, turning the corner. 'He's just angry that he lost a customer by being greedy. The man is nothing more than a thief,' he added.

''Shoot him, father,' Kissie said, looking over her shoulder. The old man stared back with angry eyes. Kissie pulled her tongue at him.

'We won't need to shoot him, Kissie,' Kalu said, rubbing her hair. 'We're not in any danger, are we?'

'No, father,' she said, shaking her head. 'We're not in danger.'

Esse and Kalu exchanged glances. Kalu looked sheepish. Neither of them chastised Kissie. It wasn't her fault. It wasn't anyone's fault. They walked back the way they came until they arrived at the arch, tired and disheartened. Kalu looked around for inspiration. None of the signage made any sense to him. A young man approached him.

'Are you people lost?'

'No. We know where we are.'

'Did the old man try to rob you?' he said, pointing in the direction they had been. Kalu nodded. He was short on trust. This man was a stranger just the same as the other had been. 'We're not all bad here in Tripoli. He's a villain.'

146

'We found that out.'

'How much was he asking for a room?'

'Too much,' Kalu answered, guarded.

'He tried to charge a family, a thousand US dollars for a week,' the man said, shaking his head. 'He's giving us all a bad name.'

'He's still trying.'

'Did he ask you for your passports?'

'Yes,' Kalu said, frowning.

'Don't give anyone your passports in this city.' The man leaned closer and whispered. 'They will take them and then bribe you to get them back. That man is a thief and if you complain or threaten him, he calls the police and they come and take you away to the camps. You don't want to be in a Libyan camp, believe me. Anyone who asks for your passports is a thief. Remember that.'

'We will. Thanks,' Kalu said.

'I'm Hassan,' the young man said. 'I have a place nearby.' Kalu held his hand to stop him. He carried on regardless. 'I charge fifty-dollars a night, per room not per person,' he joked. 'You can pay me one day at a time, no deposit and I don't need your passports.' He smiled and shrugged. 'You will not get a better offer.' Kalu and Esse looked at each other and nodded. The girls looked exhausted. 'It's a good price. The sheets are clean. I have WIFI and my wife is the best cook in Tripoli,' he added

'Thank you. We need to eat and sleep,' Kalu could feel the tiredness seeping into his bones. He felt like he had grit in his eyes. Getting to the coast had been his main priority, now they were there, the adrenalin that had fuelled him was on the wane.

'Follow me,' Hassan said. The old man returned to the street, looking for other migrants to scam. He noticed that Hassan had bagged his customers. Kalu saw him and thought that he looked annoyed. He could be as annoyed as he liked, Kalu thought. Ripping off desperate people was a dangerous game to play. 'What's your name?'

'My name is Kalu. This is my wife, Esse and my daughters, Oke, Isime and Kissie.'

'Your daughters are like flowers, Esse,' he said, bowing his head a little.

'Thank you,' Esse said, a thin smile on her face. He eyes were tinged with sadness. Hassan lingered on them a moment too long and she looked away.

'Come along,' Hassan said, cheerily. 'It's not far; Are you hungry?' he asked the girls. They nodded in unison.

Hassan was true to his word. The guesthouse wasn't far away; they were inside and organised within half an hour. The walls were painted white with a powdery feel to them and the linen and towels were clean and fresh smelling. His wife warmed up a goat curry with spiced rice. Kalu ate two helpings and drank a pint of water. He could feel the energy entering his bloodstream, although sleep was calling him. Hassan sat with them and chatted but he waited for Esse to take the girls upstairs before digging too deep.

'May I speak frankly,' Hassan asked.

'Yes,' Kalu said, nodding.

'Your wife looks very sad. Is she okay?'

'We lost our son on the journey here,' Kalu said. He didn't expand on the details. It was too raw to discuss.

'I'm very sorry for your loss.' Hassan didn't push the issue. 'The city is besieged by migrants. People like yourself, fleeing war. Unfortunately, Tripoli has become a dangerous place for foreigners but If we can help you, we will.'

'Thank you. We need to leave as soon as possible.'

'Where are you heading to?' Hassan asked.

'Europe,' Kalu said.

'That's a little vague.'

'It doesn't matter where. Once we're there, I can arrange transport to London. We have family there.'

'London, England,' Hassan said, making a thumbs up gesture. 'I like watching English football.' Kalu tried to smile but it wasn't very convincing. Hassan lowered his voice. 'Did you see all the people on the outskirts of the city?'

'Yes,' Kalu said.

'They are all trying to get to Europe just like you. It is chaos here now.' Hassan explained. 'There has been no proper government here since Gadaffi fell. Thousands of people come here every week looking to cross the sea. More people than the government can cope with.' Hassan's wife brought some sweet tea to them. 'The problem is, Europe doesn't want them.'

'Thank you,' Kalu said, taking the small glass of tea.

'You can't stay in the city long, Kalu. It is too dangerous for you. The government troops have regular purges. Especially in the old city. That's why the outskirts are full of migrants. They don't seem to venture out that far.'

'I don't intend to stay any longer than we need to. The quicker we arrange passage, the better.'

'It's not as simple to cross the sea as you think.' Hassan warned. 'As I said earlier, Europe doesn't want you. Legitimate transport across the sea has been stopped.'

'We have passports and we have money. We must be able to get passage on a ferry?'

'No.' Hassan said, shaking his head vehemently. 'This is what I'm trying to tell you. The ferries stopped running nine months ago. They ran to Italy and Turkey but they've blocked those routes now. Turkey has made a deal with Europe to turn migrants back from the coast.'

'They want to be part of it, that's why,' Kalu agreed. 'What about across the border in Tunisia?'

'You could sail to Marseille from Tunisia last year but they have stopped them all. The boats were full of people like yourself with nowhere to go. Europe has closed its doors.'

'There must be some boats sailing.'

'There are boats sailing every day,' Hassan said, nodding. He pointed his index finger to make the point. 'But they are all illegal. Nothing that sails from here comes back. It is a one-way ticket. The government are trying to stamp it out but there are so many people wanting to cross, it is a lucrative business. They'll never stop it. There's too much money involved.'

'It would make more sense to open the doors, not slam them in our faces,' Kalu sighed. 'People will always find a way around things. It's human nature.'

'So many people are trying to cross, they're climbing aboard anything that floats. Most of them don't make it. The Mediterranean is becoming a graveyard.' He paused to sip his tea. 'No one has any idea how many people are drowning out there because these overloaded boats are being launched from remote places in the dark. If they don't get there, who knows?'

'I'll find a way. There must be away,' Kalu sighed. 'I have to get my family to Europe.'

'You and fifty thousand others in Tripoli.'

'We don't have a choice. I didn't know the ferries had ceased to run.'

'It's been on the cards for years. Gadaffi made a deal with Europe, a few years ago just like Turkey has now,' Hassan explained 'He was getting pressure about human rights and they were going to impose sanctions.'

'Go on,' Kalu said, sipping his tea.

'He told the European leaders that if they took it easy on him, he would stop the flow of migrants crossing the sea, likewise, he threatened them with doing nothing if they didn't help him. He threatened to flood Europe with migrants.'

'I remember reading something about it,' Kalu said, frowning.

'He threatened to open his borders and let anyone through.' Hassan shrugged. 'The Europeans had watched a trickle of migrants becoming a flood and the ones with foresight could see it becoming a tidal wave. They took the deal. Gadaffi sent troops to round up anyone trying to cross the border to reach the Mediterranean. They patrolled the borders, picked them up, robbed them and took them back to the border and dumped them on the other side with nothing but what they were wearing. Thousands died of thirst and starvation in the desert but at least they weren't dying on European soil.'

'Of course, it doesn't matter if they died in Africa.' Kalu agreed. 'No one knows, no one cares.'

'Exactly. It worked for years but when Gadaffi went, so did the deal. Now there are virtually no restrictions and it cannot be policed anyway. It is madness. The police don't arrest anyone crossing the borders illegally anymore. They take money from them like an entry fee,' Hassan scoffed. 'Do you know who they arrest without question?'

'Go on.'

'The people who have capsized at sea. Can you believe that?'

'There's nothing that I won't believe anymore,' Kalu said.

'It is madness. They pluck them from the sea, half drowned, arrest them and put them into a camp.'

'Are the camps just for migrants?'

'Yes. They've set up camps for those they arrest, terrible places. People are beaten, raped and tortured in them until eventually, they send them back to the countries that they came from. They send them back to the things that they were running from in the first place.'

'They send them back?' Kalu said, frowning. He shook his head. The thought of being transported back to Boko controlled territory was terrifying. 'Where is the sense in that?'

'There is no sense in it but we are swamped with refugees. What can they do with them all? Sending them back means death for most of them.' Hassan sipped his tea. 'Those people on the edge of town are frightened to come into town in case they're arrested. So, they congregate on the outskirts searching for a way to cross the sea. Pirates and people smugglers mingle with them, promising safe passage across the sea for stupid prices.'

'It seems everyone is a businessman when people are desperate.'

'Criminals more like. Some of the migrants have their money stolen from them by the smugglers before they get near a boat and now they are stuck here in Tripoli with no money and no way to go home. They are broke and desperate and they can't go home.'

'I knew it was bad but I didn't know how bad,' Kalu said. 'There are thousands more coming. Boko are moving north. Thousands upon thousands are heading north.'

'And Isis troops have begun a push west into Libya. If they succeed and join up with the Boko Haram, we'll all be in trouble.'

'I didn't know Isis were moving,' Kalu said, concerned. He felt like a rat in a trap. They couldn't stay in Tripoli. He had to get them out.

'This is why the people are so desperate to leave. Things are getting worse every day.'

'It's going to get worse by the sounds of it,' Kalu agreed.

'This is why people are dying out there. They are being sold seats on boats that wouldn't stay afloat in my sink.'

'I have wondered why so many get on the boats in the first place,' Kalu said, his concern rising. 'Some of them have no choice, do they?'

'No. They take the chance, die here or die trying to reach safety.' Hassan said. 'And the weather is changing too. There are fewer days when the seas are calm enough to sail. In one month's time, only the bigger boats will make it.' Kalu felt the pressure building. When he had seen the sea for the first time, it was a massive relief. They had made it to the coast. The hard bit was completed. He was wrong. The more Hassan told him, the more it seemed like the hardest leg of the journey was still to come.

'My uncle works for the Libyan coast guard. They pulled eight hundred and sixty people from the sea last week.' Hassan paused to sip tea. 'Eight hundred and sixty people!' He shook his head. 'All of them dead.'

'It is unbelievable,' Kalu said, yawning. Hassan wasn't helping him to relax. In fact, if he listened to anymore, he wouldn't sleep a wink. 'Excuse me, Hassan but I'm tired.'

'I'm sorry. I talk too much. My wife always says this. You must go and rest,' Hassan said, standing. 'We can talk more tomorrow.'

Kalu shook his hand and finished his tea. The sugar would help fuel his depleted body. He went upstairs. The girls' bedroom door was ajar. He knocked and looked in on the girls. They were top to tail in a large double bed, the youngest two were asleep; Isime snoring like a pig already. Oke was using her phone to look at Facebook. It was charging while she used it.

'Get some sleep, Oke, Kalu said.

'I've been sending messages to my friends from Monguno, father,' she explained. 'Do you know how many have replied so far?'

'No.'

'None,' she said, sadly. 'Do you think they're all dead?'

'Maybe the network is still down there,' Kalu offered. He didn't sound very convincing because he wasn't convinced that they weren't dead. They might be alive, being forced into marriages or sold on as slaves. Kalu figured dead was better. 'Don't worry too much, I'm sure they'll be holed up somewhere safe or travelling like us.' He walked over and kissed her on the forehead. 'Try and get some sleep, if you can when your sister is snoring,' he said, smiling and gesturing at Isime, who had turned onto her back and was at full volume.

'What will we do in London, father?' Oke asked.

'Same as we did at home,' Kalu said, thoughtfully. 'I'll be a doctor and you three will go to school and pass all your exams and go to university. That's as far as I've planned.' He smiled. 'Now go to sleep.'

Oke put the phone down and turned on her side.

'Night, father, love you.'

'Love you too,' he said closing the door. He tested the handle to make sure it locked automatically. Leaving them out of his sight was going to be difficult from now on. He opened his bedroom door and stepped inside. Esse was sleeping, her mouth open, slightly. He tiptoed to the bed and laid down. The mattress and pillow felt amazing. He closed his eyes and was asleep within minutes. His dreams were dark and disturbed by encounters with thieves with guns, trying to take their money and boats awash with water, the seas around them full of dead bodies. He could hear people calling for help in his dream but he couldn't help them, just like he couldn't help Beb.

CHAPTER 28

The following day, Kalu asked Hassan to help him to find safe passage across the sea. Hassan was reluctant to let Kalu wander the old town alone, looking for a boat. He would be a marked target for every chancer and thief in Tripoli. Hassan knew some genuine pilots who were friends with his uncle at the coastguard. He figured that they would be the safest people to speak to. If anyone knew the safest route by sea, it would be the men who pulled the bodies from it. They had breakfast and left early. Esse and the girls were taking their time to get ready. They planned to wander the old town and visit the souk. Hassan's wife had said she would accompany them. If they stayed within the ancient walls and were veiled, they would be safe.

Kalu and Hassan headed for the truck. Hassan had told him that his uncle was working but his co-worker would talk to them. He lived a few miles away and arranged to meet them in a teashop. They had to park a ten-minute walk away on a strip of wasteland close to the sea. Kalu gazed at the seething blue mass as he locked the truck. It didn't seem to be so pretty when he had to take his family across it safely. The undulating waves hid the dark depths beneath them. Planning to cross it, changed the dynamic of how he saw it. They walked to the teashop, which was in the shadow of the red castle and Hassan's connection waved them over to his table.

'Hello, Hassan,' he said, standing and kissing his cheek.

'Hello Karim,' Hassan said. 'This is my friend, Kalu.' Karim nodded a greeting but didn't offer his hand. Kalu felt uncomfortable, immediately. They sat down and ordered tea. 'He needs to take his family across the Mediterranean.' Karim nodded. He looked at Kalu and sighed, shaking his head.

'Of course, he does, why else would he be here in Tripoli?' Karim said, eying Kalu with distaste. 'Where are you from?'

'A town called Monguno, northern Nigeria.' Karim nodded. Kalu knew that he didn't have a clue where that was, nor did he care. He felt the need to explain although he wasn't sure why. There were no apologies to be made for protecting his family. 'We were driven from our homes by Boko Haram; I wouldn't be here through choice.' There was an uncomfortable silence for a moment. 'Can you help us cross to Europe?'

'You know that it is illegal to help with these things.'

'I do.'

'I could be arrested for simply talking about to you about it.'

'I'm aware of that.'

'I am only here because Hassan's uncle asked me to talk to you.'

'I know.'

'I wouldn't be here otherwise.'

'I appreciate you taking the time to meet me. I'm very grateful,' Kalu said, trying to keep calm. 'I just want advice on how to cross the sea safely.'

'There are many people selling seats to cross the sea. Most of them are criminals. Boats are sinking every day, people are dying by the thousands yet you keep coming, don't you?'

'We were escaping a war. We didn't have a choice.' Kalu stood his ground but remained polite. 'I realise dishonest people are taking advantage of the situation and that's why I am here,' Kalu said, a little frustrated. He found Karim arrogant. He looked at Kalu as if he wasn't his equal. 'I am asking you for advice on getting my family safely across the sea as you're a professional, nothing more.'

'Giving advice nowadays is a dangerous business.' Karim looked around as if he was nervous of people listening. 'Giving advice is one thing but If someone were to act on my advice and do something illegal, I could be arrested and imprisoned.'

'I appreciate your concern, Karim and if you can't help, I understand.' The waiter brought the tea. They waited until he had gone out of earshot before speaking again. Hassan looked embarrassed by Karim's behaviour. 'Can you help or not?' Kalu asked, straight. He couldn't understand why he had come if he was unwilling to get involved. Karim thought about it for long seconds.

'No. I can't help you,' Karim sipped his tea. 'I couldn't jeopardise my liberty.' He looked at Kalu in the eyes. 'Not for nothing.'

Suddenly, Kalu understood. 'You want me to pay you for advice?' Kalu asked, surprised and somewhat disappointed. Hassan looked embarrassed. He spoke to Karim in Libyan Arabic. Kalu couldn't follow the brief exchange but there was angry disagreement.

'I am very sorry about this,' Hassan said, turning to Kalu.

'Don't apologise on my behalf, Hassan,' Karim snapped. 'Your friend wants advice from an expert, don't you?'

'Yes,' Kalu answered. 'That's why I'm here.'

'The advice that I can give to you will ensure the safety of your wife and children,' Karim said, shrugging. 'What is that worth to you?'

'How much do you want?' Kalu asked, resigned to the fact that nobody did anything for nothing anymore.

'A hundred US.'

'Karim!' Hassan hissed.

'Shut up, Hassan,' Karim argued, 'this is a business transaction like any other.'

'My uncle will hear about this!'

'It was your uncle who told me to make sure that I got paid, Hassan,' Karim said, grinning coldly. 'How do you think he bought his new Mercedes?' Hassan blushed. He had wondered where his uncle had found such wealth. 'We spend our days pulling these people out of the sea, piling their stinking bodies onto the decks. If we tell them how to get to Europe alive and we make a little money on the side, then there will be less bodies in the water.' He glared at Hassan angrily. 'I'm doing him a favour being here.' He turned to Kalu. 'One hundred US and I'll point you in the right direction. Yes or no?'

Kalu took a hundred dollar note from his pocket and slipped it into his hand, without anyone seeing. Karim put it away and looked around again.

'I am not getting involved, you understand but I will tell you the way I would go if I was crossing; hypothetically, of course.'

'Okay,' Kalu said, biting his tongue. He didn't have the time or the patience to play games. The thought of Esse and the girls wandering around the old town without his protection was unsettling him. Karim seemed to be enjoying his reluctance a little too much. For a hundred dollars, Kalu was hoping the advice was worth it. 'I'd be interested to hear your opinion.'

'The problem with crossing the sea in any boat is that the longer you are on the boat, the more vulnerable you become. Long voyages are obviously more dangerous than shorter ones.'

'Okay. I understand but I'm not sure what your point is?'

'If it was my family undertaking this journey, I would make the voyage as short as possible.' Karim sipped his tea.

'How would you achieve that?'

'You have to leave Libya and reach European soil, yes.'

'Yes.'

'And that is all you have to do. You don't have to sail all the way across the Mediterranean to the mainland.' Karim explained. 'The nearest European island is only two-hundred miles from here,' he said, pointing north across the sea. The tips of white horses on the waves glimmered in the sunlight. 'Lampedusa is the nearest European soil.'

'I've seen it on a map,' Kalu said, nodding. 'It's Italian.'

'Yes. Once you're in their waters, you are technically in Europe.' He made out an imaginary map with his finger. 'To the north, close to it is Malta, also in Europe.'

Karim gulped his tea and raised his glass. 'If I was you, I would be looking for a boat that is heading to one of those islands; any further and you are putting your family in unnecessary danger.'

'I understand,' Kalu said, nodding. 'That makes sense.'

'Where would you catch such a boat?' Kalu asked.

'There is a town called Zuwarah, sixty miles west of Tripoli,' Karim said, lowering his voice. 'It was a beach resort before the revolution but now it is an empty ghost town. I would be looking for boats sailing from that area, if I were you.'

'And would you know who to contact about boats sailing from there?'

'I might,' Karim said, sitting back, smiling. He gestured to Kalu's pocket. Hassan rolled his eyes but remained tight-lipped. Kalu sighed and took another note from his pocket, reluctantly handing it over. 'The men who organise this aren't contactable in the traditional way. They're very discreet. I will see they are approached on your behalf.'

'Okay, when will I hear from you?' Kalu asked, suspiciously.

'You won't hear from me again,' Karim said, wagging a finger. 'I am not getting involved in this but you will be contacted.'

Kalu nodded, unhappy and frustrated but accepting that it was the best he could do. He hadn't expected to be given five boat tickets in his hand but he wanted more certainty than this.

'If that is clear, then I have a busy day ahead,' Karim said. He stood and nodded a silent goodbye to Hassan. They were still annoyed with each other. 'Good luck.' He said curtly to Kalu. 'You will need it.'

'Thank you,' Kalu said, reluctantly. The words stuck in his throat. He didn't like Karim. He was just another thief along the way. He sensed the feeling was mutual.

Karim turned and lent over the table. He lowered his voice. 'A man called Omar is organising a boat to Lampedusa,' he said, nodding. 'He will contact you in the next few days.'

'Thank you,' Kalu said, offering his hand but Karim ignored the gesture and walked away without another word.

CHAPTER 29

The next three days were as normal as normal could be. The family ate well, slept well and were relatively safe in comparison to where they had been. They talked about Beb constantly. Esse was convinced that he was alive and that he would turn up somewhere. Kalu wasn't so sure. His optimistic side wanted Esse to be right but the realistic side knew that he was gone. He was walking on eggshells, trying to soften their loss as much as he could. It wasn't working. Esse could tell that Kalu was struggling too. He was distant, brooding and found it difficult to relax. When she asked him what was wrong, he would say that he was worried about getting out of the city without being arrested. He couldn't discuss the dangers of crossing the Mediterranean with Esse; they had lost one child already. He would have to make sure that their voyage would be as safe as it could be or Esse wouldn't allow the girls near it. Every day that they waited dragged for Kalu. Boko were still moving north and the ISIL militia were gathering on the east of the city. Libya was about to implode into civil war and knowing that they could be arrested for simply fleeing danger and be interned in a camp, added to their plight. The pressure to get his family to safety was enormous yet the uncertainty of what had happened to their son was tearing him apart.

On the fourth day, a man knocked on the door and asked for Hassan. He introduced himself as Omar. Hassan invited him inside and the men sat at the table, while the women made themselves scarce. Introductions were minimal and professional. Omar was a barrel-chested man with a long black beard. He was wearing a white kaftan and a black waistcoat. Kalu got the impression that Omar didn't like him anymore than Karim had. The age-old rivalry between black Africans and the Arab speaking population in the north of the continent was as prevalent as it ever was. Esse made sure that she could hear what was being said. Her trust levels were as low as Kalu's. Their boundaries had been narrowed by recent events, their thresholds shortened. A week ago, they had been well balanced individuals, patient and trusting. Those people were gone.

'I am told that you're looking for passage to Europe?' Omar asked. His eyes darted everywhere as if he was nervous and would rather be somewhere else. He was sweating and his body odour pervaded the air.

'I want a boat that is heading to Lampedusa or Malta,' Kalu said. 'Preferably from Zuwarah. Nowhere else will do.'

'How many of you?'

'Two adults and three children.'

'What is your profession?'

'I'm a carpenter,' Kalu lied. 'Does it matter?'

'Not really,' Omar answered, disappointed. It did matter. It mattered a lot. He wanted a boat full of professionals. They had more money. The Syrians had the most money but they had stopped coming to Tripoli. Passing through extremist lines to the east had become too dangerous. The thousands of black Africans in the city didn't have as much money as them. The average cost of crossing was dropping dramatically. Omar made his pitch. 'It will cost ten-thousand euros per person.'

Kalu looked shocked and shook his head. 'Fifty thousand euros to sail two hundred miles?' he asked, astounded.

'Fifty thousand euros to take your family to safety. A new life. That is what you're paying for.' He tapped his index finger on the table. 'I do not send people in dangerous vessels. It is a big boat.' Omar took a photograph from his pocket and passed it to Hassan. Hassan passed it to Kalu. It was a big boat and looked seaworthy and safe. 'The price includes passage on deck not down in the hold, transport from here to Zuwarah, accommodation, food and water while we wait for perfect conditions and the launches and your lifejackets.' It was a confident pitch. Kalu knew it was a practised script. 'The pilot is an experienced sailor; a Tunisian trawlerman. He's been at sea all of his life.' He paused while Kalu took it all in.

'Ten thousand euros is too much,' Kalu said, shaking his head. 'I'm not paying that much.'

'Ten thousand each is the going rate. Take it or leave it. My boat will be full regardless of whether you're on it or not.'

'I'm getting a little tired of being told to take it or leave it,' Kalu said, sighing. He took a deep breath and thought about it. 'Here's what I'll do,' he said. 'We'll make our own way to Zuwarah. We don't need your food or water and we'll buy our own lifejackets. There seems to be plenty of them for sale. Once we sail, you can have my truck as part payment and I'll pay five thousand US dollars each.' He paused while Omar frowned. 'Twenty-five thousand US, plus my truck. That's my final offer.'

'Make it thirty-thousand and you have passage on my boat.'

'Twenty-five thousand and not a dollar more,' Kalu said, stony-faced.

'No deal,' Omar said, standing. 'You won't get a better deal than that.' He turned to walk to the door.

'I've heard that a lot lately too,' Kalu said, smiling. He shrugged. Hassan looked on concerned. 'Usually when I've been told that I won't get a better deal, there is a better deal. Twenty-five thousand dollars, plus my truck. Take it or leave it,' Kalu said, confidently. The words rolled off his tongue and felt good. Omar was hovering between the table and the door.

'Twenty-seven fifty,' Omar countered. 'Meet me halfway.'

'My price is twenty-five,' Kalu said, offering his hand. 'I'm not going any higher, Omar.'

'I need five-thousand as a deposit,' Omar said, shaking Kalu's hand. He wasn't happy but he had realised that all the posturing he could muster, wasn't going to improve the price. 'You need to be in Zuwarah tomorrow afternoon.'

'I'm not giving you any cash right now,' Kalu said, looking him in the eye. 'Give me an address where we need to be. I'll pay half when we get there and half when the boat arrives.'

'I need a deposit?'

'For what?' Kalu asked, shrugging. 'I don't know you. You come here with a picture of a boat, ask me for thousands on just your word?' he paused. Omar looked annoyed. Sweat trickled from his forehead. 'If this is a genuine offer, you'll have your money when I know that we're not being ripped off.'

'You're insulting my integrity,' Omar complained.

'I mean you no offence,' Kalu said, calmly. 'If you have integrity, then you'll understand my position. I will be there tomorrow and I will pay you half on arrival and the other half on our departure on the boat.'

'Give me two thousand as a down payment,' Omar protested.

'Now you're insulting me,' Kalu said. There was quiet for a few seconds. Kalu wondered if he was pushing too hard but he was sick of being a victim. They only had one chance of crossing, he had to get it right. 'I'm not paying for anything until I'm sure.' Omar swallowed hard. He looked defeated. 'Where do we need to be tomorrow?'

'Take the Quarji road along the coast to Zuwarah,' Omar said, seething. He knew that Kalu wasn't going to give him any cash. 'When you get to the Radisson, you will see an unfinished building next door. Park behind it. Someone will come to you there.'

'What, you won't be there?' Kalu asked, smiling thinly.

'I will be somewhere else tomorrow,' Omar answered, mumbling.

'With my deposit?'

'Just be there on time,' Omar snapped.

'What time?' Kalu asked.

'Be there before five o'clock.'

'We'll be there,' Kalu said, standing. He didn't offer his hand and he didn't say goodbye. Omar was going to steal his money; he was sure of that. He was just another snake in the grass and Kalu had to learn quickly how to spot them and stop them biting him. This time he had.

CHAPTER 30

The following day, the family said goodbye to Hassan and his wife, packed up the truck for the final time and headed west along the coast road to the deserted beach resort, Zuwarah. Long sandy beaches hugged the coast all the way and it was easy to see why Libya had become a holiday destination for a short time. The beaches ran along the coastline, joining those in Tunisia to the west. Cobalt blue seas, touched with emerald, rolled onto the sand. In the distance, it was difficult to distinguish were the sea stopped and the sky began. The horizon was the brightest blue, melting into green and silver. It was hard to believe the country was literally a warzone.

Despite the idyllic views, the drive was tense. Esse was weepy, crying one minute, chatting to the girls the next. The girls were understandably nervous and she was trying to keep them calm. Kalu felt cautious yet grateful that they had an opportunity to sail to Europe. He was anxious about how vulnerable they were. They were carrying a lot of currency, which anyone with the firepower could take from them at any time. He had a gun but there were lots of guns in Libya. There were still hurdles to jump before crossing the finish line in Europe. The feeling of being in constant peril didn't lift, despite the views. He was tired of being frightened for his family.

When they reached Zuwarah, the abandoned resort had an apocalyptic feel to it. Five-star hotels stood empty; their windows broken and their parking bays littered with burnt-out vehicles. Restaurants were boarded up, their chairs and tables stacked high outside, covered in sand and dust. There were residential areas behind the rotting tourist area but there was no sign of any locals. As he was driving, Kalu started spotting armed militiamen on some of the corners. They were communicating via walkie-talkies and mobiles but payed little attention to their truck as they passed by. Nevertheless, the presence of men with machineguns made his stomach twist.

'Who are they?' Esse asked, following his gaze. Her hands were trembling a little. The girls were craning their necks to see out of the windows. Kalu could see the fear on their faces in the mirror. They had seen a lot since fleeing Monguno to escape men with machineguns and here they were again, surrounded by them. The uniforms were different but the effect was the same.

'Are they Boko, father,' Oke asked, putting her arms around Kissie.

'No,' Kalu answered. 'They're militiamen here to protect the traffickers.'

'Protect them from who?' Esse asked, nervously.

'The police, probably,' Kalu speculated. 'Government troops, other traffickers. These boats are big business. They're protecting their operation.'

His answer seemed to satisfy them although it had done nothing to put them at ease. They drove a mile along the coast road until they reached the Radisson. It was fifteen storeys high, painted white with balconies outside every room. The paint was weathered and peeling and vegetation had started growing from the roof and windowsills. Kalu turned into the car park of the building next door and steered the truck around to the rear. There were other vehicles parked there, many of them covered in sand. It looked like the place motorcars went to die. He brought the truck to a stop and looked up. The building in front of them was half finished and overgrown with shrubbery. He could see through it to the sea. Movement from the Radisson to his right, caught his eye.

'Look at all those people,' Kissie said, pointing to the balconies. There were black faces staring down at them from every floor. Hundreds of people were sitting or leaning on the railings, watching them arrive. 'Who are they?'

'People waiting for a boat, just like us by the looks of it,' Kalu guessed. A bad feeling descended over him. He knew there would be others waiting but he hadn't anticipated how many. 'Wait here and I'll make sure we're at the right place.'

'Be careful,' Esse said, touching his face. Something familiar flashed in her eyes. Something that he hadn't seen for a while. Not since Beb had gone. It twisted his stomach in knots.

'I will,' Kalu said, kissing her cheek. He smiled at the girls. 'I won't be long and then we're going on a boat.'

They nodded but looked apprehensive. He was too but he tried not to let them see it. As he opened the door, three Libyan men exited the ground floor of the Radisson. They walked towards the truck. Kalu was relieved to see that none of them had a weapon. None that he could see, that was. He approached them and smiled.

'I was told to come here by Omar,' he said. 'We want to be on the boat to Lampedusa.'

'Omar who?'

'I don't know his full name.'

'There are lots of Omar's but none of them work for us.'

'He was sent to me by Karim.' Kalu tried again. 'Karim the coastguard.'

The men looked at each other and spoke briefly. It seemed to be a positive result. They knew who Karim was.

'You want to cross to Europe?'

'Yes.'

'How many of you?' one of the men asked.

'Five, two adults and three children.'

'How are you paying?'

'American dollars,' Kalu answered, concerned that the details of their deal hadn't been communicated. It was becoming clear that Omar was just another thief. He couldn't trust anyone. 'I made a deal with Omar.'

'There is no Omar,' the man who appeared to be in charge said. He was wearing khaki combat pants and a plain black tee-shirt. He was stocky and strong looking. 'Any deal that you made with him means nothing to me. It will cost you seven-thousand each and another five-hundred for the accommodation and lifejackets.'

'That isn't what we agreed.'

'That's the price.'

'We have lifejackets and your accommodation is an empty hotel that doesn't belong to you.'

'That is the price; take it or leave it.'

'I made a deal with Omar. He was sent by Karim.' Kalu argued. 'You know who he is.' Kalu pointed with his index finger. 'We agreed on twenty-five thousand dollars and the Land Cruiser as part payment.' One of the men walked to the truck and looked around it. He kicked the tyres like a proper mechanic 'I'll give you the keys and pay you half the cash now and half when the boat arrives.'

'That's ten-thousand less than I asked!' he scoffed. 'You're in no position to negotiate. Do you see any other boats here?'

'I haven't seen any boats yet,' Kalu said, standing his ground. 'I don't even know if you have a boat.' He shrugged. 'No offence but there an awful lot of crooks around.' Kalu watched his expression change. 'I made a deal and I'm not paying any more than twenty-five thousand. That is a lot of money.'

'It's not enough.'

'It's all I'm willing to pay; We can take the truck back to Tripoli and give our money to someone else.' The trafficker looked at the burning sun and wiped sweat from his brow with the back of his hand. 'Do we have a deal or not.'

'Okay, okay, deal,' the leader said, without any further argument. He shook hands with a very surprised Kalu. Kalu had expected to pay thirty-thousand, minimum. 'My name is Ahmed,' he said, smiling. He gestured to the truck. 'Get your family out of my truck and I'll show you where you're staying,' he joked. He pointed to the Radisson. Hundreds of eyes watched their conversation. 'You can pay me the money inside. Don't count your money in front of all those people. Some of them are criminals,' he said, winking. Kalu was sure that some of them might be criminals but he was positive that Ahmed was.

'When does the boat sail?' Kalu asked, walking to the truck.

'Tonight, or tomorrow night, depending on the weather,' Ahmed said. 'The waves are high today but the forecast is good. As soon as the wind drops, we'll sail.'

'Okay,' Kalu said, relieved. They would finally be sailing for Europe. He didn't feel elated but it was another tenuous step in the right direction.

'Come on, come on, let's get you inside and show you where you'll be staying.'

Kalu walked back to the truck and opened the door. The girls looked at him expectantly. Esse looked at Ahmed and his men, suspiciously.

'Grab your stuff,' Kalu said, smiling. 'We've made a deal.'

'When does the boat sail?'

'Tonight, or tomorrow, depending on the weather.'

'How much?' Esse asked, grabbing her bag.

'What we agreed,' Kalu said, smiling. 'Twenty-five thousand plus the truck.'

'I thought they would ask for more,' Esse said, raising her eyebrows.

'Me too,' Kalu agreed.

'Can we trust them,' Esse asked.

'Not a chance,' Kalu said, shaking his head. 'We cannot trust anyone.' He looked at the girls. They looked concerned. 'Did you hear what I said?' they nodded. 'We cannot trust anyone no matter how nice they seem, understand?'

'Yes, father,' they answered in unison.

'Okay, then,' Kalu said, closing the door. 'Let's go and see what our room is like. Don't get your hopes up. It might say Radisson on the outside but it looks a little rundown to me,' he added with a wink. The girls smiled. It was good to see them smile.

They gathered their things and walked towards Ahmed and his men. Kalu handed the keys to the truck to one of them. He spoke to Ahmed in Arabic and then jogged to the cruiser. Kalu felt a tinge of sadness as it was driven away. The vehicle had carried them as far as it could on their journey. It had been a reliable asset in a time of unreliability and chaos. He glanced at the sea. The sun was glinting from the waves as they crashed onto the shore; white foam sprayed into the air. It seemed to be flexing its muscles, demonstrating its awesome power. Kalu steeled himself against the negative shroud around him. Something felt wrong. Very wrong.

'What are your names?' Ahmed asked. He smiled and waved at the girls. The girls nodded and half smiled but didn't speak. Father had told them to trust no one. 'I'm Ahmed.'

'This is my wife, Esse, and this is, Oke, Isime and Kissie,' Kalu introduced them. 'I'm Kalu.'

'Okay, nice to meet you all. Follow me,' Ahmed said, turning towards the derelict hotel. They walked across a car park that was littered with tins and bottles. Kalu had to wonder where the litter came from. There were no supermarkets or fast-food outlets here. Some of the tins were bright and shiny, obviously new but some, where faded and rusty. The litter had been dropped over a long period of time. 'You're on the tenth floor. The views are great.'

The family followed Ahmed into the reception. It was like a time capsule from a more peaceful time when Libya was trying to westernise itself by inviting sun-worshipers to her northern shores. The resources for tourism were there but the stability wasn't. The desk was intact; it was made from dark oak with brass footrails attached. A bank of pigeonholes was fixed to the wall behind it, gossamer webs spanned the gaps where letters and keys would have been stored. There were huge planters spotted around the entrance hall at regular intervals, the plants had long since died from thirst. The false ceiling had collapsed at the far end of the room, blocking the light in that area. Small trees had pushed their way through the concrete and had reached waist height but they looked wizened and pale. Bricks and breeze blocks had been stacked up here and there and were being used as seats and tables by armed men, who eyed them with contempt.

Kalu thought about what he had seen. He wondered why no one was outside, enjoying the beaches and the sea. The resort was a ghost town but the nature of it hadn't changed. Why were all the migrants inside or on their balconies? Omar weaved his way through the debris and headed up a concrete stairwell. Wires and pipes had been stripped from the walls by metal scavengers and a warm breeze whipped in through the broken windows. It carried the smell of food cooking to them; spices and herbs lingered on the breeze.

When they reached the first floor, the scale of the operation became clear. Three rows of gas stoves were filled with metal saucepans of food, simmering away. Half a dozen men were chopping and cutting, stirring and tasting, preparing food on an industrial scale. Steam climbed to the ceiling and drifted out of the windows. The smell of turmeric and coriander was overpowering. Bottled water was piled a dozen crates high along a wall of what was once, a conference hall. Thousands of litres were stored there. Kalu glanced down a hallway, which led to the rooms on that floor and saw dozens of black faces looking back. The hotel room doors had been removed, probably stolen but it appeared that every room was occupied. As they climbed higher, every floor was the same story. There were people in every room; hundreds of them. As they ascended higher, the smell of urine and faeces replaced the smell of cooking. It hung heavily on the breeze. Kalu reckoned the number of people in the hotel ran into the hundreds. The chatter of voices filled the air, languages from all over the sub-Saharan continent reached them. Cigarette smoke drifted through the corridors and stairwells. People were lying in doorways and sitting on the stairs, surrounded by luggage. Kalu was becoming increasingly concerned. The boat he had seen on the picture was a big one but not big enough to carry so many people on one voyage. To carry everyone in the building, an oceangoing liner would be required and he didn't think that Ahmed had access to one of those. This was trafficking on a massive scale. A million-dollar business, without a doubt.

When they reached the tenth floor, the stench of confined humans was thick but there were less people there. Ahmed guided them down a corridor past rooms that had only a few people in them. Most appeared to be sleeping or resting on the balconies, their bags and cases strewn everywhere. He stopped outside an empty room and gestured to them to enter. Kalu stepped in first. The room was spacious and bare; the sun glared in through sliding balcony windows. He peered into a tiled bathroom that had been impressive once. The mirror was smashed and the toilet bowl was filled to the rim with human excrement. People had continued to use it, despite the lack of running water to flush it. He recoiled from the stench and walked to a broken window for some fresh air. Looking down, he could see a mountain of rubbish, plastic bottles, tins, cans and cardboard. There hadn't been a refuse collection for decades. Little wonder the building stunk, Kalu thought. He also thought about how many migrants had passed through this building on their way to Europe. Looking at the setup and the amount of waste, the answer was in the tens of thousands. They had manufactured a human conveyor-belt, carrying refugees across the sea for vast amounts of money; opportunism at its worst.

'Make yourselves comfortable,' Ahmed said. 'You can give me the money now, Kalu,' he added, looking furtively down the corridor. Kalu nodded and walked into the bedroom. Ahmed followed him. He took a roll of notes from his pocket and took a second from his rucksack. Kalu counted out twelve thousand five-hundred dollars and handed it to Ahmed. It disappeared into the cargo pockets on the side of his pants without checking it. He patted Kalu on the shoulder. 'Okay, you have yourself five seats on the next sailing. Feel free to go downstairs to eat and drink. The food is available twenty-four hours a day. If you need anything, anything at all, ask someone else,' he joked. 'There's plenty of water. Help yourselves.'

'Thank you,' Kalu said with a half-smile.

'We'll let you know when we're boarding. Until then, relax and enjoy the view.' Ahmed left the room, waved a hand to Esse and the girls. 'Just one other thing,' he popped his head back around the door. 'Don't go outside until we are ready to board.'

'Why not?' Kalu asked, disturbed.

'This is Libya, my friend,' Ahmed said, the smile gone. 'Our government doesn't want hundreds of refugees wandering around and attracting attention from the police is bad for business. You won't be here long, so follow the rules and everybody is happy.' There was an edge in his voice now; the hint of a threat tinted his tone. He disappeared again and headed off down the corridor.

'Well, here we are,' Kalu said. Oke walked to him and put her arms around his waist, her head on his chest. He rubbed the back of her head. 'Not long now,' he said, trying to convince them everything was okay.

'How long will we be on the boat, father?' Oke asked.

'I'm not sure,' Kalu said, shaking his head. He had worked out a rough calculation in his head the day before. Most trawlers could make headway at about nine knots, which meant two-hundred miles would take over twenty-something hours. That was a long time to be at sea in an open craft but he didn't want Esse and the girls dwelling on that. 'It depends on how fast the boat is and how rough the sea is.'

'How fast will the boat be?' Kissie asked. 'Will it be a speed-boat?'

'I don't think so,' Kalu answered. He wished it would be. 'As long as there are no holes in it and the captain knows where he's going, we'll be fine.'

'Kalu!' Esse said, hiding a smile. 'You'll frighten them.'

'I'm only joking.' Kissie made a fist and play punched him in the leg.

'I can't believe we're actually here, waiting for a boat to Europe,' Esse said, her voice almost a whisper. 'It doesn't feel real. It all feels like a bad dream.' She looked at Kalu. He knew what she was thinking. Beb. 'Will you call the colonel, Kalu?' she wiped a tear from the corner of her eye. 'You never know, there might be news.'

'I think he would have called if anything had changed but I'll call him to make sure.' He looked at the girls. Oke poked her head around the bathroom door and recoiled quickly. 'I wouldn't go in there,' Kalu said, taking his mobile from his bag. He switched it on and dialled the colonel. Esse leaned against the wall, closed her eyes and said a silent prayer.

CHAPTER 31

The call had been answered by a junior officer. He asked Kalu to wait while he checked if the colonel was available. Kalu waited for the phone to be answered before taking a breath, his heart racing in his chest. Esse was frozen like a statue. He heard the phone being handed over and then heard a familiar voice.

'Hello, Kalu,' the colonel said, flatly. He didn't sound pleased to hear from him. 'Where are you?'

'Libya. A coastal resort called Zuwarah, near Tripoli,' Kalu replied. 'We're waiting for a boat.'

'Are you all well and in one piece?'

'Yes.' He looked at Esse and his girls. They were far from well. 'We're all as well as can be expected.'

'Good. that is good news,' the colonel said. There was an awkward silence. Kalu didn't want to ask and the colonel didn't want to tell. The colonel broke the deadlock. 'Kalu, there is some bad news, I'm afraid.'

'What bad news?' Kalu asked, his fists clenching around the phone. Esse slid down the wall and Oke ran to her, holding her. Isime held Kissie.

'One of our patrols came across a Bedouin caravan south-west of where the truck was found,' the colonel began. 'They told my men that they had discovered the bodies of two males a week before north of their position. The same day that we found the truck.'

'Was it Beb?' Kalu asked, his voice cracking. Esse began to shake, covering her eyes with her hands. The girls looked like they were going to breakdown too. 'Colonel, was it our son?'

'We think so.'

'What do you mean, think so?' Kalu asked, frightened to hear the answer. 'I don't understand.'

'The Bedouin said one of the bodies was a young black African boy, possibly Nigerian.' He paused to choose his words carefully. 'They said that the other body was an Algerian soldier.'

'One of yours?'

'We think so. There are so many deserters, we can't be sure.' The colonel sounded apologetically. 'Beb was taken by our soldiers. I have to assume the boy was Beb.' He paused. 'The chances of another Nigerian child being in the desert near to where we found the truck are a million to one, Kalu.'

'How was he killed?'

A groan came from deep inside Esse.

'They were shot.'

'Shot,' Kalu repeated.

Esse screamed and beat her fists on the floor.

'Where is he, colonel?' Kalu wanted to see his body. He wanted to take his boy and bury him properly. The danger of the journey back didn't matter right then. He couldn't think clearly. He wanted to see Beb.

'The Bedouin buried the bodies in the sand,' the colonel said, reading his thoughts. 'They didn't mark the graves.' There was silence again. Kalu couldn't speak. Esse took her hands from her eyes and looked at him; tears were flowing freely now. Kalu bit his bottom lip and shook his head. Beb was dead. She cried out his name, over and over. Beb, Beb, Beb. 'I'm very sorry, Kalu. I didn't want to give you the news until I knew you were safe.'

'I understand,' Kalu said. 'Take care, colonel.'

'You too, Kalu. Let me know when you're safe.'

'I will.' The colonel hung up.

Kalu walked to Esse, who was sobbing so hard that he thought she would suffocate. The girls sat next to their mother and cried with her. Kalu had no words. There was no way of numbing the pain. Beb was dead and they couldn't bury him. Their son had been taken and shot in the desert and he would lie where he had died for eternity, alone. The thought of him out there alone was too much. Kalu broke and the sound of weeping drifted from their room and echoed down the hallways. Their neighbours covered their ears and were grateful that they had never had to encounter such grief and they hoped that they never would.

CHAPTER 32

For the next three days, Kalu felt like he was in a Groundhog Day. Every morning Ahmed would come to the hotel with excuses and every day more migrants would arrive. The tenth floor was filling up and they were starting to use the eleventh. Tempers were fraying and fights had broken out on the floors below. People were complaining that their property was being stolen at night. The atmosphere was oppressive. On top of that, the food was barely edible and people were becoming ill. The stench of human waste pervaded the entire building. Children were crying day and night and the heat was stifling. Many migrants had been there for a week before Kalu had arrived. They had heard enough excuses and they asked for their money back, threatening to leave.

Kalu had gone down to the first floor for water and heard arguing from the reception on the ground floor. He walked down the stairs to see what was going on. A group of thirty or so migrants were gathered, their luggage next to them, ready to leave. Kalu recognised some of their faces from the rooms on the first floor. They had been there the longest time. Ahmed was fending off their complaints; armed militia blocked the exits. The temperature was rising and the discussion was becoming hostile.

'I'm sick of your excuses,' one man said, pointing his finger into Ahmed's chest. He was a big man, probably Nigerian, Kalu thought. His bone structure was common in that region. He appeared to be acting as the group's spokesman. 'Give us our money back and we're leaving!'

'Your deposits are non-refundable,' Ahmed said, calmly. 'That is what a deposit is.' He shrugged. 'Besides that, you've been given food, drink and accommodation. There will be no refunds.'

'You've kept us cooped up here like animals and your food has poisoned most people!' the Nigerian man pointed his finger again, poking Ahmed to reinforce his point. He was an intimidating figure. 'We want our money back, now!'

'There will be no money returned,' Ahmed said, taking a step back from the big man. 'And if you poke me again. I'll cut that finger off and stick it up your backside,' he added with a cold smile. 'Go back to your rooms and wait there until we're boarding. The weather is still too rough to sail safely.'

'You're not listening to me. We're leaving here,' the Nigerian shouted. He poked Ahmed again. Ahmed moved quickly. He stepped away and a blade flashed in the sunlight. A black index finger landed in the dust next to Kalu. The Nigerian grabbed the bleeding stump, his face a twisted mask of anger and pain; he lurched forward at Ahmed. A single gunshot rang out and echoed through the building. The crowd shuffled back and fell silent. The Nigerian man seemed to teeter for a moment before toppling forward onto his face, his eyes wide open staring at the wall. Shafts of light pierced the reception, dust drifted through them like tiny planets floating through space. The standoff was tense. Kalu thought about running upstairs but he didn't want to be the first to move. The shooter still had his rifle to his shoulder, ready to find his next target and drop them.

'Pick up your luggage and go back to your rooms,' Ahmed barked. 'Move, move, move!' he clapped his hands loudly.

The migrants moved as one, picking up their bags and cases and running for the stairs. Kalu moved aside before he was trampled. He made eye contact with Ahmed for a second. He was ice cold. Killing the Nigerian meant nothing. He shouted orders to the militiamen and they headed upstairs to ensure order was kept. More armed men came in from outside; Ahmed gave them instructions and they followed the others. Another man came in and spoke to Ahmed in panicked tones. Kalu slid behind a fallen ceiling panel and listened.

Ahmed took his mobile from his pocket and made a call. Kalu hovered near the stairwell and listened. The call was made in English. Ahmed had a good grasp of the language, which didn't surprise Kalu. Anyone who could organise a trafficking operation on this scale was smart. Speaking several languages would be essential.

'Things are becoming unmanageable here,' Ahmed said, angrily. 'We need to sail today before it is out of control.' He listened for a moment. 'I don't care about the weather. Bring the boats. I want them out of here tonight!'

Kalu waited until they he had gone and then began walking up the stairs. The building was virtually silent, fear tinged the atmosphere. He watched as one family from the first floor tried to run. They were related to the Nigerian man. That was the point when the traffickers became ultraviolent and people were grabbed and beaten into submission. Another man was shot dead in the reception area, his body dumped on the refuse pile at the rear of the hotel alongside the big Nigerian. That changed the dynamic completely. The migrants were no longer customers, they were prisoners. Armed militiamen were positioned on the entrance doors and others were stationed on the stairwells. No one could leave their floor without a good reason. The Radisson felt like it was going to explode. There were hundreds of refugees and only a dozen or so militia. Kalu could hear people discussing rushing the guards and killing them. He didn't want to kill the guards. He didn't want to kill anyone. He just wanted to get on a boat to Europe. Things were getting out of hand. Once again, Kalu feared for their safety.

****

Esse was oblivious to her surroundings. The confirmation of Beb's death had destroyed her completely. Oke stepped up to the plate and looked after her sisters, bringing the family food and water, which Esse didn't touch. She was grief stricken. The next few hours were fraught with tension but Kalu was worried about what Ahmed had said. He was forcing the voyage to go ahead, against the advice of whoever was on the phone. They were going to sail, despite the inclement conditions. It was cloudy and a strong breeze was blowing. Kalu knew that a breeze on the shore could mean a gale at sea. The wind was a different beast out at sea.

Later that afternoon, there was a lot of shouting from upstairs. The traffickers began to empty the hotel from the eleventh floor down. When it was their turn, Kalu paid the balance for their places, organised the girls and guided Esse down the stairs. The migrants were herded like sheep, out of the hotel and along the promenade to a concrete pier, that had been built for tourists to go on boat trips. Anyone who objected, was beaten savagely. A couple broke free of the herd and sprinted for the beach. A volley of shots from an automatic dropped them both. The traffickers weren't taking any prisoners. Disobeying them was fatal. People were screaming and crying as they were forced towards the pier.

Kalu could see two rigid-hulled inflatable boats ferrying people from the pier to a larger vessel. It was anchored a few hundred yards from the pier. From its shape, Kalu was sure that it was a trawler. It wasn't the boat that Kalu had been shown by Omar. It was older and much smaller. Attempting to sail two hundred miles through stormy seas in it was folly. Many times, he had wondered why migrants risk their lives aboard such vessels. Now it was clear. They were given no choice. He was beginning to think that things were about to get much worse.

CHAPTER 33

K alu made sure the girls had their lifejackets fastened tightly and guided Esse onto the rib. The gap between the boat and the pier was too far for them to step. He reached back and then lifted the girls from the stairs. The inflatable rocked dangerously as they slid over the seats to an empty space. Waves rocked the boat, soaking the occupants and filling the rib with water. As more people were forced on, the boat sunk lower in the water. Militiamen shouted instructions in Libyan. Nobody could understand a word that they were saying. The migrants were in a state of panic. Fifty people were herded onto a dingy designed to carry ten. It was so low in the water that even the smallest waves lapped over the bow. Kalu couldn't do anything but watch what was happening around him. The crowd on the pier was being forced into the second rib. Panicked refugees were being forced down moss covered stone steps, which were dangerously slippery. Cockles clung fiercely to the stone, forming a surface like a cheese grater. It was difficult for the migrants to keep their footing. The militiamen pushed them, beating them into a crush. Many of them fell painfully, breaking bones and scratching exposed flesh on the shells.

One man tried to argue with a guard who was screaming at his wife. He slapped her across the face and she crumbled to her knees, slipping on the seaweed. She tipped over the edge of the pier, falling thirty-feet into the sea. The splash was deafening. Once again, the herd was stunned into silence. Fear gripped them. Her husband rushed to the edge to help and the militiaman kicked him over. The man hit the water a few yards from his wife, who was clearly drowning. He paddled to her, struggling to keep his head above the swell. The peaks and troughs were becoming steeper as the wind picked up. The couple disappeared from his view each time a wave hit them. The woman grabbed her husband around the neck, desperately trying to stay above the waves. They rose with the deep swell for a minute or so. The husband was kicking his feet furiously, trying to keep their heads above water. A wave hit them and they vanished from Kalu's vision. They surfaced twice, coughing and spluttering and then disappeared completely.

Esse grabbed his arm, her fingers digging into his skin. The girls were wet and cold and terrified. Their eyes were wide with fear as they huddled together, shaking from the cold. Wave upon wave hit the rib as the pilot opened the throttle. The outboard motor drove them through the swell at a pace. It bounced violently as they approached the bigger vessel. Kalu was astounded at its condition. It looked worse close-up. He wasn't a sailor of any description but the old trawler didn't look seaworthy. Its paint was cracked and peeling and it was sitting low in the water. The rib floated alongside it and the migrants scrambled aboard, tossing their belongings over the gunwale before clambering across the deck to an empty space. Kalu grabbed Esse and the girls and headed towards the stern of the boat behind the bulkhead.

'Where are you taking us?' Esse asked in a daze.

'It will be drier at the stern,' Kalu said. He settled them down against the bulkhead. The girls were clinging to each other, Oke next to her mother. 'Don't move from there while they're boarding. People will try and steal you space, okay?' The girls looked at him, wide eyed. They were traumatised. He knelt and spoke to them. 'Don't be afraid. Once we set sail, we'll be safe.' Kalu lied. He looked around and watched as another two boatloads were herded on deck. Every inch of space was covered by a seething mass of human cargo. Men were forced to sit atop the wooden bridge, where the pilot was standing next to the wheel, smoking a cigarette. He looked worried as more people were forced onboard.

There was no space remaining when the next two loads arrived. The occupants were forced below decks into the hold, kicking and screaming. Militiamen beat them brutally with their rifles. Nobody wanted to be below deck but they weren't given much choice. Kalu and the girls watched in horror as load after load were delivered and forced below decks. When they couldn't fit anymore in, they closed the doors and padlocked them shut. Kalu could hear the muffled cries of men, women and children from below. The conditions would be rank, the air unbreathable and thick with diesel fumes. It was a horrific situation. Kalu and the family were cold and wet and frightened but at least they could see the sky and breath fresh air.

When the last two boatloads arrived, there were no militiamen in them. Frightened migrants held the tillers. Kalu was baffled as to how they were going to board. There simply wasn't an inch spare. The boat was dangerously low in the water and it was rocking violently with the swell. Water lapped over the gunwales. He realised what was happening when the occupants of the rib tied their boats to the sides of the trawler, as they had been ordered to do, making a ridiculously unstable raft, hideously overloaded with humans. Kalu wasn't sure who he had more sympathy for, the poor souls in the flooded ribs or those crammed into the darkness of the suffocating hold. Their predicament was unimaginably frightening and uncomfortable.

The trawler shook as the engine rumbled into life. Kalu looked at the people around him. They all had a bewildered expression, as if to say, 'is this really happening to me?'

CHAPTER 34

The boat turned starboard and headed north into the waves. Its progress was sluggish at best. Kalu reckoned it was making five knots against the wind. A knot is nearly two miles an hour, he thought. They were travelling at ten miles an hour roughly; It would be over twenty-hours until they made European waters. He huddled against the girls, using his body heat to keep them as warm as possible. Esse had her eyes closed as the boat rocked side to side; the roll exaggerated by the ribs tied to the sides. The pilot steered his makeshift craft skilfully through the waters, trying to cut through the oncoming waves to keep splashing to a minimum. The humming of the engine was steady and as day turned to night, Kalu began to settle a little. He tilted his head back and looked at the stars, searching for the constellations and thinking of the times he had studied them with Beb. Tiredness took over and he fell into a troubled sleep.

A loud bang woke him. He instantly knew it was a gunshot. A bright light illuminated the deck from the portside. It dazzled him. Another gunshot rang out. Kalu got to his feet and looked out to port and saw a speedboat was cruising on the same course as the trawler. It had two powerful outboard engines and could easily outrun the trawler. At first, Kalu thought it might be the coastguard, trying to make them turn back to Libya. It crossed his mind that they might be government troops coming to arrest them and force them into a refugee camp but he thought again when he saw the three men, who were standing in it. Kalu could see that they weren't Libyan. They were black. Two held rifles and one held the searchlight. Another warning shot was fired, hitting the bridge, sending sharp splinters of wood into the passengers. One of the men in the speed boat raised a loudhailer.

'Stop the boat or we'll fire!' he shouted. The demand was backed up with a volley of bullets fired over the heads of the migrants. Some of the migrants started to stand up, panicking, causing the boat to rock violently. Kalu thought it was going to capsize. 'Stop the boat and hand over your money!'

'They are pirates!' the trawler pilot shouted. 'Everybody, stay still. Don't move or you'll tip us over!' he shouted over the engines. The older migrants on the deck reiterated his orders.

'Sit down' fools,' one shouted.

'Keep still or we'll capsize, you idiots!'

'Stop the boat!' the pirates called, their boat stalking the trawler.

'Everybody, hold tight. We're not stopping for anyone,' the pilot shouted. He put the engine onto full-throttle and the trawler began to shiver and shake as it picked up speed. The old timbers vibrated violently. Migrants vomited as the trawler pitched and rolled, seasickness spread through the passengers. The trawler picked up speed, dragging the inflatable ribs with it. The occupants in the inflatables were complaining loudly as waves swamped them, filling the ribs with water, saturating the freezing migrants inside. Another gunshot sounded and a bullet ricocheted of the bridge. The speedboat accelerated, keeping pace with ease. It circled them like a shark waiting to pounce but the trawler pilot held his course and his nerve. The trawler sailed into the wake of the speedboat and it pitched and rolled, threatening to tip the migrants into the sea. The passengers shouted and screamed like riders on a rollercoaster.

'What are they doing?' Esse asked, panicked. Her expression was childlike. Her emotions were shattered. 'Kalu! What's going on?'

'Pirates,' Kalu answered over the engine noise and gunshots. A large wave hit the front of the trawler, making it lurch to starboard. The screaming from below decks was deafening. They were in the dark, not knowing what was happening, being choked by engine fumes as it ran at full-throttle. 'They know everyone on this boat is carrying everything they own. It must be easy pickings stopping old boats like this, robbing the migrants.'

'Stop the boat!' the pirates hailed again. They fired at the rib, which was tied to the starboard side. The occupants were screaming that someone had been hit. Another bullet pierced the inflatable and there was a loud popping sound as it burst. The rib was sinking fast, pulling the trawler with her. The trawler began to list dangerously to starboard.

'Stop the boat!'

'Untie that rib! Cut that rib free!' the trawler pilot shouted to the migrants on the starboard side. He was in a panic. 'It's going down!'

'What about the people in it?' someone shouted.

'It's going to drag us down with it!' the pilot screamed. He was struggling with the wheel. Steering was almost impossible. The trawler was being pulled over. 'Untie it now or we'll go down!'

Kalu watched as men rushed to the starboard gunwale, trampling on anyone in the way. Three of them struggled to undo the knots. The occupants of the rib were desperately trying to climb onto the trawler, tipping the boat further. Water was gushing over the side, saturating everyone aboard and flooding through the deck into the hold. The noise from below became unbearable to listen to. People were hammering on the door, threatening to shatter the planks.

Suddenly, the knots were untied and the rib was cut free of the trawler. The sudden change of weight sent her into a deep roll, throwing the migrants from one side of the deck to the other. People were rolling from port to starboard and back as the boat lurched violently. Kalu held on to his family and tried to shield them from the impact of others falling.

'Stop the boat, now!' the pirates hailed again but they seemed to be further away. Kalu looked to starboard. They had gone after the rib. It was sinking in the water and easier to attack. There were enough people with money onboard to make it worthwhile. They pulled a man from the water, emptied his pockets, removed his lifejacket and tossed him back into the sea. He sank below the waves in seconds. The pirates didn't leave witnesses behind. After a few minutes, Darkness swallowed up the scene and he could no longer see them. He heard gunshots and screaming for a while and then the sounds of the sea and the engine drowned them. The trawler sailed on and put distance between them and the pirates. It made steady headway into the darkness, rising and falling relentlessly. The engine had gone from a hum to a grinding roar, hard on the ears above deck, deafening for those below.

Kalu could only imagine what it was like below decks. The thudding on the door had lessened, which wasn't a good sign. He wondered what condition they would be in, medically. As the trawler sailed on unhindered, the migrants settled, stunned by the attack, while the pilot kept the trawler going at full tilt.

CHAPTER 35

The sun was up but hiding behind rainclouds when they heard the engines slowing. The pilot had zigzagged through the night, making it impossible for the pirates to find them again. They were too far from shore now. He had made good speed throughout the morning. Esse and the girls were sleeping in a huddle. The migrants were battered and dazed, cold and frightened. A light rain began to drizzle down, soaking them. Kalu saw storm clouds brewing to the east and the swell was growing and the troughs were deepening. The trawler climbed and fell sharply with each wave. There was no chatter onboard as the trawler made steady progress until mid-afternoon. The passengers were in shock, exhausted and miserable.

Shortly after two o'clock, the drizzle turned to heavy rain. It hammered down, soaking the migrants again. The rain was accompanied by a strong wind from the east. Large waves were hitting the boat, side on, swamping the deck. Each wave was bigger and more powerful than the next. The boat seemed to have come to a standstill, making no headway against the storm. It pitched and rolled and the pilot opened the throttle to full, trying to power through the relentless waves. The engine reached its maximum revs and the trawler vibrated and threatened to shake itself apart. There was a grinding noise from below. The engine was dangerously overheating. It was on its last legs and the pilot knew it. Checking the gauges, he decided that their position was critical. He checked their position and then picked up his radio phone and called the two numbers he had programmed into it. The first was the Rome Rescue Coordination Centre. He gave them his position and told them he had four-hundred passengers, including a hundred children aboard a sinking trawler. His second call was to the Maltese search-and-rescue centre. That call was cut off but he was sure he had done enough for them to know where they were.

Below decks, the nightmare conditions had reached a new low. The water was knee high and rising, full of vomit, urine and excrement. Many of the passengers had food poisoning from the meals at the hotel and diarrhoea was rife. The conditions were so cramped that they had to go to the toilet where they stood. Children were crying, their anguish impossible to listen to. People were beginning to collapse and pass out. When the pilot pushed the engine to maximum once more, the aging sump cracked, spewing fumes and burning oil into the already unbreathable air. When the trawler began to pitch violently again, some of the men took their attempts to breakdown the doors to a new level, taking it in turns to work on the joints with belt buckles and a spoon. They managed to make a crack wide enough to get their hands through. The aging timbers splintered. They pulled and pushed with all their combined weight and the doors cracked open.

Kalu saw the hold doors burst open and he knew what would happen next. The panicked hoard below decks rushed onto the stern, spilling to port and to starboard. The already crowded deck, turned into a free-for-all. The strongest stood their ground while the weaker ones fell and were crushed. Fights broke out and the migrants tried to move away from them, rushing to the portside as a mass. The trawler tipped, the keel showing as it lurched. Others ran to the starboard, trying to right the listing vessel, just as a massive wave hit the bow. The force of the wave and the stress on the wooden hull from the weight of the passengers, was too much. It lurched at the stern, the sound of timber groaning then splitting and then the hull cracked in half.

CHAPTER 36

There was a deafening crack and then the boat separated. The bow slipped beneath the waves in seconds, spilling hundreds of migrants into the sea. It disappeared for a minute and then resurfaced upside down. The stern reared up like a stallion on two legs, catapulting the migrants into the sea. It teetered for a moment and then toppled upside down, floating on the mountainous swell. Kalu took a hard blow to the back of the head from the bulkhead, which stunned him. He was thrown from the stern, somersaulting in the air before landing in the freezing water, which took his breath away. He was stunned for a few minutes and could only tread water. The lifejacket kept him from sinking. When his senses cleared and he realised what had happened, he looked around desperately for Esse and the girls. The sea was awash with brightly coloured lifejackets but he couldn't distinguish his family.

'Esse!' he shouted. There were calls for help, crying and screaming but none of the voices were Esse. A wave hit him and drove him down beneath the surface. The salt water stung his eyes and filled his nose and mouth, making him gag. He surfaced, coughing and choking. His eyes were sore and his vision was blurred. 'Esse!'

'Esse!' he screamed. He turned three-hundred and sixty degrees but couldn't see anything but a writhing human soup.

'Kissie!' he shouted. She was the youngest, weakest and couldn't swim. 'Kissie!' he swam to the hull and clung to it, looking around at the bodies in the water. Some were moving, some were not.

'Esse!' he clambered along the upturned hull, searching frantically. He pushed the floating bodies away from him and pulled those alive towards the hull. 'Hold on to the boat,' he told one woman. She clung to it, her eyes wide with fear. He couldn't stay with her.

'Oke!' he called at the top of his voice. Nothing.

'Isime!' He listened for their voices but heard nothing but the sound of people drowning, searching for their loved ones.

He clawed his way up the hull and looked over the other side. Hundreds of brightly coloured lifejackets bobbed up and down on the surf but he could not see Esse or his children. They were nowhere to be seen. Dropping back into the water, he swam fifty yards to the wrecked bow and clung to it for a moment to catch his breath, looking around, desperately trying to find his family. He shuffled along to the other side, making a complete circuit of the hull but there was no sign of them. The water was seething with migrants, some floating, some sinking, some already dead but there was no sign of Esse or the girls. There was floating wreckage everywhere, migrants clung to them for dear life. Suitcases and clothes floated on the waves. He spotted the pilot climbing onto the wrecked hull and felt nothing. It wasn't his fault they had sunk.

'Esse!' he shouted again, looking over the scattered debris for any sign of life. 'Esse!'

He searched through the floating dead, checking everyone wearing red lifejackets. Some were face down in the water and he had to turn them over to see their faces. He swam around the wreckage for four hours. None of the hundreds of bodies he checked was Esse or the girls. Kalu was becoming numb with the cold and he was becoming exhausted and hypothermic by the time two commercial ships arrived on the scene. He was slipping in and out of consciousness as they pulled him onto a Maltese vessel. He was wrapped in a silver insulation sheet and given fresh water. There were dozens of survivors around him. He stared at their faces, one at a time, looking for Esse, Oke, Isime and Kissie. When he had checked them all, he closed his eyes. He felt his muscles spasm with cramp and then he fell into a black abyss as his mind switched off.

CHAPTER 37

The voyage to Malta was a blur. Kalu could hardly remember any of it. There were flashes of people asking him questions, black faces crying, people wrapped in silver foil. So many different languages that he couldn't count them. He remembered a helicopter hovering above the deck, taking a critically injured child away. No one knew where her mother was. He remembered slipping in and out of sleep, his dreams panicked and choking. There were some lucid memories of when they arrived in Valletta. They were examined and clothed and placed onto buses before being driven to an army base in the town of Safi. He remembered being taken to a medical centre where he had become agitated and incoherent, ranting about his children. They injected him with something and then he didn't remember anything, until two days later.

When he came around, he was desperate for news of Esse and the girls. He was shown a list of the survivors and a list of the dead, who had been identified. They weren't on either. He was also shown photographs of the dead that they had recovered who couldn't be identified. Searching through them was one of the worst things that he had ever had to do. Looking at each face in turn, praying that he didn't recognise any of them. Thankfully, none of the dead people in the pictures were his family. Every day he returned to check the updated lists and every day he left with no answers. He was dazed by grief and felt empty inside. Not knowing where they were, was torture.

The camp at Safi was nothing more than a migrant prison. The Maltese guards were cruel and indifferent to the suffering of those in it. Many had lost loved ones to the sea. The immigration process was long and detailed and the Maltese made it difficult. Their government felt that the rest of Europe had abandoned the Mediterranean migrant crisis and let the burden fall on the Italians and the Maltese to deal with. Dead bodies were not washing up on the shores of Brussels, so no one cared. Out of sight, out of mind. Kalu was lucky, and he was granted refugee status. His brother, Dapo flew from London and visited him at the camp, when he was due to be released. Their reunion was an emotional one. When Kalu explained what had happened to Beb, he was broken and when he told him what happened to the trawler, he broke down again. An aid worker saw how distraught he was and brought them some tea. Eventually, he composed himself and the aid worker chatted to them about his experiences. She introduced herself as Anna, an Italian student on a gap year.

When she asked how long he had been there, Kalu wasn't sure but he knew that he had been picked up by a ship called the Valletta Queen with over a hundred others.

'I heard about that ship breaking up. That's terrible,' Anna had said, 'Over two-hundred people died.'

'It's more than that,' Kalu disagreed. 'There were many more aboard.'

'The pilot made a distress call and stated that he had four hundred passengers, including a hundred children,' she had said. 'Only one hundred were brought here and another ninety were taken to the Italian camp at Foggia.'

'What Italian camp?' Kalu had asked, shocked. He had seen the second ship but just assumed it was Maltese. 'What are you talking about?'

'Two vessels came to the rescue,' Anna said. 'The Valletta Queen and an Italian vessel called the Actios. Both picked up survivors.' She saw the shock on his face. 'You didn't know the second ship was Italian?'

'No, I didn't know!' Kalu freaked. He had no idea that there were survivors in an Italian camp. His heart nearly stopped and there were butterflies in his stomach. Hope returned like a rush of blood to the head. 'Anna, my family could be in that camp!'

'Wait here,' Anna had said. 'I'll contact them for you.'

Dapo and Kalu had waited patiently, pacing the room. Kalu felt hopeful, anxious, angry, elated, shocked, stunned and terrified. His emotions had been in turmoil. Anna was gone for nearly an hour before she returned. One of the camp directors was with her, carrying papers and photographs. Anna had a mobile phone.

'Someone needs to talk to you,' she said. Her eyes were deep and when she looked at him, Kalu saw sympathy in them. Sympathy and anguish. She handed him the phone.

'Hello,' Kalu said, his hand shaking.

'Father?' a frightened voice replied.

'Kissie!' he said, excited. A tear fell from his left eye. 'It's so good to hear your voice.'

'I missed you, father,' Kissie sobbed.

'Oh, I missed you so much!' Kalu said, trying not to let his emotions break his voice. 'Is your mother there?' he asked, excited to talk to Esse.

'No one else is here, father,' Kissie answered, her voice trembling. 'I'm here alone. I thought they were with you.'

Kalu felt his knees buckle and remembered falling to the ground. He remembered Dapo taking the phone, talking gently to Kissie, trying to calm her, telling her that they would come and get her and he remembered losing his mind.

CHAPTER 38

TEN YEARS LATER

T he sandstorm had been blowing for weeks, making navigation impossible. The camels were becoming restless, as were the women. Cooking was difficult and everything they ate had sand in it. They had been wandering into the storm for a week now, trying to reach the other side of it. It had showed no sign of weakening so they camped down for the night. He had seen many such storms but this one was brutal. Some of the elders had said it was the most intense that they had experienced. He had broken sleep that night.

He woke with a jump. Something had changed. The wind had dropped and the sand was thinning. It hadn't stopped, it was just a lull. He could see lights twinkling in the distance to the west. Not just a few lights, thousands of lights. It was a town, a big one too. He hadn't seen a town since he had been sold to the Tuareg by the Bedouin tribe who had taken him. The Tuareg made sure that they were never in view of civilisation, painstakingly navigating the desert so that their slaves could never run away. They tried to make it impossible to escape. If they ran, they would die in the sand. The sandstorm had disorientated the tribe and they had strayed close to a town. He looked at the stars that he could see and gauged roughly where they were. The town below them was Figuig. He could reach it in a few hours and be gone by the time the tribe awoke. They had taught him to use charts and compasses and the stars to navigate as there are few landmarks in the desert. It was a skill that they needed to survive. He had picked it up quickly and slotted into Tuareg life, becoming a useful member of the tribe. He worked, ate and slept with them, learning more about surviving in the desert every day. He was a fast learner but then again, he was the son of the cleverest man in Monguno.

EPILOGUE

Kalu had been working in the accident and emergency at Guy's hospital when he'd received a phone call from the British embassy in Rabat, Morocco. They explained that a twenty-year old man had walked into a police station in the town of Figuig, claiming that he'd been kidnapped by a Bedouin tribe ten-years ago and sold to a Tuareg tribe. He had bribed the police officer to take him to the embassy, in the hope that his family had made it to London. Beb had hidden his gold coin on his person for years, waiting for the opportunity to use it to escape. Kalu had been overwhelmed when he spoke to Beb, the man. Beb the boy was gone. His voice had changed and was deeper and touched with an accent but it was still Beb. They had talked for an hour about his childhood; Beb's memories were a little vague but mostly correct, if a little out of sync. They laughed and they cried as they talked. The news that his mother, Isime and Oke had died on the voyage to Europe was difficult to take. It was difficult for Kalu to tell him and it was just as difficult to hear. Beb had sounded stunned by the news but didn't break; he was a little distracted.

Three days later, he had been flown to London, Stanstead and the family was reunited. Kalu thought Beb was huge and had turned into a man. He had grown as tall as he was but still had his gangly physique. His features had changed a lot but it had been ten years. It was hard to see the boy in the man before him. Kalu questioned himself for a moment. Is that really Beb? He could have been a stranger until he mock-saluted, just as he had as a boy. Seeing that melted his heart. Of course, this was his son. Kalu thought Kissie would never let him go. She had started university that year and didn't shut up about it all the way home. Beb had looked bamboozled as they drove through the city; everything was new to him. They'd stayed up late that first night, talking into the early hours of the morning. Kalu explained that the Algerians had questioned a Bedouin tribe, who had claimed that they'd found and buried a Nigerian boy close to where the truck had been found. It became clear that they had said that because they'd kidnapped him and sold him to a Tuareg tribe and didn't want the soldiers to find him. Kalu carried a lot of guilt about accepting the news of his death as the truth, without questioning it but Beb held no grudges. He explained how the Tuareg moved and convinced Kalu, that they would never have found him, no matter how hard they looked. It was pure chance that he had escaped.

Beb had described his life with the Tuareg and Kalu and Kissie had listened with sadness. At first, he had cried every day for weeks, missing his family and begging the elders to let him go. They had no sympathy for their workforce and ignored their pain. Emotions were rare in the Sahara. They put him to work, teaching him the different daily tasks and beat him frequently until he learned to do things properly, first time around. Eventually, he stopped crying as often and he had resigned himself to his tasks. The years went by and he learned their language and practised their traditions but he always hoped there would be an opportunity to escape and he'd waited and waited. He thought it would never come until the night that there was a sudden lull in the sandstorm. When the chance had come, he'd taken it.

They talked about their escape from Monguno and how they had never found anybody who had escaped. Kissie had spent weeks looking online, Facebook, Twitter and Instagram, but never found any survivors. Esse's sister and her family had been found murdered in the bush along with hundreds of others. Boko Haram were still entrenched in the border regions and they had had a lucky escape.

After six months of readjustment, Beb began a college course to try to gain the basic qualifications, maths, English and computer studies. He spoke to Kalu often about going into the medical profession, aiming to become a nurse first and then to see where the job took him. Pictures of Esse, Oke and Isime took pride of place in the family home and they talked about them every day. On their birthdays, they took a trip to Brighton and placed three wreaths of red roses into the sea. Then they would eat and toast their lives and talk about where they would be, had they survived. Kalu grieved in private for his wife and children; the pain never faded, not for him. He questioned the decisions that he had made and tortured himself with what ifs. Having his son returned to him was some compensation and he doted on Kissie and Beb every day. Leaving them to go to work was a trauma and he rang them often, making excuses as to why he was ringing. He just needed to know that they were okay. Life became as normal as normal could be for them. They knew it would be a long hard road for all of them to move on and come to terms with things but they also knew they would get there together. The journey still hadn't finished for them, it never would.

What Kalu and Kissie didn't know was that Beb had had a special friend in the tribe. Beb and Damilola had been sold to the Tuareg at the same time and they spent all their time together, working the herds, cleaning, eating and sleeping. They became close; two peas in a pod. They were from the same area and spoke the same dialect and after some confusing family-tree discussions, they decided that they were distant cousins. They talked incessantly about their lives before the tribe and learned everything about their childhoods. The Tuareg called them the twins because they looked so alike and after years of being together, even their mannerisms became alike. They began to mimic each other. Beb told Damilola about his family and how he had disappointed his mother on his last day with them. He told him how his father was a doctor and that they were heading for London when Beb had been kidnapped. He said that one day, he would escape and find them there and be reunited again.

Damilola had watched his family being slaughtered and had nowhere to escape to. He had asked Beb how he would get there and Beb had showed his best friend his gold coin. It was his last resort, his parachute and when the time came, he would use it to bribe somebody to help him get to his family.

Damilola had been consumed by envy. His friend had a family and a gold coin to help to get to them. Damilola had nothing and no one, but Beb. He dwelled on the situation for weeks and then decided to act. One night when they were tending the goats, the main caravan had gone over the border to Morocco for supplies, Damilola stamped on Beb's neck while he was sleeping. Beb was paralysed but still breathing when Damilola dug a shallow grave in the sand, stole his coin and buried him. Beb suffocated slowly in the sand. When the tribe returned, he told them that Beb had told him that he was going to escape across the desert and had run away. They didn't send anybody to look for him and the years rolled by until the sandstorm gave him the chance to escape. Beb was no longer Beb. Beb was Damilola, who had killed Beb five years earlier in the desert.

Damilola fitted into family life with Kalu and Kissie and they never questioned him. If they ever did, he would leave and would still be a thousand times better off than where he was and infinitely better off than Beb. When Kalu had given his children the coins, he had told them to hide the coin but to be careful as people would kill them for gold. On this occasion, Beb had let his guard down and paid the ultimate price. He should have listened to the wisest man in Monguno.

THE END

The sequel to the Journey will be released in 2022

The Journey

Printed in Great Britain
by Amazon

12220223R00109